SAS

The Illustrated History of the SAS

Also by Joshua Levine

Beauty and Atrocity
Forgotten Voices of the Blitz
Forgotten Voices of Dunkirk
Forgotten Voices of the Somme
Operation Fortitude
On a Wing and a Prayer
The Secret History of the Blitz
Dunkirk

SAS

The Illustrated History of the SAS

JOSHUA LEVINE

WILLIAM
COLLINS

William Collins
An imprint of HarperCollins*Publishers*
1 London Bridge Street
London SE1 9GF

WilliamCollinsBooks.com

HarperCollins*Publishers*
Macken House
39/40 Mayor Street Upper
Dublin 1
D01 C9W8, Ireland

First published in Great Britain in 2023 by William Collins

1

Maps by Martin Brown

A catalogue record for this book is available from the British Library

ISBN 978-0-00-854995-4 (UK)
ISBN 978-0-00-864087-3 (US)

Set in Arno Pro

Printed in Bosnia-Herzegovina by GPS Group

This book is produced from independently certified FSC™ paper to ensure responsible forest management

For more information visit: www.harpercollins.co.uk/green

To Mike and Peggy. Bold souls from different eras.

CONTENTS

PART THREE – EUROPE

FOREWORD

I was born in London, in 1920, while my family was passing through the city. Two weeks later, with me a babe in arms, we moved to Gloucestershire where life was hard – but we didn't see it that way. Today, of course, everyone's lives are so different, but one thing remains similar. People have always had dreams of one kind or another, and from a very young age mine was to have an interesting life and see the world. I was looking for adventure.

When I was fifteen I cycled around Germany with a friend, staying in youth hostels. We visited little cafés and, in one, the waitresses discovered we were English and they thought it was a great joke to stand around saying 'Heil Hitler' to us, laughing. They took no mind of our startled faces. There were clear signs of what was going on: our youth hostels had 'Jews not welcome here' signs, and out in the countryside we saw young people working on the land, marching together with their spades over their shoulders in a militaristic way. We were struck by the level of organisation. People seemed to know what they were doing and where they were going. It was a stark contrast with Britain at that time.

None of us knew what the forthcoming war would bring. But long before that, in 1937 when I was just seventeen, I boarded a ship and set out for Rhodesia where I worked on a farm. I joined the Rhodesian artillery when the war began and became an anti-tank gunner in the Western Desert. On leave in Cairo, I met some members of the Long Range Desert Group who asked me if I would be willing to join them. That was how I learned the magic art of navigation and began working with the SAS.

The SAS was born in the hot and unforgiving deserts of North Africa. Based on a simple yet revolutionary idea that small groups of highly trained and determined men operating deep behind enemy lines could wreak untold damage on the enemy, the SAS were to prove themselves time and again one the most potent 'pound for pound' forces throughout the rest of the war.

The SAS has a fearsome reputation nowadays, but I never remember wanting to kill anybody. But I found a life in the SAS that suited me. I got a bit of an education – albeit an unorthodox one. I enjoyed the organisation's unusual kind of discipline. And I became friendly with all sorts of people from all manner of backgrounds. In fact we captured a few Italian prisoners in central Libya who were agreeable chaps. They became, in a way, friends – so that when a German aircraft came over, they hurried to help us get out mountings for our guns. When we got back to Cairo we took them for a drink in one of the bars before handing them over. It was quite difficult to see these Italians as being on the other side but, at the same time, they knew very well that we would have shot them had they tried to escape.

Of course the technical context then was quite different. We had no support from satellites or other wonders of communication that people take for granted today. We were wholly dependent on each other and our mental and physical resources and aptitudes. Looking back, I suppose the war in the desert was quite different to the war in Italy and France. Once we were in France, we were fully aware of the Nazi evil and the Gestapo-style grip on German behaviour. Hitler had issued his instructions that people like us were to be shot. Our attitudes changed. And I ended up investigating the murders of friends in France. This wasn't a good time as far as I was concerned.

Much has been written about the early formative years of the SAS – years that I still remember clearly – but now, for the first time, this book provides a compelling photographic record of that period. Drawing on previously unpublished material from the SAS Regimental Archives, these pictures of the SAS fighting across North Africa, up into Italy and through Western Europe, tell their own captivating story. I can no longer see, but I know these pictures would bring back memories of hardship, danger, sacrifice and loss, as well as great friendships and much laughter. For you, I hope they serve as an interesting and illuminating reminder of a small group of young men who, by daring all to win all, played their small part in defeating the tyranny of Nazi Germany.

Who Dares Wins.

Mike Sadler, 2023

PART ONE

THE IDEA

Troopers and horses of the Staffordshire Yeomanry in Palestine, 1940.

1

BEFORE THE SAS . . . CAME THE SAS . . .

In 1939, Mick Gurmin, a trainee engineer living in Wolverhampton, was nearing the end of his apprenticeship. Like millions of other Britons, he was following a carefully considered path which allowed for few surprises. As boys and girls of the Depression, his generation of youngsters knew the dangers of straying from their path; work and economic security could never be taken for granted.

Yet the world was about to erupt under these young people's feet. Before 1939, Gurmin had never travelled abroad – and nor did he expect to. His life was settled; his expectations were limited. But over the next few years he would find himself in Albania, Austria, Belgium, Bulgaria, Czechoslovakia, Egypt, France, Germany, Greece, Hungary, Iraq, Italy, Libya, Malta, Palestine, Syria, Tripolitania, Tunisia, Turkey, Transjordan and Yugoslavia. He rarely knew where he would be going next, and he *never* knew when – or if – he would see Wolverhampton again.

Mick Gurmin's deviation from the path began when he joined the Staffordshire Yeomanry, a cavalry regiment, as an ordinary trooper. On the very first day of 1940 he arrived in Palestine where his primary job, in the area known today as the West Bank, was to keep the peace between local Jews and Arabs.

Gurmin spent much of his time on horseback – at a time when most British cavalry units had converted to tanks and armoured cars. Serving as mounted policemen in flashpoint areas was one of the few remaining tasks better suited to non-mechanised cavalry. 'We thought we would be better off doing the job than the infantry on their feet,' remembers one yeomanry officer, 'and we were right!'

But in April 1941 Gurmin's life took its least predictable turn yet. He was plucked out of Palestine and sent to Cairo on a strange secret mission. In Gurmin's army file the mission is described only as 'special escort duty'. In fact he was to be provided with a carefully crafted backstory, dressed in a fancy-dress uniform pasted with parachute badges, and sent into bars, restaurants and other public areas where he had to engage random strangers in awkward conversations. And in the process he was to become the first member of the SAS, months before the SAS actually existed.

Mick Gurmin's mission was the central part of a plan dreamed up by Dudley Clarke, the unorthodox visionary who headed the army's special deception section in the Middle East. Clarke was a dynamic little man with carefully slicked blond hair whose job, simply put, was to mislead the enemy. An unusual mix of playful creativity and cold determination, he was amply suited to the role.

Clarke's iron-and-velvet nature was well known. He had once choreographed a particularly enjoyable Royal Tournament yet was equally capable of suppressing the 1936 Arab Rising. In the immediate aftermath of the Dunkirk evacuation, he had suggested the formation of a force that

Mick Gurmin.

Dudley Clarke.

Yeomen engaged in horseplay.

could 'hit sharp and quick, then run away to fight another day'. In the days that followed, the Commandos came into being.

In December 1940, Clarke arrived in the Middle East, summoned by his friend and champion, the commander-in-chief, Sir Archibald Wavell. Here Clarke turned his attention to strategic deception, seeking the best means of fooling enemy commanders into doing exactly what he wanted them to do. There was no template for this work. Clarke was breaking new ground – and the capture of an Italian officer who had kept a careful diary presented him with an exciting opportunity.

One of the diary entries revealed a belief that British parachute troops were present in the Middle East. In fact there were none, but Clarke spotted the chance to exploit an existing fear. He would set about convincing an already nervous enemy that five hundred parachutists, all specialists in the sabotage of enemy vehicles, had recently arrived and were ready to cause mayhem. These fake parachutists had to belong to a unit – so Clarke would invent one: 1st Special Air Service Brigade.*

* The SAS name was not chosen at random. As Clarke was inventing his brigade, a genuine British unit was mounting a parachute raid on an aqueduct in southern Italy. This unit, 11th Special (Air) Service Battalion, had only recently been named – by Clarke himself. The raid was an initial success, although the damage caused was promptly repaired and the parachutists were subsequently captured. The operation had a number of notable effects, however. It unnerved the Italians, it popularised the idea of airborne raiding in Britain, and it amounted to the first publicising of the Special Air Service name. A few months later the unit was renamed 1st Parachute Battalion.

A feature in *Parade*, a Cairo magazine (left) depicts supposed Abyssinian parachutists. In fact, they were local laundrymen. More unpublished pictures of the fake parachutists (below).

The scheme, he understood, was key to unlocking his bigger plans. The Special Air Service Brigade could become the first in a chain of fake units. If the enemy believed in them, then the British Army would seem stronger and more adaptable than it really was. This would deter attacks and prompt the enemy to waste resources on unnecessary security. And when a sufficient number of units had been faked, they could become the basis for large-scale offensive deceptions.

So much for the theory; how was the enemy going to be convinced that the Special Air Service existed? The answer was Operation Abeam.

Dudley Clarke, ever the showman, decided to give himself a leading role in the operation. Dressed in a parachutist-style uniform, carelessly dropping incriminating documents, he would share a railway sleeper car with a Japanese diplomat who, it was hoped, would spread the fake news. Specially stamped documents and receipts, meanwhile, would be 'discarded' in carefully chosen spots around the Middle East.

At the same time, an area in Transjordan would be conspicuously closed off due to supposed 'parachute training'. And a group of local Cairo laundrymen, posing as Abyssinian parachutists training with British troops, would be photographed alongside a Bristol Bombay aircraft.

All these plans were duly carried out. But the central element of the deception was Mick Gurmin's mission. Joining up with a fellow member of the Staffordshire Yeomanry, Gurmin was to spread the story around Cairo that he was a member of 1st Special Air Service Battalion undergoing training in Transjordan.

There were clear problems with the story. Neither Gurmin nor his colleague, Lance Corporal Smith, had any parachute experience or technical knowledge. Yet they were now expected to convince everyone they met that they were highly trained parachutists about to embark on sabotage operations. Not only that, but they had to convey this information while seeming reluctant to do so. It was a difficult acting exercise with genuine risks involved, as Dudley Clarke was keen to remind them in his last-minute instructions:

> You must understand that the duty for which you have been detailed is one of very great importance. Any carelessness or indiscretion on your part may well upset carefully arranged and important plans and have far-reaching consequences. Please keep this in mind all the time.

Dispatched with these unnerving words, Gurmin and Smith donned their crisp new uniforms, with bright parachute badges sewn onto both arms, and set off. They wandered around the Pyramids, attended a football match and went to a cabaret. They sat in a cinema watching Chaplin's *The Great Dictator* and danced at the Services Club. They walked around the zoo and travelled north to Port Said, where they hoped to be spotted by a known enemy informer. All the while, they popped in and out of cafés and restaurants. Wherever they went they attracted attention. 'Are you real live parachutists?' they were asked, the most direct of many similar questions. '*Bonne chance*!' said a Greek restaurant owner, tapping their badges ominously. The longer their performance lasted the more confident they grew, until they found themselves chatting easily to a pair of army warrant officers as though they were real members of a real parachute battalion. They were starting to believe their own patter. Their time, perhaps fortunately, was now up.

At this point we might expect the principal actors in this drama to retreat back into the shadows. Certainly Gurmin and Smith returned to the Staffordshire Yeomanry. But a glowing review followed them, penned by Clarke in a letter to their strikingly named commanding officer, Gordon Cox-Cox:

> I do not think it would have been possible to make a better choice for that particular job . . . Both men have done extremely well under really very difficult circumstances. It was by no means an easy task which they were set and the way in which they carried it out reflects a great deal of credit on them.

In Mick Gurmin's case, this letter had career-changing consequences. Marked out for better things, he was sent on an officer training course.

Left: Mick Gurmin: a tourist in Cairo.

Below: Trooper Gurmin and Lance Corporal Smith posing in fake uniforms as Gunner Gurmin and Lance Bombardier Smith of 1st Special Air Service Battalion.

Above: Dudley Clarke's fake SAS stamp.

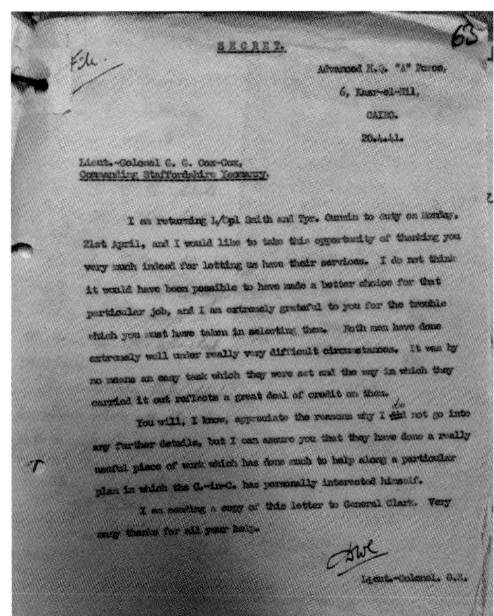

SECRET.

Advanced H.Q. "A" Force,
6, Kasr-el-Nil,
CAIRO.
20.4.41.

Lieut.-Colonel G. G. Cox-Cox,
Commanding Staffordshire Yeomanry.

I am returning L/Cpl Smith and Tpr. Cumming to duty on Monday, 21st April, and I would like to take this opportunity of thanking you very much indeed for letting us have their services. I do not think it would have been possible to have made a better choice for that particular job, and I am extremely grateful to you for the trouble which you must have taken in selecting them. Both men have done extremely well under really very difficult circumstances. It was by no means an easy task which they were set and the way in which they carried it out reflects a great deal of credit on them.

You will, I know, appreciate the reasons why I do not go into any further details, but I can assure you that they have done a really useful piece of work which has done much to help along a particular plan in which the C.-in-C. has personally interested himself.

I am sending a copy of this letter to General Clark. Very many thanks for all your help.

Lieut.-Colonel. G.S.

Right: The congratulatory letter from Dudley Clarke to Gordon Cox-Cox.

He received his commission in September, before being posted to the newly reformed Middle East Commando. A year on, as we shall see, he would rejoin the SAS story.

Operation Abeam seems to have been a success. Rumours began to spread. A Cairo resident reported being told that if parachutists were seen coming down over Cairo there was no cause for alarm 'because they would be British'. The German handbook on the British Army, meanwhile, added 1st SAS Brigade to its list of formations. And Clarke's deception organisation – now known as 'A' Force and situated in offices beneath a Cairo brothel* – began to grow in size and substance. His chain of fake units soon lengthened.

Yet even as his plans were progressing, Clarke almost brought about his own downfall. In October 1941, he was arrested while on an apparently unnecessary visit to neutral Spain. His arrest alarmed the British authorities – but his state of dress positively bewildered them. 'At the time,' wrote Guy Liddell, head of MI5's 'B' Division, 'he was dressed as a woman complete with brassiere. Why he wore this disguise nobody quite knows.'

* This was an ideal location because Clarke did not want attention paid to his unit – and little attention would be paid to a succession of male visitors to a brothel.

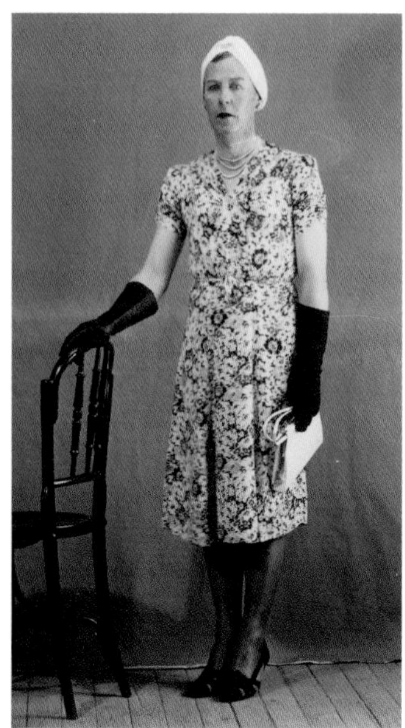

At the time of his arrest, the Spanish police took these striking photographs of Dudley Clarke. His gender contrasts are interesting. As a man his legs are spread; as a woman he faces the camera at a slight angle.

Clarke was extremely fortunate to be handed over by the Spanish police into British custody. He could just as easily have been passed to the Germans. In the event he was free to continue formulating his rules of strategic deception that would bear fruit in operations such as Mincemeat and Bodyguard.

By this time, however, one of his creations was already taking palpable shape. The Special Air Service was far too valuable a concept to remain fake for long.

2

THE WHISPERERS

In June 1941, several weeks after Mick Gurmin wandered around Cairo introducing the Middle East to British parachute troops, a small article appeared in the *Daily Mirror* and various other newspapers worldwide.

Small groups of British paratroopers, flying from southern England, had dropped onto Berck-sur-Mer airfield in the Pas de Calais. Taking the Germans by surprise, they destroyed 30 aircraft on the ground and took prisoners, before boarding motor torpedo boats moored nearby and speeding home to England. This was a brilliantly successful Special Air Service-style parachute raid – but the SAS did not yet exist. So who had carried it out?

The answer was nobody. The raid never took place. It was a story invented by a secret government organisation designed to create fake news. The Sib Committee (from the Latin *sibilare,* to whisper) was a group of bowler-hatted British worthies who met regularly in the incongruous splendour of Woburn Abbey. They received ideas from spy chiefs before working them up into full stories to be passed around the world by rumour-spreading agents or friendly news agencies. They worked with 'a mixture of bureaucratic solemnity and schoolboy zest' to turn fictions like the Berck-sur-Mer raid into apparent facts that might enhance the British war effort.

Fact or fiction, the story's existence suggests that much of the thinking that would inform the soon-to-be-real SAS was already in place. Dudley Clarke's carefully curated Middle Eastern scheme was only one link in a chain leading towards the development of 'Stirling's Mob'.

An extract from the *Daily Mirror*, 19 June 1941.

PARATROOPS HIT NAZIS

—New York Report

How daring British parachutists destroyed a Nazi airport, thirty aeroplanes and took forty German pilots prisoner was told yesterday in a cable to the *New York Post* from Zurich.

Parachutists crossed the Channel in bombers and baled out over the airport in the French town of Berck-sur-Mer

They split into three groups. The first group rushed the control room and seized the occupants before the alarm could be given; the second attacked the barracks and took the prisoners, and the third scattered over the airport and destroyed the planes.

The parachutists then went to a nearby port where torpedo boats waited to take them and the prisoners to England.

The men were home before the Nazis knew what had happened.

3

LAWRENCE IN ARABIA

A vital early link in the chain was T.E. Lawrence and his band of Great War desert guerrillas.

The adventures of 'Lawrence of Arabia' became the stuff of popular legend after the First World War. A presentation, playing to 10,000 people a day at the Royal Albert Hall, followed by the publication of Lawrence's exotic memoir, spread the word. With its mix of military adventure, colonial confidence and spice-scented Arabian Nights,* Lawrence's story

T. E. Lawrence.

* Not to mention a whiff of Tutankhamun's tomb, discovered by Howard Carter in 1922.

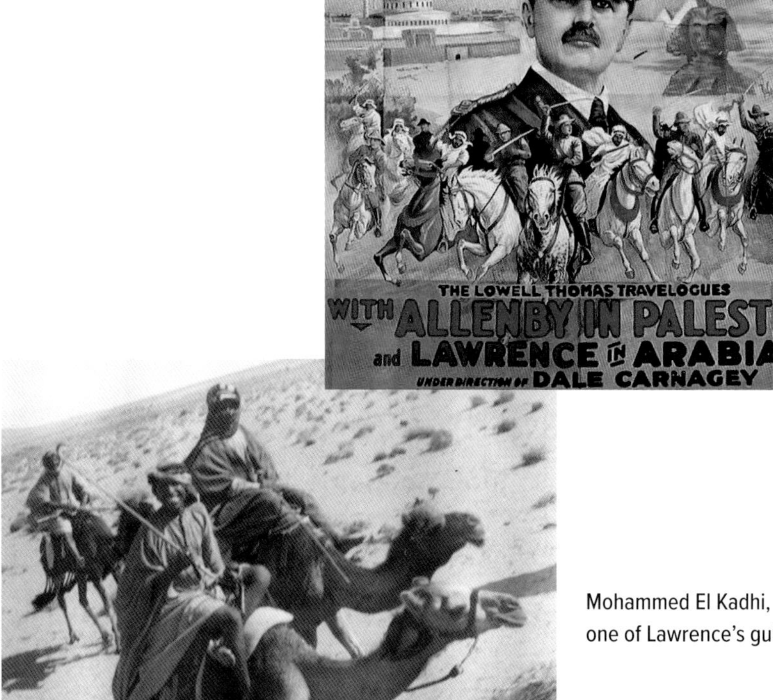

Mohammed El Kadhi, one of Lawrence's guides.

served as an antidote to the folk-memory of misery and mass slaughter on the Western Front.

By the start of the next war, any mention of 'the desert' was liable to turn British thoughts to the legend of Lawrence and his free-spirited warriors. Influential figures were keen to cite him as an inspiration, among them Sir Archibald Wavell and Winston Churchill.

Yet there was plenty of truth behind the legend. Seated on camels, as the SAS would later use trucks and jeeps, Lawrence led self-supporting units of carefully chosen men. His groups were small, though larger than the subsequent four- or five-man SAS teams. And he preferred – at least, usually – to avoid pointless risk or loss of life. 'To me,' he wrote, 'an unnecessary action, or shot, or casualty was not only waste, but sin.'

In November 1917 Lawrence mounted a sabotage raid on a railway line passing over the Yarmuk Gorge near the Sea of Galilee. This was a dangerous mission, far behind enemy lines, but it would greatly assist the coming British assault on Beersheba. The plan was to blow a bridge supporting the railway line. Gelignite was to be attached to the girders and a thousand yards of lightweight electric cable were to lead from the explosive to a hand-operated detonator. In the event, however, Lawrence was provided with a much shorter length of inferior cable which would place the detonator just 250 yards from the bridge. But even this was never used. As the raiding party edged towards the bridge, a rifle was dropped with a loud clatter. Enemy guards reacted quickly – and Lawrence's men had to run for their lives, leaving behind most of their precious cable.

Desperate to salvage something from the botched raid, Lawrence moved south to another stretch of railway line. Near the village of Minifir, explosive was laid beneath the track. Only 60 yards of cable now remained, reaching a solitary bush. As a train passed, Lawrence, hidden

Left: The railway bridge across the Yarmuk Gorge, which Lawrence and his men tried to destroy in November 1917.

Right: The railway passed through a deep cutting near El Akhthar.

behind the bush, pushed down the handle of the detonator – and nothing happened.

Adjustments were swiftly made until, after an agonising wait, another train appeared. This time the explosion was huge. All manner of debris rained down on Lawrence, perched behind his bush:

> Between my knees lay the exploder, crushed under a twisted sheet of sooty iron. In front of me was the scalded and smoking upper half of a man. When I peered through the dust and steam of the explosion the whole boiler of the first engine seemed to be missing.

As he came to his senses, under fire from soldiers further down the train, a sentence appeared in Lawrence's head: 'Oh, I wish this hadn't happened.' Chanting it aloud in the style of a Buddhist mantra, this most unorthodox of British officers stumbled away to safety. His men shot up what they could, suffering casualties in the process, before finally making off into the desert.

For all his obfuscating legend, Lawrence was a truly inventive military thinker. His operations almost invariably took the enemy by surprise. Rather than engaging and attempting to deliver a knockout blow, his men would materialise suddenly to harass lines of communication. This led to opponents being pulled from forward positions to protect the flanks. And in the process, the enemy would come to fear the shapeless threat 'drifting about like a gas' somewhere in the silent desert. The psychological effect was profound.

The remains of Lawrence's sabotaged train, photographed in 2017.

Lowell Thomas, an American journalist who popularised Lawrence's story after the Great War.

A 1922 portrait of Lawrence by William Roberts. By now, Lawrence was in the Royal Air Force under the name 'Ross'. The following year he changed his name to 'Shaw.'

There were fundamental differences, of course, between the Arab force and the SAS as it later developed in the desert. Lawrence's focus, for example, was on tactical operations while the SAS was intended as a strategic force. But Lawrence's influence on the wartime SAS would be demonstrated many times in its future activities. From his emphasis on surprising the enemy to his experimentation with new kinds of explosives, the parallels are marked.

Lawrence, for example, was not a man who blindly followed the existing rules. He always looked to adapt theories and practices – as would the SAS throughout its wartime existence. (Although the SAS, as we shall see, would sometimes find itself reacting to the enemy, and sometimes to interference from its own side.)

Yet, similarities aside, Lawrence had another, less obvious but very real impact on the creation of the SAS. He was, as Lord Carver – chief of the general staff and wartime tank commander – has observed, a strong

Colonel Blimp as drawn by David Low.

influence on Wavell and Churchill's preference for irregular methods. Sir David Hunt, a former private secretary to Churchill, goes even further. He notes that the attitudes of senior army officers towards irregular operations in the early part of the Second World War were strongly influenced by memories of two colonels – Lawrence and Blimp. 'They were like two figures in an allegory,' writes Hunt, 'representing Hope and Fear.' Senior figures knew that, courtesy of Lawrence, the British public approved of unorthodox officers. And they knew that, thanks to the fuddy-duddy cartoon character Colonel Blimp, the public believed regular officers to be alarmingly stupid. These two cultural totems, argues Hunt, made it dangerous for High Command to turn down *any* unorthodox project.

On this reading, by 1941, the late Thomas Edward Lawrence (or Shaw, as he became to distance himself from celebrity) was practically holding the door open for the SAS.

4

MOSQUITO ARMY

Clearly the SAS was not the first irregular British unit – or 'private army' – to operate in the Middle East. But it was not even the first to operate there during the Second World War. In 1940, Ralph Bagnold (another man heavily influenced by Lawrence) had formed the Long Range Patrol.*

During the 1920s, Bagnold, a signals officer stationed in the Nile Valley, drove off into the desert, and fell in love with it. He was soon leading regular desert expeditions to unmapped regions, culminating in a series of epic motor journeys into the heart of the Egyptian-Libyan desert. He crossed the Great Sand Sea, an arid wilderness of shifting dunes almost as large as Ireland, dismissing it as an area 'where the careless might well get lost'. Such muscular understatement, reminiscent of a John Buchan hero, obscures the reality. Bagnold and his colleagues were true pioneers whose imagination and hard-won expertise would shape the war in the Middle East and beyond.

During their explorations, Bagnold's team developed numerous desert tools and techniques. They reduced their tyre pressures, and stripped their cars of unnecessary weight, such as canopies, bonnets and radiator covers. They condensed steam as it boiled out of their radiators, ensuring that engines needed little supplementary water (making more available for drinking). Bagnold even developed his own 'sun-compass' to plot a course through an environment without landmarks where no life existed beyond a few lost, starving birds. This daylight compass, which allowed the party to remain on a course set each night by starlight, proved extremely accurate.

* The original name of the Long Range Desert Group. It was changed in November 1940.

After a hundred-mile trek, following the shadow cast by the needle, the expedition would seldom find itself more than a mile off course.

Bagnold also developed a specialised style of driving. The Sand Sea consisted of endless sandy waves, similar in appearance and behaviour to ocean waves. Noticing regular gaps of tightly packed sand between them, Bagnold found that these could be climbed if charged at high speed. He described the experience to armchair explorers in a series of features in *The Times* newspaper:

> Once upon this firm sand all feeling of motion ceases, and even the eye fails, through lack of any detail in the great golden curves, to register speed, direction, or gradient. Only the speedometer, creeping up steadily to 50 or 60 miles an hour tells one to beware. Then – crash! The car stops up to its axles in sand . . .

The group had to learn how to free their vehicles using metal sand channels and canvas sand mats. They had to work out the most suitable clothes to wear and the best rations to carry for weeks away from

Ralph Bagnold.

A Second World War-era sun-compass as originally designed by Bagnold.

Stills from a film documenting Bagnold and his team's 1929 explorations into the Great Sand Sea.

civilisation. Taken together, these tough lessons gave Bagnold and his colleagues a remarkable degree of self-sufficiency. They would also give the Special Air Service a platform from which to build.

Bagnold was captivated by his surroundings from the earliest days. He recalls the thrill of 'driving into unknown and unmapped country where perhaps no one had been since Stone Age people left due to lack of water [and] finding oneself alone among their implements and the ashes of their ancient hearths'.

Many other desert travellers and soldiers shared this excitement. Some were struck by the freedom, others by the romance. George Lloyd, companion to T.E. Lawrence and future colonial secretary, effused in his diary about meeting an Arab sheikh who, in the moonlight, reminded him of 'some modern Saladin out to meet a crusade'. Ahmed Hassanein, an explorer of the Sand Sea, felt a passion that alternated between joy and despair:

> It is as though a man were deeply in love with a very fascinating but cruel woman. She treats him badly, and the world crumples in his hand; at night she smiles on him and the whole world is a paradise. The desert smiles and there is no place on earth worth living in but the desert.

Yet, captivated as he was, Bagnold remained a practical soldier, able to view the desert in level-headed military terms. One evening he found himself camped hundreds of miles south of Cairo alongside an Italian army detachment. Over dinner he chatted with Major Orlando Lorenzini about

Bagnold's dinner in the desert with Major Orlando Lorenzini.

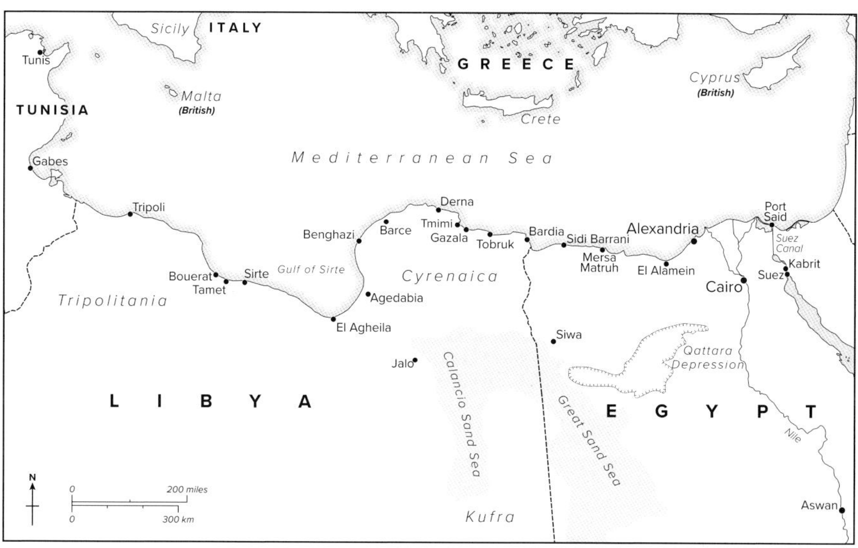

their shared passion for desert motoring. At the time there was no prospect of war, so Lorenzini felt able to tease Bagnold. What fun it would be, he said, if he were to drive his battalion directly across the southern part of the desert to capture the Aswan Dam. Britain's command of the region would be jeopardised – yet what could the British possibly do to stop him?

Bagnold knew that the answer was *nothing*. The Egyptian-Libyan desert below the coastal corridor, an area almost as large as the Indian peninsula, was of no interest to the British military authorities. There were no plans to set foot in it. And there the matter rested for almost a decade, until the outbreak of war and the now-retired Bagnold's recall into the British Army.

It would have made sense, in 1939, for Bagnold to be posted to Egypt, but he was sent instead to East Africa, an area about which he knew nothing. On his way to Kenya, however, his troopship was involved in a collision, and he was landed temporarily at Port Said. Taking advantage of the opportunity, Bagnold made a quick detour to Cairo to catch up with old friends. While there, he was recognised by a news reporter who filed a report:

> Major Bagnold's presence in Egypt at this time seems a reassuring indication that one of the cardinal errors of 1914–18 is not to be repeated. During that war, if a man had made a name for himself as an

> explorer of Egyptian deserts, he would almost certainly . . . have been employed digging tunnels under the Messines Ridge. Nowadays, of course, everything is done better.

The piece (possibly more ironic than it appeared) was spotted by the *Daily Telegraph* in London, which published its own version. More important for the sake of British wartime prospects, it was spotted by Wavell, the recently appointed Middle East commander, who summoned Bagnold to the shortest of meetings. The result was a posting to a signals unit in Egypt – where Bagnold found the military authorities just as indifferent to the desert as they had been years before.

Given its scant resources, the army's lack of interest was perhaps understandable. If the Italians were ever to attack Egypt, they would likely mount an assault from Libya along the coastal corridor. Their forces, vastly outnumbering those of the British, would then be met by a single armoured division. But what if Lorenzini, or a similarly desert-minded officer, had *already* drawn up plans to attack along the southern frontier? Bagnold was disappointed, but hardly surprised, to find that the army had given no thought whatsoever to the vulnerable south. He quickly came up with a plan inspired by his old expeditions. A small force, using adapted American vehicles, could patrol large, otherwise unobservable parts of the desert.

Bagnold's force would cost very little in financial or manpower terms yet promised to keep a watch on a large area. He sent his plan up the chain

Mussolini declares war on Britain and France from the balcony of the Palazzo Venezia in Rome.

Archibald Wavell (far right) makes a point in the desert.

of command in late 1939 and again in early 1940, but on both occasions it was rejected before reaching Wavell.

In June 1940, however, Italy entered the war in alliance with Germany. The Mediterranean Sea was all but closed to British traffic and the only practicable means of reaching Egypt from Britain was an epic sea voyage around the Cape of Good Hope. An Italian attack on Egypt seemed inevitable.

Leaving nothing to chance, Bagnold now exploited a mutual contact to make sure that a copy of his plan was placed directly in front of Wavell. An hour later, standing in front of the commander-in-chief, Bagnold finally had the chance to sell his idea. He began by explaining that his vehicles could travel anywhere in the desert to observe the Italians. Wavell was unconvinced – so Bagnold tried another approach. 'How about some piracy on the high desert?' he asked. Wavell smiled. 'Can you be ready in six weeks?'

Archibald Wavell, cutting through giant knots of red tape, had just issued Ralph Bagnold, a man who had landed in Egypt by accident, with his own private army. But how would it function, given the likely oppos-

New Zealand members of the Long Range Patrol (as it was still known in the Autumn of 1940).

ition of the army establishment, and the inevitable obstructions that would be placed in its way? The answer came at once.

Wavell issued Bagnold with a magic charm in the form of a typed memo. 'To all heads of department and branches,' it read, 'I wish any request made by Major Bagnold in person to be granted immediately and without question.' Bagnold was astounded by Wavell's gesture. 'What a man!' he later wrote.

Bagnold began to assemble his force straight away. Chevrolet trucks were found and adapted. Tough, eager volunteers from the Second New Zealand Division were recruited. And every crumb of knowledge from Bagnold's previous expeditions (from headdresses and radiators to sandals and sun compasses) was applied.

The result was that, on 15 September 1940, as Italian forces invaded Egypt from Libya, a much quieter invasion was underway several hundred miles to the south. This tiny incursion, heading in the opposite direction, consisted of two of Bagnold's patrols driving across the border into the Libyan desert.

Bagnold's men were mainly focused on reconnaissance, but with an eye always open for 'piracy'. Frank Jopling was a New Zealander with one of the patrols. Against regulations, he kept a diary, which forced him to hide himself away at intervals to record his thoughts. They reveal, above all, immense excitement to be involved in a unique adventure: 'The map of this part of Africa is just a white sheet of paper with no markings on it at all – so I don't suppose there has ever been anyone here except Major Bagnold in 1932.'

Jopling's thoughts were confirmed when he spotted tyre tracks in southern Libya which turned out to be the imprints left by Bagnold's expedition eight years before. As time went on, Jopling became enthused by many of Bagnold's old enthusiasms. He was excited to find stone artefacts in the remains of an ancient village. And he could barely contain his wonder at the strangeness of desert driving:

> Talk about thrills, it was great!! Travelling at 80kph up and down smooth sand dunes. I had to keep looking at the speedo to see if we were moving, to look at the sand in front you would think that we were standing still.

A feature of the diary is how strikingly, in its descriptions of the patrol's daily existence, it anticipates the SAS. When a truck was stuck deep in the

Long Range Desert Group life in 1941. Note the man asleep on the truck.

Chevrolet trucks on their way to attack Murzuk.

sand, for example, all ranks were encouraged to come up with a solution. The men were not sidelined. Eventually an ordinary trooper improvised a method for setting the truck free. In this unit, everyone had to be able to think for themselves, as Jopling understood: 'When Major Bagnold decided on who to have on the trip, he wanted good daring drivers who could use their heads.'

The result was increased responsibility, greater self-respect and less distinction between ranks. Jopling was surprised, one morning, to be served his morning tea in bed by his troop leader. 'What a war!' he marvelled. Traditional relationships and behaviours were shifting. The SAS would become noted for its relaxed, self-imposed discipline – but this was really an inherited trait.

The Long Range Desert Group (LRDG) also anticipated the SAS in its willingness to attack. A year before the SAS began operations, desert raiding was underway.

Twice in September, Jopling's patrol tried to ambush Italian desert camps, only to find them abandoned. A number of trucks were captured, however, together with prisoners. Jopling's patrol then raided an Italian fort on the western edge of the Great Sand Sea at Awjila. But the most ambitious attack came when Wavell gave Bagnold free rein to pick his own target. Bagnold chose Murzuk, an Italian garrison and aerodrome near the south-west corner of Libya, well over a thousand miles from Cairo.

Jopling took part in the assault, which inflicted serious damage and heavy casualties. He then watched as enemy aircraft were soaked in petrol and set on fire.

By the spring of 1941, Wavell's 'mosquito army' (as he privately described the Long Range Desert Group) was watching enemy movements, attacking their positions, capturing men and vehicles, destroying aircraft, transporting spies, rescuing lost souls, and ranging freely across unexplored desert. It would shortly accept another role – transporting Special Air Service men to and from raids.* This is how the LRDG and the SAS are most widely thought to have been connected, but their relationship was in truth more fundamental. Had Ralph Bagnold never formed his private army, it is very difficult to imagine how David Stirling's could have taken shape as it did.

In fact, their earliest incarnations even shared a duplicitous purpose. Writing years after the war, Bagnold claimed to understand why Wavell had wanted the LRDG to be formed so quickly:

> I remembered that [Wavell] was the leading exponent of strategic deception. Faced with the probability of being attacked in overwhelming numbers, he was going to delay the enemy by bluff ... The small unit I proposed, with its extraordinary mobility and endurance, could create ... the impression of British ubiquity throughout the interior of Libya.

In other words the Long Range Desert Group, like the Special Air Service, was originally created as a deception unit. The more successful they became, of course, the better they served this purpose – until they both became so well known that they failed to serve it at all.

Sharing so much military DNA, it is probably unsurprising that when, in January 1941, Sergeant Johnny Cooper of the SAS revealed the existence of the Special Air Service to an American reporter in Tunisia, he was equally quick to speak about the Long Range Desert Group. 'They're very

* This role led to the poaching of members. The SAS's finest desert navigator, Mike Sadler, whom we will meet shortly, had been an LRDG man who impressed the SAS so much that he was nabbed.

similar to us,' Cooper told A.J. Liebling of the *New Yorker*. Yet while their intentions, and even their methods, may have coincided, we should be careful about bracketing the Long Range Desert Group and the Special Air Service too closely together. Mike Sadler, who served with both, believes that the LRDG remained true to the spirit of Bagnold, whereas the essence of the SAS lay in the very different ideas of its own founder:

> [The LRDG's] job was really about getting to know the desert. Exploring. Finding ways through it. The SAS was more on the aggressive side. That was David Stirling's idea. It was a different outlook.

That aggression came, most immediately, from another side of the family.

5

THE SMART SET

Dudley Clarke arrived in the Middle East in late 1940 to develop the art of deception under his old friend Archibald Wavell. But, several months earlier, serving as Sir John Dill's military assistant in London, Clarke had been set a more desperate task. With the country on the verge of capitulation, he was asked to respond to Winston Churchill's request for some way of hitting back at the enemy. Inspired by his early childhood in the Transvaal, he had proposed a force based on the Boer Commandos, loose-knit bands of horsemen who had struck against the more powerful British during the South African War.

Boer Commandos.

A modern equivalent of the Boer Commandos, argued Clarke, could 'hit sharp and quick, then run to fight another day'. And, given Britain's geography and her naval power, he imagined the modern version as an amphibious force, arriving by sea at the most favourable point of attack and slipping away before the enemy could summon its defences.

The desperate circumstances freed Clarke's imagination. His ideal commando, he wrote, had to have 'a dash of the Elizabethan pirate, the Chicago gangster, and the Frontier tribesman'. These were not the qualities of the steadfast infantryman, that bedrock of the British army. Clarke was calling for a different type of soldier, a man with initiative, who was willing to think and act independently of those around him.

Clarke's production quickly took shape, and, as was often the case, he gave himself a starring role. Just three weeks after suggesting the idea, he sailed for the French coast as part of the first Commando raid. One of his parties landed near Le Touquet where a firefight took place. Two German sentries were killed, and a grenade was tossed into a building. The only British casualty was Clarke himself – though he was unaware of his wound until, arriving back on his ship, a petty officer stared at his ear. 'God almighty, sir!' he said. 'It's almost coming off!'

The raid achieved little in practice, but it was reported in the press and gave the British people a sense that the nation was fighting back. It also popularised the Commando name, allowing Clarke to begin recruiting in earnest. One of his first recruits was actor David Niven, who was quickly promoted to captain and made liaison officer between the unit and the War Office. While on leave, Niven met Winston Churchill, who asked him what he was now doing. Niven excitedly described his new job until the prime minister cut him off. 'Your security is very lax,' said Churchill gravely. 'You shouldn't be telling me this!' Niven never discovered whether he was serious or not.

Back at work, Niven's most important intervention was to ensure that his friend (and future father-in-law) Bob Laycock joined the commandos.

Laycock was an immensely well-connected officer in the Royal Horse Guards who sought challenge and adventure. After a successful cavalry career he had sailed halfway around the world as an ordinary seaman on a Finnish windjammer. Now he took command of the newly raised No. 8

Dudley Clarke, David Niven and Bob Laycock: a chain leading to the birth of the SAS.

Commando, and began recruiting an unusual selection of officers. Many were Laycock's friends from White's Club in London: men such as Lord Fitzwilliam, Lord Sudeley, Lord Stavordale, Toby Milbanke, Gavin Astor and the future Earl of Munster. Abounding with wealth and titles, this group became known as the 'smart set'.

Author Evelyn Waugh joined on the recommendation of Minister of Information, Brendan Bracken, who assured Laycock that Waugh would prove an asset 'in the dreary business of war'. Waugh's relationship with the smart set would prove interesting. He occasionally viewed them with critical detachment, but more often cosied up to them, dazzled by their effortless superiority. Another unlikely officer was Randolph Churchill, the overweight, self-regarding but near-fearless son of the prime minister, who was chosen for his influence with his father. Scattered among this crowd were genuinely talented officers who would, before long, make their mark on the Special Air Service.

The great majority of the other ranks, meanwhile, were drawn from the army's most exclusive regiments. Entire troops came from the Household Cavalry, the Grenadier Guards, the Coldstream Guards and the Scots Guards. These men, including Jimmy Brough, Bob Lilley, Pat Riley, Chris O'Dowd, Jim Almonds, Ernie Bond, Jim Blakeney, Johnny Rose, Dave Kershaw, Anthony Drongin, Fred Casey, Bob Bennett and many others, were the solid foundation on which the SAS would soon be built.

Like their officers, these men were unusual, though for different reasons. Jim Almonds was a Coldstream Guards sergeant who had marched behind the coffin at George V's funeral in 1936. Six feet two inches tall and well-built, Almonds had an extremely inquisitive mind. Able to identify different stars, animals and plants, he frequently disappeared on fishing trips, and took pleasure in building things. He was deeply frustrated in his current job, that of training recruits, and was desperate for the chance to start thinking for himself. With more than a dash of the pirate about him, he was exactly the sort of soldier Dudley Clarke was looking for.

Along with friend and fellow Coldstream Guards sergeant Pat Riley, Almonds had begun applying for a variety of jobs – from trawler gunner to Finnish ski-soldier – but both of them had been consistently turned down. Their futures were sealed in the summer of 1940, however, when Riley had a chance conversation with George Jellicoe, one of Laycock's aristocratic officers. Jellicoe briefly explained what the Commandos would entail, and asked Riley whether he was interested. Riley *was* interested, as was Almonds. Within days the pair reported for training.

Above: Evelyn Waugh.

Left: Randolph and Pamela Churchill.

Jim Almonds and Pat Riley (far right).

Bob Bennett was a member of the Grenadier Guards who had grown tired of brass-polishing and square-bashing. He started applying for the same sorts of jobs as Almonds and Riley until his major warned that if he attempted to leave the guards again, he would find himself in gaol. One afternoon, without warning, he was marched to the orderly room. Fearing the worst, he was led along a line of queuing guardsmen until he reached the front. There stood his major, who said, 'You're off to the Commandos!' Bennett was surprised – and delighted.

8 Commando was sent to Burnham-on-Crouch in Essex, where the other ranks encountered a new style of soldiering. Jimmy Brough, of the Scots Guards, was told to go and find his own billet among the local population. This reflected Dudley Clarke's idea of fostering a unit of individuals thinking and fending for themselves. The men were set regular initiative tests. Brough was sent out one morning with instructions to cross a river, find a church and ask a vicar how long the war would last. (The vicar's answer, at a time when many Britons quietly expected a German invasion at any moment, was a reassuring 'six years.')

Initiative took many forms. Brough remembers a deal reached with a local pub landlord. Each day the landlord would watch out for the commandos, in the distance, as they completed a gruelling country march. As soon as he saw their outlines coming over the hill, he 'started filling pint pots and by the time we were dismissed the counter was covered with pints soon to be quaffed'.

While most of 8 Commando drank and trained in Essex, small groups of officers and NCOs were sent to a new school for irregular warfare, created and overseen by Bill Stirling – David's elder brother – at Lochailort in western Scotland. Here they were introduced to a variety of unorthodox procedures, including methods of sabotage and silent killing that would, in due course, be adopted by the SAS. Among the instructors were captains Fairbairn and Sykes, who introduced themselves to students in striking terms:

> We're police officers from Shanghai, the dirtiest, bloodiest, most corrupt city in the world. We have an average of two murders a day and we have to deal with them in our way. It's not approved by the powers that be, but it works. We want you to get the dirtiest, bloodiest ideas that you can get in your head of how to destroy a human being.

One of Fairbairn and Sykes's favoured training methods was to bring students to an abattoir, where they were asked to plunge knives into recently killed animals and then try to pull them out again. The idea was to give the students a feel for (near-human) flesh. As one man recalled many years later: 'The contraction of the sinews is such that it's very difficult to get out. It's not like you see on TV.'

In late 1940 all members of 8 Commando moved to Scotland where intensive mountain and coastal landing training began. Shortly afterwards, Nos. 7, 8 and 11 Commandos were brought together as 'Layforce', a composite unit under Bob Laycock's command. They sailed in early February for the Middle East on board the infantry landing ships HMS *Glenroy* and *Glengyle.*

Conditions on the ships were uncomfortable for the officers, particularly as some of them, reports Waugh, 'had brought luggage enough for a film star's honeymoon'. But conditions for the men were far worse: crammed below decks, many were violently sick for days as gales raged. The officers passed the time giving each other lectures. Randolph Churchill spoke about parliamentary procedure; Peter Beatty, whose horse had won the 1938 Derby, talked of racing; Roger Courtney gave advice on how to behave in Muslim countries, with emphasis on the likely consequences of ignoring sexual taboos.

Mostly, though, the officers of 8 Commando gambled for extraordinary sums of money and bullied the well-meaning naval officers, who

HMS *Glenroy*.

were laughed at as amateurs and inferiors. Waugh, glorying in borrowed prestige, scorned them as 'a pathetic collection of youths straight from insurance offices, who had nothing in common with 8 Commando'. These 'dreary fellows' were evidently the prototypes for *Brideshead Revisited*'s Hooper, a character who embodies the banality of the modern world. But if the smart set looked down on the navy, they were disdained in turn by their own men, who considered them smooth-talkers with plenty to say but not much worth listening to.

At least one 8 Commando officer took little part in the taunting of the navy. David Stirling (whose arrival at 8 Commando had been greeted with 'considerable guffaws' from his colleagues due to his questionable military record) was now spending so much time asleep in his cabin that he was dubbed 'the giant sloth'.

Layforce arrived in the Middle East expecting to be launched into action. Instead it was placed in reserve near Alexandria. This anticlimax followed the success of an Axis force led by General Erwin Rommel, which had retaken ground only recently captured by British Commonwealth forces.* When the Germans subsequently invaded Greece and Yugoslavia,

* This marked the start of the 'pendulum of war', which saw each side moving backwards and forwards over the same territory until the cycle was eventually broken by Montgomery's victory at El Alamein.

Left: Walter 'Tich' Cowan in 1919.

Below right: HMS *Aphis*.

the Royal Navy was called into urgent action. This, in turn, limited the amount of shipping available for commando raids.

Laycock, determined to find a role, argued that Layforce should be used to attack the large Axis flank along the Mediterranean coast. His cause was helped by a timely intervention from Winston Churchill demanding that German lines of communication be harassed – so Layforce was given the job of attacking the enemy-held coastal town of Bardia.

Taking part in this attack – and highlighting the extremely strange nature of Layforce – was seventy-year-old Admiral Walter 'Tich' Cowan. An unlikely individual to be serving as a front-line soldier, Cowan had never attended school, instead joining the Royal Navy as a boy. He had spent his formative years serving with the Mediterranean fleet in the days of masts and yards. He liked to describe himself as 'an old-style sailor'.

As a midshipman in his teens, Cowan had worked aloft in the rigging. It was not an easy life. 'If a man didn't prove himself a sailor in every sense of the word,' he later recalled, 'he had a dog's life.' This was a world in which duty and humility were valued above all else. Once, while trying to remedy a jammed gun, Cowan forgot about the men around him – and was given a robust reminder:

> Time was passing for the sailors to get back to their tea. The commander, F.W. Fisher, who was in my cutter, knocked me flat with his fist. None of us ever minded what he did because he never stopped our leave.

Cowan was to enjoy a glittering naval career spanning six decades before he retired in 1931 as Admiral Sir Walter Cowan, Baronet of the Baltic. He had served as aide-de-camp to Lord Kitchener during the Boer War, before commanding a battlecruiser during the Battle of Jutland. Much of his retirement was spent fox-hunting and it was on returning home, exhilarated, from the season's final hunt in 1941, that he decided to extend his own season by joining the war. He began approaching influential friends, offering to serve in any rank, until Admiral Sir Roger Keyes, Director of Combined Operations, agreed to find him a job. This was how he found himself on the Bardia raid alongside men a fraction of his age.

The raid started awkwardly for Cowan as the landing craft approached the port. He was in extreme discomfort 'because Evelyn Waugh, rather

on the bulky side, was unknowingly most of him sitting on me, but I was so pleased at being at last involved in an enterprise that I felt I had better endure it'. Once ashore the various assault parties set out to their objectives – but things quickly began to go wrong. 'It was all rather like finding a wasp's nest and stirring it up with a stick,' reported Cowan. Little damage was done to the town and the commandos had extreme difficulty getting away. Five officers and 60 men were captured, with Cowan's landing craft almost sinking as it drew off. 'At once the water surged in and the men were in process of being drowned,' he wrote. The landing craft stayed afloat – but barely managed to struggle back to HMS *Glengyle*.

Bob Laycock considered the raid a miserable failure – and the next few weeks brought no further action. Officers and men grew frustrated. For Dave Kershaw, a Grenadier Guards sergeant who had fought in the Spanish Civil War, it felt 'like wanting to get married and finding that your girl has deserted you'. People found other things to do. Some, like David Stirling and Randolph Churchill, devoted themselves to their social lives. Others increased their spending power: Jimmy Brough and a few friends got hold of plaster of Paris (used by the medics) and bottle-tops (used by everybody). When they had enough, they began melting the bottle-tops into moulds carved from the plaster. The resulting coins, remembers Brough, were so realistic that they 'passed very easily in the Australian canteen on Saturday night'.

Finally, in the middle of May, another raid was organised. Eleven officers and 99 other ranks of 8 Commando (now 'B' Battalion, Layforce) boarded HMS *Aphis*, a river gunboat, for an attack on the enemy position near the besieged port of Tobruk.

Each day for a week after the party set off, it came under attack from Stuka dive-bombers, Junkers 88 medium bombers and Italian Savoia 79 bombers. The Stukas descended almost vertically to drop their bombs before pulling up with little room to spare above the ship. Bombs were landing on one side of the ship, passing underneath, and exploding on the other. The deck was constantly cascaded with water.

The experience was hellish for all involved – except for one man. Walter Cowan was spotted walking up and down the deck calling to his batman and eagerly firing his Tommy gun at dive-bombers. It soon dawned on his fellow commandos that his ambition was not quite the same as theirs. They were hoping to survive – while he was plainly hoping to die. For a man of his generation whose life had been informed by war and service, death in battle now seemed preferable to illness and decline. A fearless life would be concluded by a glorious death. The Luftwaffe, however, failed to oblige him. Of the estimated 172 bombs aimed at HMS *Aphis*, not one achieved a direct hit, although the ship was sufficiently damaged that the raid had to be called off.

On 20 May, 'A' Battalion of Layforce was sent to Crete where, instead of mounting an attack, it covered the retreat of the battered Allied forces. This had not been Clarke's intention for the Commandos, and many men were wounded or captured. Layforce had, in truth, been dying for some time, and it came as little surprise when, eventually, the decision was taken to disband it. Its members were left homeless.

A Eureka landing craft.

'Tich' Cowan while serving with Layforce.

Some of the men, whose original regiments were present in the Middle East, went back to those units. Jimmy Brough, back with the Scots Guards, was soon driving a Lancia truck which carried a thousand gallons of petrol in leaky tins. It was not a job he relished. Dave Kershaw and Bob Bennett were sent to the Guards Base Depot near Suez where the instructors considered them little more than traitors. They had willingly transferred away from the army's finest regiments and their treatment now reflected the fact. Chased around the drill square all day, Bennett remembers it as a 'period of misery'. Dejected and abandoned, these men had taken a chance on a new style of unit, which had failed through no fault of their own. Their adventure, it seemed, had come to end.

There were, however, a few spirited individuals who tried to keep the adventure going. Carol Mather and George Jellicoe hatched a plan to repeat the *Aphis* raid on a tiny scale. The two of them would attack the same target from an American landing craft known as a Eureka boat. Three nights running they attempted to land. Each night, they failed.

Mather and Jellicoe (both future SAS officers) were unable to raise a phoenix from Layforce's ashes. But two other 8 Commando officers, Jock Lewes and David Stirling, were also coming up with ideas. These two very different men, reflecting on the situation separately, both understood. Moreover, they both knew how much could be learned from the past and from those currently achieving success in the desert.

Meanwhile, Walter Cowan remained a determined old man. On leaving the Commandos, he served with 3rd Indian Motor Brigade at the Battle of Bir Hakeim, where he made another attempt to die, this time by refusing to surrender to the crew of an Italian armoured car. Twice he was told to put his hands up and twice he refused. A machine gun was fired at him at near point-blank range, but every bullet missed. Cowan was then taken prisoner – to his apparent disappointment. He later wrote of his experience:

> I had no feeling of dread or desire to take cover but only of great interest that in a second or two I was going to be on the other side of the curtain and finished entirely with this life. It felt all very matter of fact and I had not a regret and probably owing to having just had a very good breakfast I was feeling as well as I ever could be.

Cowan would have many more good breakfasts. He survived the war, dying in 1956 aged eighty-four.

6

THE BIRTH: Jock Lewes

As Layforce ground to a sad halt, Dudley Clarke was busy with Operation Abeam, thinking up ways of convincing the enemy that British parachutists were about to deploy in the Middle East. Mick Gurmin had recently been earning Clarke's praise (and a commission) for his fully committed performance as a trooper in 1st Special Air Service Brigade. Yet Clarke had not staged any actual parachuting that might be observed. That was about to change.

Clarke had information that Helwan airfield, south of Cairo, was being watched by enemy observers. He now decided to give them 'something definite to report'. He laid out rows of fake aircraft, and demanded the enemy's attention by warning the police that parachute drops were about to take place. Then he attached parachutes to dummies and dropped several of them from RAF aircraft.

Observers were also watching Fuka airfield, further to the west. There, two entirely separate plans were about to come together, with significant consequences for the future SAS. One of the plans was Dudley Clarke's. He now wanted to drop real parachutists.

The other plan came from Jock Lewes of 8 Commando. His plan was a considered attempt to create a desert-based parachute team capable of mounting raids on enemy targets. He acknowledged the factors which the commando raids had ignored, chiefly the exploitation of surprise.

Lewes could not simply begin parachuting, however. He had first to approach Bob Laycock for permission – and his timing was good. Parachuting was the current military vogue, and Winston Churchill, ever keen to embrace the latest thing, was pushing for immediate training of large numbers of parachutists.

Yet there were absolutely no real military parachutists in the Middle East. Bob Laycock, looking to extend the life of Layforce, gave his blessing. In a boyish letter to his father, spilling over with excitement, Lewes wrote:

> I have been allotted a special task with a few picked men. I am delighted with it. We are training together all the time . . . You can imagine how exactly this is what I have been wanting, what indeed I joined this unit to find. I must not write about it, but that is what has been occupying my thoughts and hours since I last wrote to you.

It is worth noting that Lewes says the training is a special task *allotted* to him. This suggests that his plan was being co-opted by Dudley Clarke and now served a dual purpose. As well as furthering Lewes's own aims, it would reinforce Operation Abeam. As his team fell to earth, enemy observers would believe they were watching members of 1st Special Air Service Brigade.

John Steel 'Jock' Lewes.

So, in the summer of 1941, Lewes and five others took off on a trial flight in a Vickers Valentia. They carried with them a dummy made of tent poles and sandbags that was strapped to a parachute and thrown out of the aircraft. It was later found on the ground in an ominously smashed condition. Next, the men jumped from the Valentia with the very vaguest of instructions: they should all dive out, they were told, as though into water. Most of them did and landed in reasonable safety. But one man, David Stirling, 8 Commando's Giant Sloth, had jumped forward, catching his parachute on the aircraft's tail fin. It opened – but not fully. Stirling landed hard, damaging his back and legs, and he also temporarily lost his sight.

The following day, except for Stirling who was now in hospital, the jumpers tried again. This time one man damaged his ankle and Lewes himself injured his back.

So affected was Lewes by the experience that he tried to express it in verse. To jump out of an aeroplane was

> to stand and shrink from earth below and wonder
> Why ever you confide in Time's word
> That moments end and one is like another
> Then suddenly to see the face of dread.

Gazing upwards, the blessed parachute reminded him of 'an angel in panoply, guarding the skies'.

Jock Lewes evidently had a creative streak, but his defining characteristics were determination and self-discipline. Twenty-seven years old in the summer of 1941, he did not fit comfortably among 8 Commando's 'smart set' of officers. His father was a chartered accountant who had taught him, assisted by a half-inch thick cane, to observe a strict set of moral values. Each night, as a boy, he would recite his eight points:

> Love God as our father
> Keep your face to the light
> Tell the truth at all costs
> Think of others
> Forget yourself
> Stick up for the weak

Play the game
Take your beating like a man.

Lewes was no longer a boy, but the eight points still underpinned his thinking. To the playboys of 8 Commando he seemed odd and prudish – but whenever he set his mind to a task he was determined to see it through. His sole aim in the summer of 1941 was to strike hard at the enemy – and it involved the creation of a Middle Eastern parachute force.

Yet despite Lewes's determination and belief, despite the recent popularity of parachuting, despite the existence of a notional Special Air Service, the military authorities cancelled his plans. The trial drops, they decided, had not shown sufficient promise. Lewes was an immensely able officer but he wasn't a natural advocate for his own cause. He had neither the connections nor the brashness to push his idea forward. The door was still ajar for a real parachute unit to step into the fake one's shoes. What was needed was the right person to deliver the right proposal in the right way.

7

THE BIRTH: David Stirling

A seemingly unlikely member of Jock Lewes's (and Dudley Clarke's) parachute project was David Stirling, the 8 Commando lieutenant who had damaged his back and suffered temporary blindness after the first jump. Stirling had asked to join the project – but Lewes initially declined. He was not drawn to the twenty-five-year-old Scottish aristocrat whose values were so obviously different to his own.

For some time before the jump, Stirling had been living a wild drunken existence. Discovering that a dose of oxygen could ease his hangovers, he had become a regular visitor to the Cairo Scottish Hospital where he would find a quiet room to recover from 'pyrexia of unknown origin', as he described his morning-after condition.

This was not the sort of behaviour which commended itself to Lewes. Not only did Stirling seem irresponsible and unreliable, he also displayed a sense of entitlement that the middle-class Lewes disliked and perhaps envied. 'I resented the strength of his persuasion,' he wrote to his father, 'and despised a little his colossal confidence.'

If there was good cause for Lewes to exclude Stirling, there was equal cause for Stirling to want to join. He hoped to distance himself from his growing reputation for disorderly behaviour. In fact, Stirling – who had recently punched an Egyptian taxi-horse in the face while arguing with the driver – was in more trouble than he realised. After an official review of his service record, he had been placed under investigation for malingering on active service.

Yet however justified Lewes's misgivings may have been, he eventually allowed Stirling to join his project. The odd couple jumped together – and, for Stirling, the consequences were huge. In physical terms, he lost the use of his legs and eyes, albeit temporarily.* In career terms, the official investigation into his conduct was halted. In military terms, he was awakened to the true potential of a raiding group dropped behind enemy lines.

Stirling was actually a far more thoughtful soldier than he had appeared to those reviewing his military record. Self-preservation had not been his only motivation for joining Lewes. As he lay recuperating from his injuries in hospital, he asked to see Lewes to explain his ideas.

This is a hinge moment in the genesis of the SAS. Until the parachute drop, Lewes had been the innovator. But once his plan was rejected, Stirling – with the help of his brother Bill, the founder of the Lochailort irregular warfare school – assumed leadership of the project. Whereas Lewes had imagined groups of about ten men carrying out essentially tactical operations, Stirling's plan was more ambitious. His force would consist of smaller groups, dropped by parachute deep into the desert, where they would remain, carrying out reconnaissance of the target before approaching silently, striking quickly and sneaking away. This force, with its flavour of T.E. Lawrence and the Long Range Desert Group, would operate at a strategic level, doing whatever was most likely to hamper the enemy, free from any local commander's whims. Its members would be drawn from the disenchanted and underused – but extremely talented – ranks of Layforce.

Sitting beside him in hospital, Jock Lewes listened to Stirling's ideas approvingly. They were not, after all, dissimilar to his own. But he highlighted problems. How, he asked, would the men get away after a raid? It occurred to Stirling that the LRDG could pick them up at pre-arranged rendezvous. After all, the LRDG was already ferrying Allied agents around the desert; this responsibility would merely extend its taxi operation.

Lewes also wanted to know who would authorise the plan. In truth this was not an insurmountable problem for Stirling. Unlike Lewes, he was a well-connected young man with a gift for persuasion. According to his fellow officer and future colleague Pat Reid, Stirling 'did not always convince by logic, but rather by giving a strong impression that he was sorry

* Stirling's sight came back almost immediately, and he began regaining movement in his legs during a hospital visit from his friend and former Layforce colleague Evelyn Waugh. He never fully recovered, however: back pains and migraines remained with him for the rest of his life.

David Stirling.

for you if you didn't see his point'. Influential friends, such as Dudley Clarke, would happily assist. And Stirling's brother Bill was now a senior staff officer in Cairo and would have little trouble bringing the idea to the attention of the new commander-in-chief, Claude Auchinleck.

On Stirling's discharge from hospital, he went to live with Bill in a flat belonging to a third brother, Peter, who was attached to the British Embassy. There a memorandum was drafted to explain the purpose of the organisation. This was really a sales pitch aimed at Auchinleck, and it made some bold claims.

The organisation, it said, would carry out a crucial role that was not otherwise being attempted: the raiding of enemy lines of communication, aerodromes, oil dumps and similar dispositions. Its deployment of small groups parachuting into the desert at night would allow its men to lie up unobserved and collect valuable information. It would be economical in terms of manpower and supplies and would require no covering troops or air or naval support. Its prospective members, previously of 8 Commando, already had unusually high levels of 'initiative, power of observation and individual resource'. Above all, the organisation would gain the maximum effect from surprise – which Layforce, despite its best efforts, had never been able to achieve.

The memorandum demonstrates how clearly the SAS was already visualised in mid-July 1941. And from Auchinleck's perspective it was an attractive idea. 'The Auk' was an imaginative man who understood that enemy advances relied on long, vulnerable supply chains. Stirling's proposed unit, like Lawrence's in the last war, promised to weaken the chains' links at very little expense. The Auk knew, too, that the LRDG was providing him with valuable information. Stirling's unit would use comparable methods and might achieve comparable results. But the Auk was also under pressure. Churchill was pushing him to display more aggression and to encourage guerrilla warfare. And in person, Auchinleck had very recently been exposed to David Stirling's charm.

Influenced by all these factors, Auchinleck sought approval from the War Office for the formation of the new organisation. In due course, permission for a parachute unit was granted and Stirling began recruiting officers and other ranks from the remnants of Layforce. The Giant Sloth was achieving his goal.

His next task was to persuade Jock Lewes to join him. If the memorandum's claims were to be realised, he would need Lewes's discipline

A thoughtful Stirling photographed in the desert.

Parachute training at Kabrit in November 1941.

and expertise. At first, Lewes declined. In his eyes, Stirling's project was simply an extension of his own plans, and he was nervous of placing them in the hands of a half-hearted dilettante. Yet after sleeping on the offer, he changed his mind, as he explained to his father: 'I trusted in God that night . . . and when David came again in the morning I said yes though I know not why, for I had made no decision in the night.'

Whether the change of heart was prompted by God, or by a vague sense on Lewes's part that he was underestimating Stirling, it was soon vindicated. In early November 1941, Lewes wrote to his father that Stirling was 'rising up out of indifference big and strong and admirable'. He praised Stirling's 'enthusiasm, his energy, his confidence, his courage'. Indeed he went as far as to admit that Stirling 'appreciated the long-term value of my experiment more accurately than I'.

Such was their growing mutual respect that each man would champion the other as the prime mover behind the SAS. According to Mike Sadler, 'David, speaking out of court, used to say that he gave the credit for the SAS largely to Jock Lewes, who he thought knew more practical things about military organisation while he knew more about social connections and influence.'

The point, of course, was that each man had talents the other lacked.

The final word on the subject can rest with Lewes, writing to his father in mid-1941:

> Together we have fashioned this unit. He [Stirling] has established it without and I think I may say I have fashioned it within . . . And now we want to prove ourselves. This unit cannot die as Layforce died.

Yet even once the parachute unit was up and running, it was still serving Dudley Clarke's deception effort. Its existence, after all, would help to convince the enemy that Clarke's growing chain of fake units was in fact genuine. For this reason Clarke wanted members of the real unit to look as distinctive as possible. Stirling and colleagues, with their striking badges, were happy to oblige.

But Clarke's most durable contribution to the new parachute unit would be its name. A recent addition to his SAS brigade had been 'K' Detachment. (This was the unit responsible for the deployment of dummy aircraft at Fuka and Helwan.) Logically, the next unit formed should be 'L' Detachment, SAS Brigade. That next unit was Stirling's – which was how one of the army's most unusual units duly received one of its dreariest names. Jock Lewes was unimpressed: 'My ambition now is to change our name from the present absurd title to 1st (Middle East) Parachute Battalion. After all you can't go on being a detachment all your life.'

Back in April, Mick Gurmin had spent a couple of days as a member of a fake organisation. Months later, others were about to follow him into the real version. Events in the meantime had not proceeded in a straight line; plenty of people had come together at different times to help create the SAS. And 'L' Detachment would, indeed, change its title as it grew – but not, fortunately, to 1st (Middle East) Parachute Battalion. The 'Special Air Service' name was here to stay.

PART TWO

THE DESERT

Parachute training at Kabrit: SAS members climb into a Bristol Bombay.

8

GETTING OFF THE GROUND

As members of 8 Commando, Pat Riley and Jim Almonds had grown very close to Jock Lewes, judging him the best officer they had ever served under. Lewes was now about to join David Stirling in 'L' Detachment, SAS Brigade, as Training Officer, so it was not surprising that he should also try to persuade Riley and Almonds (and their close friends and fellow NCOs Bob Lilley and Jim Blakeney) to join. After a discussion they all agreed, despite having serious misgivings about the new unit's prospects. Bob Lilley says:

> We did not share Jock's view of the rosy future, as a matter of fact, we didn't think there was any future in it at all and we were all of the same opinion that any man who wished to jump from an aircraft was just damned stupid.

Not everybody felt this way. Parachuting appealed to Reg Seekings of 7 Commando. But as he was waiting to be interviewed by David Stirling at the Geneifa Guards Depot, he overheard the man ahead of him being asked why he wanted to be a parachutist. His answer – 'I'll try anything once!' – angered Stirling, who said, 'Yes! And if you don't bloody well like it, you'll just drop out! I don't want people like you!' Seekings took note of what *not* to say – and he was accepted.

All new members travelled to 'L' Detachment's camp at Kabrit, a hundred miles east of Cairo. On arrival there was little to see. The camp consisted of no more than three tents and a truck, standing forlornly on a barren stretch of sand beside the Suez Canal. It was a dispiriting sight – which, partially at least, was a deliberate choice by Lewes. Each new member's

Bob Lilley (left) and Reg Seekings.

reaction to the starkness would reveal how much he *really* wanted to be a parachutist.

Lewes's zealous approach soon left him facing a near-mutiny from disgruntled men who, after being forced to dig holes in the sand, threatened to return to their units. Instead of trying to reason with them, Lewes confronted them. He accused them of having 'a yellow streak a yard wide'. He challenged them to prove him wrong. 'I'll do anything that you do,' he said, 'and you do anything that I do!' The men, some of the toughest and most resilient in the British Army, were so taken aback that they gave in. 'Christ,' recalls Reg Seekings, 'I don't know how he survived.'

Almost every part of 'L' Detachment's early existence at Kabrit amounted to some kind of test set by Lewes. The food, for example, was extremely poor. A hapless orderly had a jam roll shoved in his face after handing Reg Seekings a portion that contained no jam and not much roll. 'Poor little bugger,' recalls Seekings, 'it wasn't his fault.'

The men's first raid was launched soon after their arrival – but not against the enemy. It was another test that, if carried out successfully, would dramatically improve their lives. Three miles away was a well-established

New Zealand camp, guarded by sentries, whose occupants were away on exercise. Stirling and Lewes ordered the men to sneak past the sentries and steal at least 15 tents and whatever else they fancied. The only rule was that no one was allowed to get caught. The next morning, the SAS camp had acquired tents, tables, chairs, jugs, mirrors, hurricane lamps, a gramophone, a table tennis table, a bar and a piano. The men respected the New Zealand troops and had no wish to deprive them, but when they saw how comfortably the Kiwis lived, their concerns quickly faded.

'L' Detachment's training programme, devised by Lewes, was tough and wide-ranging. Time was scheduled for everything, recalls Bob Lilley, except sleep. Training lasted for nine or ten hours every day and carried on into the night. Blair 'Paddy' Mayne, an ex-11 Commando officer, took early morning physical training. A solicitor and rugby international from Northern Ireland, Mayne was shy and watchful, with a barely concealed rage that sometimes spilled over into violence. At six foot three and fifteen and a half stone, he was a match for the toughest of the men. An often-repeated story, almost certainly apocryphal, has it that Stirling had to secure Mayne's release from detention to allow him to join 'L' Detachment. Once a member, however, it seems that his physical training regime was based on his pre-war rugby training – with a difference. Any idlers were invited to spend three rounds with him in the boxing ring. Few idled.

Lewes, whose rigid outlook governed everything the men did, sent them on long desert marches. Water was a precious commodity and strictly allocated; just four bottles were allowed for a hundred-mile march between Kabrit and Cairo. Sharing was prohibited as it invariably led to resentment. And anybody caught stealing other men's water could not expect to remain a member of the SAS, as Reg Seekings remembers: 'One old chap joined us and did everything fine, but he couldn't do without his water. On one trip I caught him with a length of tubing, pinching the water. So he had to go.'

The men responded to the marches with differing levels of acquiescence. On one occasion, the grumbling reached such a pitch that Paddy Mayne seized a particular man, held him one-handed over a two-hundred-foot drop, and asked him what exactly he was moaning about. The grumbling ceased. On another march, Douglas Keith silently carried his pack 40 miles across the desert, wearing only socks after his boots had given way.

There was more to training, though, than fitness and endurance. 'L' Detachment had a firing range unlike any other in the British Army. The men were free to draw any firearm – including German and Italian weapons – from the armoury whenever they liked. Bob Bennett appreciated the fact that 'there was no one hollering and shouting behind you. So you became a much better shot.'

The men also participated in memory tests in which they had to stare at a table full of objects for half a minute, walk out, and accurately list what they had just seen. Lewes believed that this would improve reconnaissance and map reading. Even the dreaded marches had a purpose beyond fitness. That purpose was, says Jimmy Brough, to become what he calls 'S-minded':

> It was hammered into us by [Stirling] that . . . we had to become 'sabotage-minded'. Instead of admiring a nice bridge or building we had to weigh up the best place to plant the explosives to blow the bloody thing up. That was what we were trained for.

The men learned tricks associated with sabotage. On an airfield, for example, it was better to target the same wing of every aircraft, port or starboard, as any unbroken remains could not then be cannibalised to produce a working plane. Similarly, a curved stretch of railway track was much more difficult to replace than a straight stretch.

And what explosives would be used for these attacks? The only bombs available in the Middle East were unsuitable for 'L' Detachment's purposes. Very small groups of men would approach their target, typically an airfield, on foot. They would need to destroy every aircraft they found. A light and simple bomb was needed that could explode and then ignite, guaranteeing the destruction of each aircraft. It was a tall order – and the ordnance experts were convinced that such a bomb was impossible.

Jock Lewes, who, as a boy had spent so much time experimenting with explosives that he had almost lost a hand, was determined to prove the experts wrong. 'All you could hear around the camp,' says Bob Bennett, 'was bangs all over the place,' as Lewes tested combustible materials in hopeful combinations. And when this most taciturn of young men suddenly started screaming and hugging passers-by, everybody understood that he must have succeeded. His mixture of plastic explosive, thermite and engine oil – quickly dubbed the Lewes bomb – could be shaped into small balls, carried in large numbers in linen bags and placed easily on aircraft wings or inside cockpits. It turned 'L' Detachment from a promising idea into an excitingly radical unit with the potential to cause severe damage to the enemy.

This was not the end of the story, of course. 'L' Detachment was a parachute unit – even if some members had little desire to jump out of an aeroplane. But it soon became clear that Lewes was going to receive no help from the RAF parachute school at Ringway, leaving the responsibility for day-to-day training with him. This was unnerving considering the failure of his previous attempt to organise parachute training, and his anxiety was exposed as he was giving a lecture to the men. Reg Seekings, who had been paying close attention, asked a valid question about the workings of static lines.* 'What the hell do you know about it?' snapped Lewes. 'You've never jumped!' Seekings was hurt – and Lewes's sensitivity was noted.

In a makeshift fashion, ground instruction began. The men made practice jumps from large stands built by Jim Almonds. They leapt from a truck on rails that had been stolen from a quarry. And at Lewes's instigation, they jumped facing both forwards and backwards from a lorry travelling at speed until so many bones were broken that the exercise was halted. Jimmy Brough, who often considered Lewes's training methods too extreme, was particularly relieved. He was convinced that the exercise would have killed him before he had a chance to face the enemy.

On 16 October, the men made their first actual parachute jumps in Bristol Bombays of 216 Squadron. Douglas Arnold was the first man out of his aircraft. He was scared before jumping and euphoric on landing. 'Is there anything greater than knowing you landed safely?' he wondered many years later. As a Bombay flew overhead for the third time that day, Bob Bennett stood watching with Dave Kershaw. Bennett thought he saw something falling out of the aircraft. Kershaw told him he was wrong as they had seen no parachute. But Bennett was right. He had, in fact, just witnessed a colleague falling to his death.

* The cord attaching the jumper to the aircraft.

Joe Duffy (left) and Ken Warburton (above). Friends in life, they were found next to each other on the ground.

There had been ten men on that particular aircraft, all waiting to jump. The first, Ken Warburton, a veteran of the Dunkirk evacuation, jumped, but his canopy remained in its pack. Joe Duffy was the next to go. Sensing a problem, he turned round to look at his static line, but others were impatient, and he too jumped – with the same result. Before any more men could go, the dispatcher woke up to the problem and the Bombay was brought in to land. Warburton and Duffy, close friends in life, were found next to each other on the ground, as though laid out for burial. Duffy had made visible efforts to pull his parachute out as he fell.

A lot of cynical comments were made that afternoon about having joined the sort of organisation that kills its own men. Jock Lewes quickly called the men on parade, reassuring them that the Royal Air Force was rectifying the problem, and that jumping would resume the next day. But he added that anybody who wanted to leave 'L' Detachment was free to go. Despite the earlier cynicism, nobody spoke. Everybody wanted to continue. 'This,' says Bennett, 'is when I found out I was with a unit that meant something.'

The problem had been a fault in the clip attaching the static line to the aircraft's rail. It was remedied and the men jumped again next morning. Either Stirling or Lewes jumped first – accounts vary. But the lesson was the same: in 'L' Detachment, everyone had to be prepared to take the same risks.*

As training continued, 'L' Detachment retained the confidence of Auchinleck, but many Cairo staff officers seem to have considered the unit an eccentric folly that was bound to fail. Indeed an RAF group captain, visiting Kabrit, told Stirling to his face that 'L' Detachment's chances of success were practically nil. Irritated, Stirling countered that the SAS's biggest problem would be getting the RAF to drop them in the right place. After some more banter, Stirling bet the group captain £10 that his men could penetrate the British airfield at Heliopolis and place stickers on aircraft in place of bombs. The group captain took the bet.

This was a clever move from Stirling. The raid would serve as a controlled dress rehearsal before the start of genuine operations – and it would give the men some genuine excitement as the strain and monotony of training took its toll. The march from Kabrit to the foothills behind Heliopolis lasted almost four days, with the men laying up during the day, camouflaged by strips of hessian. Moving on to the airfield, they found it very easy to avoid the sentries and place stickers on dozens of aircraft before slipping away. Stirling duly received his £10.

It later transpired that one group, led by Eoin McGonigal, a solicitor from Dublin, had cheated outrageously. Instead of marching across the desert like everybody else, McGonigal and his men had thought laterally. First they stopped the Suez–Cairo Express train by shining a red torch at the driver. They climbed on board and rode to Cairo, where they 'borrowed' transport from Middle East Headquarters and drove to the foothills behind the Heliopolis airfield. They lay up there for two nights until joined by their colleagues, and were only rumbled a fortnight later when GHQ

* Another accident almost occurred the following day when Ralph Lazenby's parachute split after catching the Bombay's tail fin. Fortunately he landed safely; a third fatality in two days might have had a serious effect on 'L' Detachment's future.

A watercolour sketch by Lieutenant Charles Bonington (painted in a POW camp) of Eoin McGonigal's adventure on the Heliopolis raid.

started asking questions about the disappearance of their transport. In another unit, such behaviour might have brought severe punishment, but it was hard to deny that McGonigal's actions reflected the spirit and purpose of the SAS.

In the end, the raid on Heliopolis was more than an initiative test for McGonigal and a side bet for Stirling. It was a genuine boost to 'L' Detachment's morale. It showed members why they had put up with Jock Lewes's trials, his almost literally backbreaking training and the deaths of their comrades. For months these men had languished in Layforce, hoping for action, excitement and a chance to strike a real blow. That chance was about to arrive.

9

BADGE OF DISTINCTION

When some of the men had time off in the early days, they would travel from Kabrit into Suez, where they would routinely cause trouble. According to Reg Seekings, 'we were a tough mob of ex-Commandos' who 'just took our fun where we could get it'. Once the SAS badges arrived, however, Seekings claims that their behaviour improved: 'We developed an honour of regiment, which in the early days we didn't have.' The badges, in other words, helped foster an identity in which the men could take pride.*

The original parachute badge was designed by Jock Lewes, whose ideas guided so many facets of 'L' Detachment life. The military establishment would ordinarily have to authorise any new insignia, but Lewes, in a letter to his father, explained that he did not want to involve the authorities 'because we have trained this unit without the least assistance from home or trained instructors'.

Lewes was to find his inspiration at Shepheard's Hotel in Cairo. Shepheard's was one of the most famous luxury hotels in the world, and, during wartime, the favoured Cairo haunt of British officers, including those of the SAS. Its interior resembled a particularly lavish set for a Victorian production of *Aida*. Sphinxes, palm fronds and oriental rugs vied for supremacy throughout its public spaces.

* Stirling notes, in a memorandum on the SAS's origins, that there had grown in the Commandos a tradition that 'to be a tough regiment it was necessary to act tough all the time . . . We insisted that with "L" Detachment, that toughness should be reserved entirely for the enemy. The introduction of the badge underlined what was expected of the men.'

The interior of Shepheard's Hotel in Cairo – a theatrical pastiche of styles.

An Egyptian-style ibis with outstretched wings sits above the hotel reception desk. Jock Lewes saw this . . .

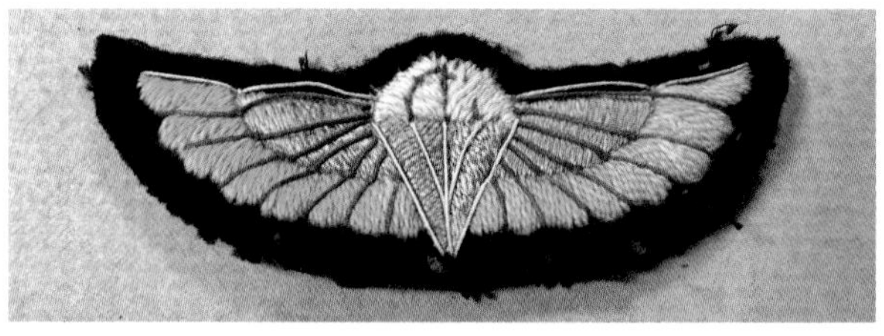

. . . and came up with the design for the parachute wings.

Lewes's attention was drawn to an Egyptian frieze above the hotel's reception desk, depicting an ibis with outstretched wings. He based his group's parachute badge on it, but replaced the body of the ibis with a parachute. He also coloured the inner part of the wings dark blue to represent Oxford University (for whom he had rowed in the Boat Races of 1936 and 1937) and the outer part light blue to represent Cambridge.

It is worth noting that a teammate of Lewes's in the 1936 and 1937 Oxford squads described him as a charismatic man who inspired confidence and 'refused to recognise any possibility other than victory'. For Jock Lewes, war was the continuation of varsity rowing by other means.

An unusually light-hearted Jock Lewes joking with teammates before the 1936 Boat Race.

The cap badge, designed by Sergeant Bob Tait, represents a flaming sword of Damocles hanging downwards. The motto 'Who Dares Wins' was coined by David Stirling.

10

THE EYE OF THE STORM

As 'L' Detachment prepared itself for action in November 1941, Kabrit camp was visited by General Auchinleck and a Pathé film crew who recorded the men parachuting for a two-minute newsreel. No opportunity was missed to demonstrate that parachuting really *was* taking place in the Middle East.

The men were filmed learning to control their parachutes while hanging from one of Jim Almonds's frames. They were shown leaping from moving trucks (though not at full speed and not facing forwards). And there was footage captured of the entire process of jumping, from climbing into the Bombay to landing.

'A leap into space for the first time takes some doing,' declares the voice-over, 'but once the big silk canopy opens out, you feel like a lift boy at Blackpool.'

The men were also filmed meeting General Auchinleck. The Auk's visit was timely as 'L' Detachment's first operation – codenamed Squatter* – was about to be launched in support of Eighth Army's first offensive, Operation Crusader.

Crusader was an effort to drive German and Italian forces out of Libya. Squatter would assist by sabotaging airfields and destroying aircraft that threatened the assault's success. This was a chance to lay the ghost of Layforce to rest and make a name for 'L' Detachment as a dynamic organisation brimming with fresh ideas.

* The name 'Squatter' seems to refer to the fact that the SAS would soon be squatting where it wasn't wanted.

Days after being filmed by Pathé, members of 'L' Detachment were flown in 216 Squadron's Bombays from Kabrit to a forward landing-ground at Bagoush, 300 miles to the west, where the Royal Air Force treated them to a surprisingly good meal. The men were waited on by officers, offered beer, and given games to play and books to read. The unaccustomed treatment unnerved Bob Bennett: 'Quite honestly, with all these people running around us and an operation the next evening, it seemed to me like The Last Supper.'

As the operation approached, a problem arose. Parachuting was vulnerable to the weather, and forecasts were predicting heavy storms. Official advice was to cancel the operation, but to do so might have severe consequences for 'L' Detachment. One of Stirling's boasts in his memorandum to Auchinleck had been that 'weather will not restrict [the SAS's] operations'. If it were to prevent the very first mission, there might be no second chance. The men understood this and were desperate to go ahead. Reg Seekings remembers:

> We – the men – insisted . . . This is one thing you've got to remember – that we were the product of Commandos, and in the Commandos we had cancellation, cancellation, cancellation. And when the first job came up, in spite of all this rough weather and rough conditions, everybody wanted to jump – they insisted. Otherwise it was cancelled, that was us finished.

Stirling and his officers agreed, and the second British parachute raid of the war went ahead. In the early evening of 16 November, the Bombays took off once again, carrying 55 men to be dropped in five groups, ten miles inland of their targets. Charlie West, of 216 Squadron, was piloting one of the Bombays. The weather was good initially. The forecasters, it seemed, had been mistaken – but then the cloud thickened, the wind got up and the rain started to fall.

Members of 'L' Detachment were disconcerted by the weather but also by increasing flak. Johnny Cooper was impressed – and frightened – as his pilot flung the aircraft into dives and turns to escape the glare of the searchlights. Jimmy Brough was amazed that a lumbering old Bombay could be thrown around like a Spitfire.

A Bristol Bombay.

As the weather worsened, West found it difficult to maintain speed and direction. Descending to look for a visual fix, he emerged from the cloud at just 200 feet near anti-aircraft gunners who were gifted a target. West's instrument panel was smashed and fuel started to gush from one of the engines. He climbed back into cloud and flew east until he was virtually out of fuel. After a rough landing in the desert, the SAS men on board, led by Charles Bonington (father of future mountaineer, Chris), climbed out of the Bombay, believing themselves in friendly territory.

It did not take long to realise, however, that they were still behind enemy lines. Reaching a road, Bonington and his men ambushed an Italian fuel lorry, whose startled driver told them that they were 45 miles from Allied-held Tobruk. The fuel (and the lorry driver) were put inside the aircraft, and West took off again, hoping to reach Tobruk. He followed the coastline for a while, before flying into at least one Messerschmitt ME 109 which shot away his engines and controls. West managed to close the flaps and throttles before the Bombay crashed into low sand hills.

A number of men were trapped under the Bombay's wreckage, which then came under fire from enemy troops. It is remarkable that only one 'L' Detachment member – Barney Stone, who had taken part in Jock Lewes's parachute experiment at Fuka – was killed. The others (including Ernie Bond, a future deputy assistant commissioner of the Metropolitan Police) were captured, as was Charlie West, who woke up days later in hospital. The Italian lorry driver survived – and was only saved from summary execution when the SAS men explained that he had been their prisoner and not a willing passenger.

This was the only aircraft that failed to reach its drop zone. The other four dropped their parachutists, but the landings were difficult and dangerous. Once on the ground, the men struggled to release their harnesses as they were dragged by gale-force winds across stony ground. Dave Kershaw bounced along helplessly until his canopy caught on a boulder and he was able to free himself. By this time, his arm had been scraped raw. Reg Seekings had a similar experience. 'My hands and arms were completely skinned,' he says, 'and my face was a hell of a mess.'

Some were left unable to move after the drop. Jock Cheyne broke his back and there seemed little that could be done to help him. Jimmy Storie shook his hand, Jock Lewes said a few words, and the group moved on. Cheyne was never seen again. Douglas Keith also injured his back, but he was luckier than Cheyne, initially at least. He was left with another injured man, Douglas Arnold. In the morning they spotted a figure on the horizon who turned out to be an Italian soldier. Arnold and Keith were taken prisoner, but they concealed their identities as parachutists by claiming to be British engineers who had fallen off the back of a lorry.

They then asked, rather hopefully, to be repatriated to join their fellow engineers. The request was refused. Douglas Keith was killed the following year when his prison ship, *Sebastiano Venier,* was attacked by a British submarine.

For those men fit enough to move, the plan now was to march north and lie up overlooking the target airfields until the time came to attack. But, in these conditions, many of the men were struggling to find each other, let alone the airfields. The situation grew worse as a torrential downpour began. 'L' Detachment had experienced rain once or twice at Kabrit, but this was the most extreme rainfall the region had seen in decades. 'Suddenly we were up to our knees in water stretching as far as the eyes could see,' remembers Brough, who could feel his suede desert boots shrinking around his feet. 'The rain really hurt, it was so heavy,' says Reg Seekings.

Several men in Paddy Mayne's group, including Seekings, Kershaw, Bennett and Mayne himself, tried to keep the rain off. 'We had a blanket and we spread it over and above us,' says Kershaw. Mayne shared some rum with the others, before suddenly announcing that he was going to set off alone to carry out the operation. 'We had a hell of a job talking him out of it,' says Seekings. It was an early intimation of the eagerness for action that would make Mayne one of the most heavily decorated soldiers of the Second World War.

In truth the operation was no longer possible. The Lewes bombs were waterlogged and useless. Weapons and equipment were lost and scattered over the desert. The men could do no more than head to the rendezvous point, where members of the Long Range Desert Group were waiting to ferry them to Siwa Oasis near the Egyptian border. But the rendezvous was not easy to find. As Mayne's group was moving back, Kershaw spotted several men in the distance. Getting out his binoculars, he recognised them as members of Stirling's group, including Sergeant Yates and Stan Bolland. They were all heading in the wrong direction. Kershaw started whistling loudly and firing off rounds, but the men simply carried on walking. All would eventually be taken prisoner, except for Bolland who disappeared in the desert.

The plan was for the LRDG to light a beacon to advertise its position. After Mayne's group had been walking for a day and a night, Bob Bennett shouted, 'Look! There's a light over there!' Dave Kershaw, an amateur astronomer, said that it was probably the planet Mars. Somebody else wondered whether the LRDG would even be waiting after all this time.

Paddy Mayne after the first raid.

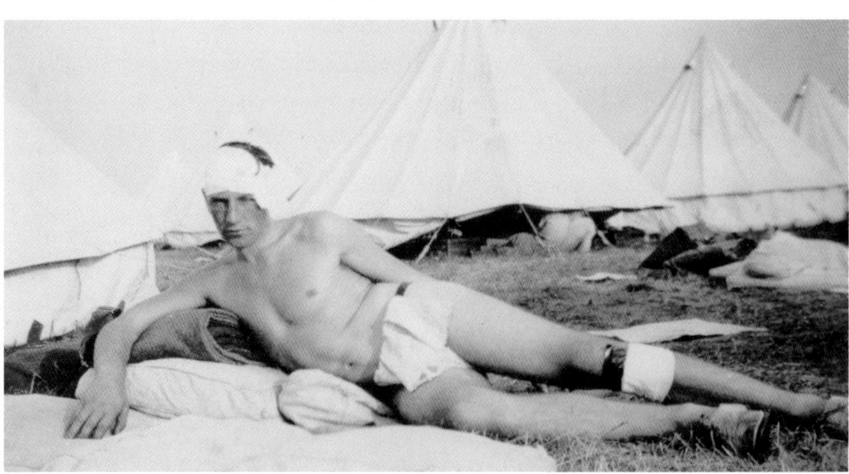

Unable to agree, the men slept for a few hours – but when they woke at dawn the light was still there and a plume of smoke was rising beside it. As everybody marched towards the light, a truck containing members of the LRDG drove towards them. They were brought to the LRDG's temporary camp, where they were given tea, cigarettes and food. The relief was overpowering.

Jimmy Brough, a member of Jock Lewes's group, stumbled onto the LRDG position some time later. He and his colleagues realised they were safe when 'we heard a most welcome sound. Someone whistling "Roll out the Barrel". We joined in, as this tall figure with a substantial black beard came out of the darkness. Hot mugs of tea all round was the order.'

David Stirling and Bob Tait, meanwhile, chanced upon a separate LRDG hideout manned by David Lloyd Owen, the organisation's future leader. But not everybody was so fortunate. Not only had Charles Bonington's group crash-landed in Charlie West's Bombay, but another group led by Eoin McGonigal, the officer who had held up a train before the Heliopolis raid, could not be found. None of the 11 members would ever be seen again.

In the end, Operation Squatter achieved nothing. It had been a failure as complete as anything suffered by Layforce. Of those who jumped, only 22 remained. Most of those who featured in the Pathé newsreel were killed or captured just days after it was filmed. On the long drive to Siwa Oasis,

'THE FIASCO!' Charles Bonington's comment on Operation Squatter, written in a POW camp.

20 THE FIASCO! The operation was a total failure owing to very bad weather, high winds, and rain the heaviest for years in Libya.
5 a/c (Bombays) left DABA aerodrome after dark. 4 dropped their parachute secs, – the 5th (LT. C.J. BONINGTON.) was shot down by three M.E. 109 near GAZALA.
LT. McGonigal was killed on landing. His section had other casualties such as broken legs.

The majority of the men recovered from Operation Squatter. Stirling is in the centre wearing sunglasses. Mayne is believed to be behind him to the right; Bill Fraser is two across to the left.

the survivors' relief gave way to melancholy as they contemplated the loss of friends and regretted that another exciting prospect had turned sour. It would not be long, they believed, before they met the dreaded instructors at the Guards Depot once again.

'L' Detachment, it seemed, was finished.

11

HANGING BY A THREAD

David Lloyd Owen was impressed with David Stirling when they met at the LRDG rendezvous. 'Failure,' writes Lloyd Owen, 'meant nothing more to him than to generate fierce determination to be successful next time. He was convinced that he had only been thwarted by bad luck.'

Stirling found good reasons to remain positive. The chief cause of 'L' Detachment's failure had been freak weather conditions, yet Paddy Mayne's group had still come close to its target without being spotted by the enemy. The greatest problem facing the SAS, Stirling felt, was its many enemies at headquarters who, for reasons of jealousy or lack of imagination, would be delighted to see it killed off.

As Stirling and Lloyd Owen sat together, they discussed the limitations of parachuting. It was more vulnerable to the weather than Stirling had appreciated. And there were other potential issues relating to the

David Lloyd Owen.

availability of aircraft and accuracy of dropping. The solution, Lloyd Owen suggested, was straightforward. As well as picking up SAS men *after* an operation, the LRDG could convey them *beforehand*: 'I assured David that we could guarantee to take them exactly where they wanted to go, and precisely when they required to be there.'

Stirling did not initially respond to Lloyd Owen's offer. (Perhaps he was annoyed that the idea had not previously occurred to him.) Later that night, however, during the long drive to Siwa, he raised it with Jock Lewes, describing the LRDG as a possible 'taxi service'. And by the end of the two-hundred-mile journey, Stirling seems to have been fully converted to Lloyd Owen's suggestion. Once the agreement of other senior LRDG officers had been secured, the Special Air Service would find itself rooted to the ground (operationally at least) for the remainder of its stay in the Middle East and North Africa.

'L' Detachment's other pressing problem was solved by Stirling's social connections and persuasive charm – those traits so recently deplored, but now appreciated, by Jock Lewes.

Among his many military contacts, Stirling was on good terms with one brigadier who had introduced him to another brigadier who had recently captured Jalo Oasis from the Italians. Jalo, near the western edge of the Great Sand Sea, was the perfect spot for 'L' Detachment to hide away, safe from the prying eyes of its enemies, until it was ready to start raiding again. Not only did Brigadier Denys Reid, the commander of 'E' Force, allow Stirling to move his entire unit from Kabrit to Jalo (without the knowledge of headquarters), but he was also able to offer the SAS its next operations. The Germans, he said, were mounting damaging attacks on his men from a series of airfields at Sirte, El Agheila and Agedabia. Clearing them of aircraft would be much appreciated. Reid had originally offered the job to the LRDG, which had suggested it be given instead to 'L' Detachment. Jalo was already a forward base for two of the LRDG's most effective patrols, which could now convey Stirling's men to the airfields.

The SAS was being kept alive by a mix of Stirling's pragmatism, his social connections and a measure of luck. An association with the LRDG, kindred relations in theory, outlook and spirit, promised much. But the test would come with the next series of raids. Stirling had been offered a path to his unit's redemption. But he could not afford any more failures.

12

REDEMPTION: Sadler

One of the LRDG groups based at Jalo was the Rhodesian 'S' Patrol, led by Gus Holliman. A twenty-year-old sergeant with this patrol, Mike Sadler, would become one of the most iconic individuals in the story of the wartime SAS.

Raised in Gloucestershire, Sadler was an adventurous young man with a desire to see the world. After leaving school, he travelled to Rhodesia and worked as a farm assistant. He was about to start running his own farm in the Savé Valley when war broke out. Instead, he joined the Rhodesian artillery and was sent to the Western Desert as an anti-tank gunner. While on leave in Cairo, he visited a hotel popular with Rhodesians where he met members of the LRDG:

> They told me about the lovely life they had. It interested me and they asked me if I would be willing to join. I didn't want to spend my time

Mike Sadler.

> being bitten by fleas in the Abbassia Barracks so I found myself in the LRDG.

Sadler became a navigator. 'I was so tickled,' he says, 'by the idea of being able to find where you were by looking at stars.' He was taught the basics by a merchant navy officer at LRDG headquarters. 'I was not too far removed from school and algebra and geometry at the time,' he says, 'so I acquired my alleged skills.'

Sadler was working in the tradition of Ralph Bagnold and his fellow desert explorers. Using a theodolite and a wireless receiver by night and Bagnold's sun-compass by day, he found himself so intrigued by his job that he never minded having to work while everybody else was asleep. Part of the attraction, in fact, was the level of involvement. Sadler was not simply keeping to a bearing. He was in a constantly evolving relationship with the landscape:

> You were trying to follow a compass course on the ground but you were continually shoved off course by hills or rocks or boulders or things like that. A great deal of the art was making due allowance for turning off and then getting back onto the same course. That was a sort of knack.

Sadler remains very modest about his ability, describing it as 'nothing special'. Many SAS members down the years, including Reg Seekings and Carol Mather, have strongly disagreed. But before his reputation was confirmed, Mike Sadler of the Rhodesian Patrol of the Long Range Desert Group was tasked with guiding a party containing David Stirling, Paddy Mayne and others from Jalo to Sirte. It was a crucial journey for the future of the SAS.

13

REDEMPTION: Stirling and Mayne

Stirling's basic plan, based on Brigadier Reid's suggestion, was to send one group, led by himself and Mayne, to Sirte,* another, led by Jock Lewes, to El Agheila, and a third, led by Lieutenant Bill Fraser, to Agedabia. These were all coastal fishing communities with Axis airfields nearby. Their aircraft were now threatening Eighth Army's advance, as well as ships supplying the island fortress of Malta. 'L' Detachment's job was to destroy these aircraft.

Mike Sadler was to guide Stirling, Mayne and others 350 miles north-west to Sirte. He remembers the difference, at this stage, between the SAS and the LRDG: 'I think the impression was that they [the SAS] were still quite clean-looking soldiers. And we'd all got long beards and we looked very scruffy.'

On the third day of travel, while Sadler was establishing his position, the drone of an Italian aircraft was heard. The men opened fire with machine guns and the pilot veered away, dropping his bombs harmlessly, but he called in reinforcements. By the time three more aircraft arrived, the men had thrown camouflage netting over all seven trucks and dived into a nearby patch of scrub. The planes flew up and down, firing for 15 minutes that seemed like a great deal longer.

When they finally flew off, everybody got up, looking around to see who was still alive. To Jimmy Brough it seemed miraculous that nobody

* Several months after the first raid, Muammar Gaddafi was born to a Bedouin family near Sirte.

was wounded and that none of the trucks were damaged, although one LRDG man – Cecil Jackson, known as Jacko – had a lucky escape. He stood up to find his head and shoulders neatly outlined by a curve of machine-gun bullets.

The men brewed some tea to calm their nerves and began to chat. Brough remembers a member of the LRDG saying 'that he owned shares in a gold mine and that in the event of his being killed we could have his share'. But as Brough pictured his future prosperity, Mike Sadler interrupted to say that they were now 20 miles from Sirte. They drove on until, after another halt, they heard voices and revving engines ahead. They were now beside the coast road and it seemed that they were expected.

Stirling, Mayne and the LRDG commander, Gus Holliman, held a hurried conference and decided to split the party up. Stirling and Brough would attack Sirte airfield as planned, while Mayne, with Reg Seekings, Edward MacDonald, Tom Chesworth and others would attack a previously undetected airfield at Tamet where aircraft had been seen landing. The attacks would go in simultaneously. Their arrival in the area might no longer be a complete surprise, but one or other of the airfields might still be caught unawares.

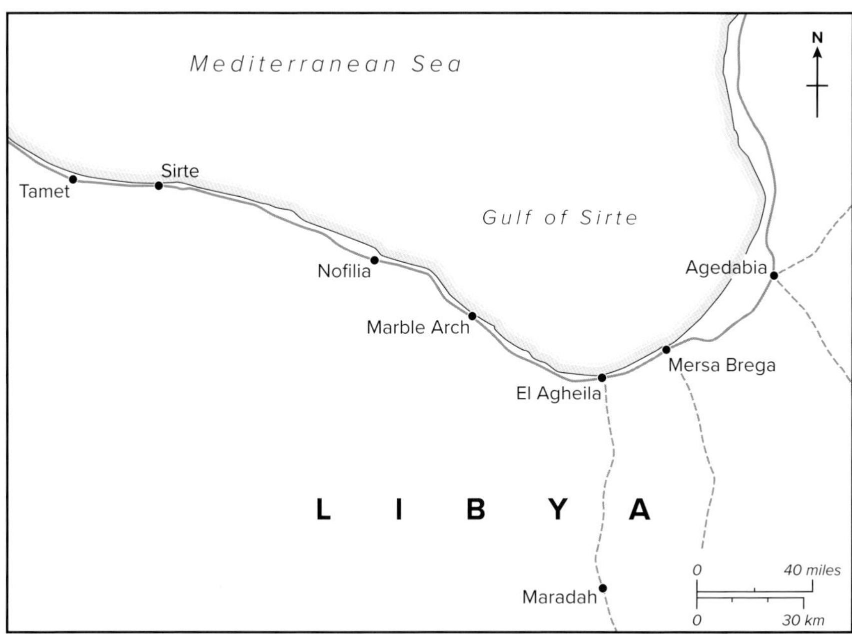

The LRDG told Stirling and Brough how to mark their pick-up spot after the raid. They should place a bush on the road and the trucks would know to stop. With this information, the pair set off on foot for the ridge overlooking Sirte airfield. They were not due to attack until 11 p.m. the following night, but they wanted to have a look around first. Brough was heavily weighed down with rations, a large supply of Lewes bombs and a Tommy gun. Stirling was somewhat less burdened.

They moved carefully forward until they suddenly found themselves on the airfield. In the dark they could see the outlines of enemy aircraft. There seemed to be no sentries about, and they were heavily tempted to plant their bombs straight away, but Stirling knew he had to stick to his own plan. If they attacked now, they would prejudice Mayne's assault.

As the pair crept around, Stirling seems to have trodden on a sleeping Italian soldier who shot his rifle off into the darkness. This led to panicked gunfire across the airfield, interspersed with Italian cries. A large gun began firing out to sea. In the midst of the mayhem, Stirling and Brough quietly made their way back to the ridge where they dug themselves into the scrub.

The following morning they woke to find that the airfield was protected by sentries. They stayed where they were, well hidden, and watched local life unfold beside them. First two Arab women arrived to work the ground with mattocks. Then a gazelle started feeding on the scrub. Brough was quietly concerned that it might eat away their hiding place. Suddenly they heard noise coming from the airfield. To both men's horror, the aircraft had started taking off in pairs. Soon there were none left. Their targets had fled.

That night they made their way back to the road. They set a bush down as instructed. Brough recalls what happened next:

> We were feeling pretty miserable when suddenly there was a white flash and explosion ... The sky to the west lit up ... [We] sat at the side of the road watching this beautiful sight and exactly at 12.45 the trucks of the LRDG came roaring past us, then braked, and slowly came back to us, having seen the bush. After our reunion we decided to mine the road and had the satisfaction of seeing an enemy truck blow up.

Paddy Mayne.

Stirling and Brough had at least survived their raid. Mike Sadler, meanwhile, had led the trucks to Tamet airfield, where Paddy Mayne and his men were set down. At the planned hour, they slipped onto the airfield in single file and spotted the outlines of aircraft. Mostly CR42 biplanes, these were the same planes that Stirling and Brough had seen taking off from Sirte. The pilots, spooked by the disturbance they had caused, had flown off to the apparent safety of Tamet, where they now rested at Mayne's mercy.

Yet just as the headstrong Mayne had wanted to march off alone during the first raid, so he now decided to put his own stamp on this one. Spotting a large hut at the edge of the airfield, he moved towards it. The closer he came, the louder grew the sound of people enjoying themselves inside. This was the pilots' mess in which Germans and Italians were drinking and relaxing. Mayne kicked the door open, said 'good evening' to the occupants and began firing his Colt .45 while others joined in with Tommy guns. Once the massacre was complete, Mayne and his men moved across to the aircraft and began planting their Lewes bombs. When he ran out of bombs, Mayne is supposed to have climbed up onto the wing of an aircraft and torn out the instrument panel with his bare hands. In total, two dozen aircraft were destroyed, and at least as many airmen were shot dead.

Mayne and his men were still on the airfield when the bombs started detonating. A particularly large explosion was caused when a petrol dump blew up. This was the 'beautiful sight' that Jimmy Brough observed 30 miles away at Sirte. Mike Sadler, too, was watching the fireworks display. He recalls that 'they arrived back full of euphoria with their success and then we zoomed off into the desert before anybody could catch us.'

Steering trouble on one of the trucks would hold them up, and they only rejoined the Sirte group at 11 a.m. the next morning. Jimmy Brough remembers:

> Paddy's party came rolling in to a victory salute . . . We all fired our weapons into the sky. They had cause to celebrate. 24 enemy planes had been destroyed and not a single casualty on our side. We then headed back to Jalo to await the return of Jock Lewes and Bill Fraser.

David Stirling and Paddy Mayne had, on this occasion, benefitted from a stroke of luck that went some way to counteracting the misfortune of the first raid. Stirling, a keen shot, had flushed out the birds into the path of Mayne's guns. Nevertheless, Stirling was unhappy with Mayne's behaviour in shooting up the mess. It was, he felt, closer to an execution than an act of war. 'He spoke to Paddy himself privately,' says Mike Sadler. 'Paddy got a severe rocket for it.'

But for a British public hungry for heroes, Mayne's actions were welcome. A near-contemporary newspaper cutting, quoted in the SAS's wartime diary, reads like a children's adventure:

> Suddenly the door flew open. A burst from a Tommy-gun swept the card players and drinkers at the bar. German drinking songs turned into shouts of horror. Those who weren't killed or wounded tried to make for the doors or windows. They were mown down before they had gone a yard . . . It was all over in a minute. They threw a time-bomb onto the roof of the mess 'for luck', then onto the next job.

This was the night that the legend of Paddy Mayne – soon to spread among British and Commonwealth troops in the Middle East – was born. But Stirling and Mayne were not the only officers leading parties on this raid. Jock Lewes and Bill Fraser were there too. And Fraser's contribution would, arguably, prove to be the most important of all.

14

REDEMPTION: Lewes and Fraser

While Stirling and Mayne's groups were heading towards Sirte, another party, led by Jock Lewes, was leaving Jalo and heading for an airfield near the coastal settlement of El Agheila.

Lewes had Jim Almonds, Dave Kershaw and Bob Lilley in his party, as well as an Italian Lancia truck with solid tyres. Lewes did not at first reveal why the Lancia was needed, but the men quickly grew to hate it. 'We damn nearly carried it all the way across the desert,' remembers Lilley, 'every few yards it would get bogged down in the sand.' Refuelling it involved sucking oil from a large drum: 'Whoever had to suck the tube to get it started invariably got a bellyful of oil.'

The Long Range Desert Group left the group 35 miles from the airfield. They marched the rest of the way. But, on arrival, Lewes found that the enemy was simply using the landing ground as a ferry station. Aircraft would stop briefly to refuel but none remained overnight. There was nothing to attack. Now at last, Lewes revealed the Lancia's purpose. He and his men were to drive it onto the coast road where they would join the end of an Italian convoy, breaking off when they reached a particular rest stop beside the road. They would capture an Italian general who was supposed to be staying there, bomb the roadhouse and hurry back to the rendezvous to meet the LRDG.

Events did not quite go to plan. The group managed to join an enemy convoy and successfully reached the roadhouse. Dave Kershaw opened the door to find an enemy soldier ready for him:

> There was a blue flash . . . he just fired as I opened the door. Well I had a .45 . . . and I just pressed the trigger and pointed it upwards . . . The

> bullet must have caught him on the bridge of the nose or the bottom of the forehead because his face split open all the way down.

Lewes and his men quickly escaped back onto the road. They had managed to plant bombs around the building and they now stopped to mine the road itself. But the first vehicle to come along was an Italian mobile brothel, which had earlier tried to tempt Lewes's men inside. 'Up they went on the mines,' remembers Lilley, 'I was very sorry about this.'*

The final raid sent out from Jalo was led by Lieutenant Bill Fraser. Fraser was far gentler in nature than many of the other members yet would prove himself an immensely effective fighting man, twice winning the Military Cross. Mike Sadler describes him as 'an extremely nice chap and a brave fellow too, and about the most Scottish Scotsman I ever knew'.

Some of the men clearly sensed an insecurity in Fraser. He was given the nickname 'Skin' to reflect his supposed homosexuality. And in the early days, having been taunted by an inebriated Paddy Mayne, he often preferred to spend time on his own rather than socialising with others. Nevertheless, he earned the respect of his men – even before leading the remarkable raid on the airfield at Agedabia.

Like the other groups, Fraser's party, consisting of Bob Tait, Jeff DuVivier, Arthur Phillips and Jack Byrne, was driven from Jalo to the target. The men were set down 15 miles from the airfield and marched towards it noiselessly across the sand in their rubber-soled desert boots. They wore battledress covered by sand-coloured boilersuits topped off with stocking caps. Each of them had a revolver and eight Lewes bombs, while Jack Byrne, carrying a Tommy gun, brought up the rear.

After hours of slow marching, they lay up in a likely spot and waited for the dawn. There they stayed throughout the day, watching aircraft taking off and landing on the airfield, which was just beyond their view. Once it was dark again they moved slowly on and stepped over a two-strand wire fence, the airfield's only barrier.

* Prisoners were taken, including a Libyan soldier named Ali who was brought back to Kabrit. He was handed over to the military police, who began mistreating him – until Dave Kershaw stepped up and furiously defended him. After this Ali was given a job in the 'L' Detachment canteen where he became a favourite of the men.

Bill Fraser (left) with Jim Chambers and Bernard Schott.

Now they were moving quickly. They reached the runway and found, in the darkness, a profusion of aircraft in front of them, gathered together in clusters. They walked around each cluster, placing Lewes bombs on the noses of fighters and the wings of bombers, until they ran out of aeroplanes. Throughout this strange exercise in reverse husbandry, sowing lethal seeds on an enemy field, the men remained unchallenged. Only when the time-pencils had run their course, and the bombs began exploding, did the enemy reveal themselves. Machine-gun fire raked the edges of the airfield and anti-aircraft fire opened up in the belief that the airfield was being attacked from the sky.

As the men moved away from the field, the light from burning aircraft revealed eight brand-new Messerschmitt Bf 109Fs, separated from the rest of the aircraft. Fraser called to Byrne to collect up all remaining bombs from the other men. Then, as the others waited, they placed them on the planes' wingtips, one by one, and activated the bombs' pull-switches, reducing the explosive time delay to just 14 seconds. The first planes blew up while Fraser and Byrne were still running to join the rest of the group. As Jack Byrne remembers, 'The whole area was light as day, and we must have been clearly visible to anyone who wanted to see. Spreading out in one long line, we marched off the airfield in style, taking giant strides.'

Meanwhile, three Royal Air Force bombers were arriving overhead to drop their own bombs, adding to the overall chaos. Fraser and his men set off for their rendezvous with the LRDG at a particular roadsign on a desert track. They arrived three hours late, expecting the LRDG party to have disappeared, but, as they arrived, they heard a voice. 'This way, men!'

After an hour's drive, the LRDG trucks ran into an Eighth Army battle group. These were the vehicles and men directly threatened by the aircraft Fraser and his men had just destroyed. As their trucks joined the battle group, Brigadier Denys Reid, the man who had proposed the raids, appeared.

'How many aircraft did you destroy?' asked Reid.

'All of them,' replied Fraser.

'How many is that?'

'Thirty-seven, sir.'

Reid, a large man, was so pleased that he thumped Fraser hard on the back. The smaller Fraser was visibly stunned. The brigadier smiled and shook his hand, saying, 'I'm proud to take the hand of someone who has done something so worthwhile.'

Fraser subsequently received the first of his Military Crosses. And as a result of the raids, Neil Ritchie, Eighth Army commander, commended the SAS and the LRDG. Their attacks had actively assisted the offensive. But, as with T.E. Lawrence's force, they were achieving a more subtle result. 'L' Detachment was a shapeless threat, drifting about like a gas in the silent desert, 'causing the enemy to waste much time, personnel and valuable fuel in fruitless hunts for their tormentors'.

Bill Fraser's raid on Agedabia deserves to be remembered as the classic 'L' Detachment desert raid. The destruction of all 37 aircraft present, a comprehensive feat that the Royal Air Force would have struggled to achieve, was a true turning point for the SAS in the Second World War.

15

AN OFFICER AND A GENTLEMAN

It must have been clear to everybody who had taken part in the raids on Sirte, Tamet, El Agheila and Agedabia that 'L' Detachment's chief weapon was surprise. The more unexpected the raid, the more likely its success. And what would be more unexpected than to raid exactly the same airfields in the days that followed? And so, on Christmas Eve, groups under Stirling and Mayne set out again for Sirte and Tamet, guided by Mike Sadler. And, just as last time, Stirling's party failed to destroy any aircraft while Mayne's group destroyed 27.

At a professional level, Stirling was delighted at Mayne's success. It ensured, after all, the continuation of his organisation. At a personal level, though, it aggravated him, as Mayne pointed out the contrast between their achievements. 'They were in competition with each other,' remembers Mike Sadler, 'they had quite a rivalry. Paddy's stories made David feel the need to do something aggressive.'

On Boxing Day, Jock Lewes, with Jim Almonds, Bob Lilley and others, set out for a raid on Nofilia airfield. On arrival, Almonds counted 43 aircraft before retiring to wait inside a large buried water container. They returned at 2 a.m. and made their way silently to the first aircraft, careful not to wake its sleeping guard. They found a second aircraft but then, according to Almonds's diary, 'disaster overtook us. We could not find another aircraft. We searched frantically, zig-zagging to and fro across the aerodrome'.

As they were searching, the first bomb exploded, then the second, and the airfield was quickly alive with troops. 'Several times we came very near to getting caught,' remembers Bob Lilley.

As his group marched back to its rendezvous, Jock Lewes demonstrated his firmness. When a corporal ran out of water, his colleagues began offering him sips from their bottles. Lewes saw this and ordered them to stop. As the corporal started to fall behind, Lewes refused to wait for him until, eventually, he disappeared out of sight. (He was later taken prisoner.) Bob Lilley notes that he and the other men subsequently ran dangerously short of water as a direct result of sharing with the straggler. 'We were just about on our knees,' he says, 'when we arrived at the RV.' Lewes's rigour made him an extremely effective, if not always a sympathetic, commander. An apparently harsh act had probably saved his men's lives.

The LRDG picked up the men and drove them on. The following morning they watched a Messerschmitt Bf 110 flying overhead. Just as it seemed to have ignored them, it turned and began attacking with its machine guns and cannons. 'It soon became obvious,' writes Almonds, 'that it was only a matter of time before we should all be killed if we stayed with the trucks.' Almonds and Lilley ran towards a mound in the middle of the desert as the Messerschmitt tried to get a sight on them. An extraordinary game of ring-a-ring-a'-roses developed as Almonds, Lilley and a German fighter-bomber found themselves moving in concentric circles around the desert mound, until, in the end, the Messerschmitt gave up. Almonds remembers: 'We

had that plane beat. It took him some minutes to get round the rock but we could do it in a few strides.'

The men jumped back into their trucks and drove on. After a few miles, tiny specks appeared in the sky, gradually growing to reveal themselves as Stuka dive-bombers. Camouflage nets were quickly thrown over the trucks and men ran into the open. Within moments, Jim Almonds's truck was hit. Almonds knew that the Stuka pilots would be able to spot any movement. His life depended on staying absolutely still. Manoeuvring himself into 'the most unnatural human shape' he could assume, he scooped sand over his hair and body to break up his silhouette. 'Time and time again I thought it was all over,' he writes, 'as the planes just skimmed over . . . to machine gun some bush or dark patch.'

Eventually, after a long and harrowing experience, the party arrived back at Jalo. Jock Lewes was not with them, however. Accounts were confused, but it seemed that he had been killed by a cannon shell fired from the Messerschmitt. He was buried in the desert by Jimmy Storie, who said that he had uttered the name of his fiancée – 'Mirren' – before he died.

David Stirling was badly affected by his cofounder's death. Not only had Lewes become a close friend, but he played a crucial role in keeping the organisation running. Who, now, would fill this enormous gap? As Jim Almonds wrote in his diary:

> I thought of Jock Lewes, one of the bravest men I have ever met, an officer and a gentleman, lying out in the desert barely covered with sand. No one will stop by his grave or pay homage to a brave heart that has ceased to beat. Not even a stone marks the spot.

16

AN IRREGULAR UNIT

On the second day of 1942, Hermione, Countess of Ranfurly* was leaving Shepheard's Hotel when a tall, scruffy officer climbed out of a taxi and asked her to pay his fare. She knew the officer well and was impressed by the length of his beard – so she paid, before asking him a question. 'How many men have you got now and what's the score?' 'Four officers and fourteen men,' he replied, 'and around ninety enemy planes destroyed on the ground.' He was now off to take a bath, he said. Would Hermione like to join him later for dinner?

The officer was David Stirling, just arrived from Jalo. As he checked into the hotel, he was mulling a series of problems. He had to ensure that his now-desirable unit remained independent and was not swallowed by a larger organisation. He had to increase its size quickly and substantially. He had to find somebody to continue Jock Lewes's work. And he had to keep the raids going.

'L' Detachment would certainly grow over the coming months and, as it did, it continued to reflect Stirling's attitudes. Jim Smith, for example, was a mechanic who joined the SAS in somewhat murky circumstances. Shortly after his arrival, he and a colleague were accused of deserting from their previous unit. When a military policeman appeared with a formal charge sheet, Stirling called Smith and the other man into his office and read out the charges. He then addressed the military policeman: 'Sergeant, these are

* When her husband, Dan, the 6th Earl of Ranfurly, was posted to the Middle East, Hermione had broken army rules and followed him. She was placed on a ship back to Britain, but quickly returned. By January 1942, Dan was a prisoner-of-war and Hermione was working with the Special Operations Executive in Cairo. She had become one of the city's most celebrated society figures, and a confidante of David Stirling.

Hermione Ranfurly with a large tuna (left) and her husband (right) while living in Nassau in the mid-1950s.

your men. We asked for volunteers but these men are deserters! Now don't you think that deserters are *better* than volunteers?' He then signed and stamped the sheets before handing them back. 'There you are, sergeant!' he said. 'The men stay with me!'

Stirling clearly had an unconventional approach to discipline. He had been keen, after all, to bring Paddy Mayne into the SAS, regardless of his reputation. Beyond this, though, the unit's character seems to reflect Stirling's simultaneous belief in both hereditary status and meritocracy. As Mike Sadler notes:

> [Stirling] had the upper classes' confidence that they knew what to do and had better ideas than ordinary people. But that was tempered by the fact that he was a nice chap with a fairly democratic outlook on life who thought that other people had merits as well.

This dual outlook was transferred to the unit. Stirling was pleased to invite well-heeled friends to come on board as officers but equally happy to grant the lower ranks generous levels of freedom and responsibility. Officers and men, for example, were often on first-name terms with each other. Once jeeps were introduced, everybody seemed willing to chauffeur everybody else. And after Jock Lewes's death, Stirling actively sought the men's advice on whether 'L' Detachment should continue. From a certain viewpoint, the SAS was an unusually egalitarian organisation.

This was not entirely down to Stirling, of course. Dudley Clarke had sought an unusual style of soldier for his commandos, and these men had now graduated to 'L' Detachment. 'L' Detachment was moreover influenced by the LRDG – even more so once it began working with the New Zealand and Rhodesian patrols, many of whose members were tough, practical men used to forming their own opinions and acting on them. It is hardly surprising that Ron Cryer, an LRDG man who later joined the SAS, notes that the lower ranks of both organisations were full of 'self-starters' who did not need to be motivated by their officers.

One might expect a unit of self-starters to lack discipline. But Dave Kershaw insists that, as guardsmen, the original members had *more* discipline than ordinary soldiers. The camp at Kabrit, he says, grew to become well ordered, with a parade ground, neatly laid-out tents and military policemen. Away from Kabrit, however, things were different. Once the men were out in the desert, Kershaw admits, everyone started enjoying themselves. 'It was great!' he says. 'You'd be in the blue for six or seven weeks.* You'd have a scruffy beard on you!' But this did not indicate a lack of discipline, Kershaw implies, as an unusual lifestyle was required for unusual circumstances.

For Mike Sadler, SAS discipline was never about drill or spit and polish, even though the men were capable of military displays when necessary. 'It was a different kind of discipline,' he says. Roy Close, who joined the SAS in 1944, calls it a 'quietly understood discipline'. It was understood because every member, officers and men alike, had earned it. Anybody who failed to make the grade, or did not fit in, was returned to his original unit. If Stirling's high-born friends did not deserve their places, they went. Even the chaplain would have to prove himself worthy of being a member. The result was shared respect and a sense of unforced discipline.

* The desert was known to British soldiers as 'the blue'.

The inspection of HQ Raiding Forces, July 1945.

This could have unusual corollaries. Officers and men could become friends on an equal footing. Roy Farran and Harold 'Tanky' Challenor developed such a bond, as Challenor recalls: 'I was "Tanky" to him from the start, and we became close friends – a situation only possible in a free-booter unit such as ours.'

The atmosphere also allowed for an unusual sense of personal importance. Charlie Radford joined in March 1944 and immediately regretted his years spent with other units. He had previously 'felt like a very small cog in a very large machine'. But now that he was a member of the SAS, he 'felt like an individual and someone who was valued'.

Another result was that when outrageous behaviour did occur, it might simply be overlooked. On a training exercise in 1944, Tanky Challenor aimed two bullets inches from a sergeant's feet 'to make a joke of it'. The sergeant's men fired back, and within moments a genuine gun battle was underway between colleagues. It was only when a man was shot in the arm that 'everyone came to their senses'. It is a measure of the unit that there was no inquiry or court martial in the aftermath, Challenor recalls, merely an order posted on a noticeboard 'telling us to cut out that kind of bloody nonsense'.

Back in January 1942, however, David Stirling was still establishing his highly irregular unit. To a large degree, the problems he mulled at Shepheard's Hotel were solved by the support of General Auchinleck, who was impressed by 'L' Detachment's contribution to Operation Crusader. The

SAS had been responsible for almost a third of the enemy's total aircraft losses. The Auk duly rewarded Stirling with a generous crop of replacement officers and men, his agreement to the next operation and a promotion to major. All this, in turn, reduced the risk of the SAS being sucked into a larger organisation – but the problem of Jock Lewes's replacement as training officer remained. Stirling now had an idea. But not, in retrospect, a very good one.

17

PADDY AND DAVID: Writer and Artist

Of all the possible candidates to succeed Jock Lewes as 'L' Detachment's training officer, David Stirling picked his most successful and aggressive operational leader – Blair 'Paddy' Mayne. This, as Stirling later admitted, 'was a bloody stupid thing to do'.

Mayne, the quiet man from Strangford Lough, was a leader who inspired confidence in the toughest of men. Bob Bennett felt 'immune to danger' when with him. This sense of safety, shared by SAS medical officer Malcolm Pleydell, was 'because he took such great care of the people who were under him'. Dave Kershaw, meanwhile, appreciated Mayne's habit of consulting senior NCOs during raids, even when his mind was already made up. And when asked to compare the styles of Mayne and Stirling on operations, Mike Sadler says:

> Paddy knew what was going on with everybody. He was conscious of everything, what we were all doing. But David, I don't think was like that. He was thinking about strategy, about what equipment would be needed next time. One felt his mind was on higher things rather than what was happening to you.

Even Stirling was quick to acknowledge Mayne's leadership ability and battlefield intuition. They were the reasons why, he now argued, the Ulsterman should become 'L' Detachment's training officer. Yet this plan was fundamentally flawed. It made little sense after all, for the unit's most valuable operational asset to be sidelined in an administrative job. Indeed,

Mayne had a trait that was often hinted at but less frequently named. He enjoyed killing. Malcolm Pleydell was deeply struck by a brief conversation they shared shortly before the start of a raid:

> 'Well, good luck,' I said after we had exchanged a few remarks, to which [Mayne] replied by saying he thought there should be some 'good killing.' As I walked over to the medical tent I wondered if I could ever think of 'good killing' and felt rather weak-minded and unwarlike in my inability to do so.

On the first Tamet raid, the need for 'good killing' might, in other circumstances, have wrecked the operation. Yet far from compromising his ability to lead and motivate his men, Mayne's aggression inspired 'L' Detachment members. They wanted to live up to his example – and they wanted him to be present as they tried.

In the circumstances, then, it was hardly surprising that Mayne reacted coldly when Stirling told him of his decision. He initially suspected Stirling of professional jealousy. While he was stuck at Kabrit, after all, Stirling would be able to overtake his haul of destroyed aircraft. (There may have been some truth to this suspicion.) But, in the moment, Mayne controlled himself and refrained from violence – in part because Stirling assured him that the role would only be temporary.

The subsequent raid on enemy ships in the port of Bouerat, which Mayne missed, was chiefly notable for the involvement of the Special Boat Section, a small unit that had been part of 8 Commando. Members of the SBS paddled two-man foldable kayaks, called folbots, from which they could attach limpet mines to floating targets. The raid, however, was a failure. Rommel's most recent advance had led to enemy ships being moved from Bouerat to Benghazi, depriving the raiders of their targets. The upshot was that Stirling failed to increase his haul – and he returned to Kabrit, where he found Paddy Mayne reading James Joyce surrounded by empty bottles, looking dark and resentful.

Mayne, it soon became clear, had been neglecting his unasked-for duties. A group of recently recruited French members had been left half-trained, while a valued explosives expert, Bill Cumper, had been allowed to leave. A long and ferocious argument ensued between Stirling and Mayne,

Left: Paddy Mayne.

Right: David Stirling asleep on the wheel of a jeep.

until the mood calmed and the pair relaxed into drunken conversation. They spoke openly about loss – Mayne was missing his closest friend, Eoin McGonigal, the Irish officer killed during Operation Squatter – and each man learned something about the other.

It was already clear to most original members of 'L' Detachment that David Stirling had more than one side to his character. Jimmy Brough remembers that Stirling would give the impression of being 'a hard man' while on a raid, entirely focused on the task, scheming and planning meticulously so that no opportunity was missed to strike at the enemy. But at some stage on the journey back to Kabrit, he 'would change back into his usual vague self'. And that reversion, says Brough, would be very sudden.

This vagueness was seen in the turmoil of the Cairo flat used by Stirling as his unofficial SAS headquarters. So chaotic was it, with its stream of visitors and official papers strewn everywhere, that it became a recognised security risk. There was even speculation that the Cairene butler was in the pay of the enemy. 'It was that kind of atmosphere!' says Mike Sadler.

Now, as the two men sat drinking in Mayne's tent, Stirling revealed something of his past. Before the war, he said, he had lived in Paris, where

he had desperately tried to make a living as an artist. Dressing in threadbare clothes, passing himself off as a young man of the people, he spent his days painting in different styles, trying to discover his own. And while he had a vivid imagination and an intense desire to succeed, he became increasingly frustrated as the results consistently failed to match his creative ambition. In the end, his tutor told him the devastating truth: no amount of hard work or creativity could make up for his basic lack of drawing skill. 'It remains the most bitter disappointment of my life,' Stirling would admit many years later.*

Stirling admitted all this to Mayne, explaining that he had reacted to his artistic failure by going to the opposite extreme and pursuing the most gruelling physical ambition he could imagine. He had decided to become the first man to climb Mount Everest, a goal he was building towards when war broke out.

* The open atmosphere of the SAS may have been influenced in part by Stirling's experiences in Paris, where he lived alongside, and learned to respect, people from very different backgrounds to his own. The pre-war artists in Montmartre created a community, he later said, where 'everywhere one turned there was willing help and advice'.

By this point in the conversation, all aggression had fallen away from Mayne. Quietly, drunkenly, he admitted that he had his own frustrated ambition. All he had ever wanted to do, he said, was to be a writer.* As the pair spoke openly, for the first and last time, Stirling began to understand Mayne a little better. Everybody who knew the Ulsterman had witnessed his deep devotion and care for those around him, as well as his anger and violence, sometimes towards the same people.† It now dawned on Stirling that Mayne was a deeply sensitive person sitting on a well of unfulfilled creative energy. He was driven to all kinds of behaviour by his frustrations – and what was his sixth sense on SAS raids, after all, if not a kind of creativity, a rare ability to anticipate and communicate in an extraordinary situation?

By the time the two men parted, two things seemed clear. First, that Stirling would have to return Mayne to an operational role immediately. And second, that the SAS owed its success, at least in part, to the creative failures of two highly unusual men.

* Mayne was certainly an avid reader and was often observed with a book. Not only was he reading James Joyce when Stirling arrived at Kabrit from Bouerat, after a July 1942 raid Malcolm Pleydell spotted him enjoying *The Spanish Farm*, a novel by R.H. Mottram. He also enjoyed poetry and would often ask Mike Sadler to recite poems during evenings in the mess. 'Paddy loved recitations of any kind. He had a sentimental streak,' remembers Sadler.

† Mayne was notorious for his outbursts. Speaking to the Imperial War Museum, Johnny Wiseman, who joined the SAS in 1942, said that after a heavy bout of drinking, Mayne once pinned him down and forcibly shaved off half his beard without soap or water. 'I thought he was going to cut my throat,' said Wiseman. 'It was the most dangerous moment of the war as far as I was concerned.'

18

CHURCHILL AND SON

Randolph Churchill, son of the prime minister, had served with Layforce in 1941 until the unit's disbandment. He then became the army's press spokesman in the Middle East, but never seemed to enjoy the role. He wanted instead a front-line position with a prestigious unit, but none seemed prepared to take him on. In the meantime, he became a frequent visitor to the Cairo flat used by David Stirling. And Stirling, as we have seen, was often willing to offer SAS positions to prominent friends.

There were good reasons why commanding officers were cautious of appointing Randolph. For one thing, they did not want to be responsible for the death or capture of Winston's beloved son. For another, he was overweight; one journalist described him as being 'dressed in a Commando cover-all that fitted like a greengrocer's bag around a single onion'. But a significant problem was his personality: he was awkward, argumentative, and frequently wrong. As Stirling once said, 'I was very fond of him, but you couldn't talk to him without arguing with him. It always came out as a verbal scrap.'

Randolph had too much confidence and, perhaps, too little. Winston had raised him as an equal, entitled to speak without deference to absolutely anybody, no matter their standing. This led to toe-curling scenes as he argued with generals and contradicted statesmen. Yet he was frequently aware of being tolerated only because of his father. A quality that Randolph undoubtedly possessed, however, was physical courage. As he himself noted, 'I have no imagination – so action doesn't bother me in advance.' His father, of course, valued courage above almost all other virtues, and Randolph was always aiming to please his father.

In the spring of 1942, David Stirling ran into an old friend in Cairo, the

David Stirling at the wheel of the Blitz Buggy. His passengers are (left to right): Reg Seekings, 'Johnny' Rose and Johnny Cooper.

much-admired diplomat and member of parliament Fitzroy Maclean. After pleasantries, he asked Maclean whether he would like to join the SAS. Maclean asked him what that was. Pleased with the answer, he said, 'Yes.'

At about the same time, Randolph – also a member of parliament – joined the SAS. This arrangement seemed to be in the interests of both parties. Randolph was joining a daredevil unit with a conspicuous winged badge announcing one's courage. He'd finally be able to prove himself – particularly to his father, always capable of crushing him with double-edged thoughtfulness, as when he wrote: 'Of course I do not wish to hamper you in any way, but I am told parachuting becomes much more dangerous with heavy people . . .'

For Stirling, Randolph offered a direct connection to Winston and all the benefits that could bring to the SAS. However unfit or annoying Randolph might prove, it was surely a deal worth making.

The next 'L' Detachment operation planned was an attack on Benghazi, Rommel's chief supply port. A party brought to the edge of town by the LRDG would use an inflatable boat to plant explosives on ships moored in the harbour. Their transport in the town would be a Ford station wagon, driven by Stirling and painted to resemble a German staff car, complete with air recognition stripe across the bonnet. This car was known fondly by Stirling as the 'Blitz Buggy'.

On hearing of the planned raid, Randolph begged to take part. Stirling refused at once; six officers and NCOs were already undergoing specific training. Randolph, who was wholly untrained and entirely unfit, began to argue. Getting nowhere, he took to puffing loudly and ostentatiously around the camp on a series of early morning runs. Eventually, worn down by the display, Stirling gave in. Randolph could come – but only as far as the lying-up spot outside the town. He would not be joining the raid itself.

An officer who *was* joining was Randolph's fellow new boy, Fitzroy Maclean, who spoke enough Italian (or once had) to help the party out of tight spots. Another member of the group, intelligence officer Gordon Alston, was familiar with the layout of Benghazi. There were no equivalent reasons for Randolph's presence. Yet at the end of a five-day drive with the LRDG, a detonator accidentally blew up in Reg Seekings's hand, with, according to Maclean, the following result:

> The crack of the exploding detonator had hardly died away and the wounded man's hand had not been dressed and tied up, before Randolph emerges from behind the nearest sand dune, bristling with lethal weapons and ready to start. There could be no stopping him now.

The overgrown schoolboy *would* be coming on the raid. He climbed into the Blitz Buggy, and with Stirling, Maclean, Alston, Cooper and Rose, headed down the escarpment towards Benghazi.*

Under cover of darkness, the raid started badly. The car developed a noisy fault, Maclean had to use his creaky Italian to pass through a checkpoint into the town, and they attracted the attention of another vehicle which began following them. But the biggest problem proved to be the inflatable boat. It failed to inflate – as, devastatingly, did the spare. Without a working boat they could not sabotage any ships. The mission could no longer be described as a raid. It was reclassified as reconnaissance for a future operation.

* When the party made a stop to cut telephone wires, Stirling smelled rum in Randolph's water bottle and angrily emptied the contents onto the sand.

Day was now dawning, and the group would soon have to hide away. Told to find a shelter for the Blitz Buggy, Randolph and Johnny Rose attracted an audience of curious locals who watched them trying to push it inside a bombed-out house. The others, meanwhile, were looking sufficiently Italian in the gloom that enemy soldiers began falling in behind them. The result was a strange (and perhaps unique) assembly of Allied and Axis soldiers marching together through the centre of Benghazi.

Fitzroy Maclean, thinking of a way to avoid being exposed, decided to march everybody (Stirling, Alston, Cooper and the Italians) to the main gate of the docks, where he angrily accused the Italian security commander of neglecting his duty. How, he yelled, had his men managed to walk around the area for most of the night without once being properly challenged? 'Why, for all you know,' teased Maclean, 'we might be British saboteurs carrying loads of high explosive!'

The commander laughed nervously at the suggestion while the Italian soldiers, keen to avoid trouble, slipped away. Maclean quickly led his SAS back to Randolph and Rose, who had in the meantime managed to conceal the car inside the house. Everybody then went upstairs to spend the day hidden on the derelict upper floor.

As the town came to life, it became clear that the house sat almost directly opposite a busy German headquarters. Throughout the day, officers came and went, unaware that the son of the British prime minister – and potentially the war's greatest propaganda coup – was just out of reach.

As it was, the SAS group sat anxiously on the floor in their upstairs rooms. For much of the day Johnny Rose gazed at a patch of sunlight creeping slowly across the wall, waiting for it to reach a particular crack. At midday his attention was diverted when he heard somebody moving over the roof. 'We all got ready for trouble,' Rose later remembered, 'craning our necks up and watching the ceiling like a pack of animals.' It was a false alarm but, fed up with sitting around, David Stirling decided to recce the harbour on the pretence of going for a swim. Dressed in a polo-neck with corduroy trousers, suede boots and a towel around his neck, he headed outside – looking so English, thought the others, that they were unlikely to see him again.

Only Randolph seemed immune to the tension, talking loudly and often. As he kept watch (he had been given a particularly long shift 'to teach him not to be lazy') he heard somebody entering the house and climbing the stairs. Randolph started grunting in anticipation, 'as he always did,' says Stirling, 'in moments of intense excitement when about to gamble way beyond his means.' The intruder turned out to be a drunk Italian sailor who caught sight of Randolph and ran terrified back out into the street. The prime minister's son chased him but returned only with his cap.

After dark, Stirling (safely returned from his 'swim') decided on a final bluff. He had the group set out again, walking arm-in-arm around the town, whistling and laughing, pretending to be a band of Italian recruits. They had a good look around and almost carried out some sabotage – but, finally, after a 36-hour stay inside the enemy-held town, they climbed inside the Blitz Buggy and drove out of Benghazi to meet up with the LRDG. The group arrived 24 hours late to find their long-suffering chauffeurs (and Reg Seekings) waiting patiently.

The drama was still not over, however. Driving the Blitz Buggy from Alexandria to Cairo, Stirling took a bend too fast. He turned the car over, killing *Daily Telegraph* journalist Arthur Merton, to whom he was giving a lift, and badly injuring his other passengers. Maclean, unconscious for four days after the crash, was left with a fractured skull, while Randolph had three crushed vertebrae which brought his membership of the SAS to an end. Stirling was almost unscathed – but he was left with the shattering knowledge that the first man he killed in wartime was a Fleet Street correspondent.

Given its objectives and results, it is hard to describe the Benghazi raid as anything but a total failure. Yet a wider view is possible. Randolph, as Fitzroy Maclean writes, enjoyed himself so much on the raid that 'when he wasn't talking, he literally yelped with pleasure and excitement, like a dog following a hot scent'. Such a level of delight led him to write – as David Stirling hoped he would – a long, vivid and embellished account of the raid to his father. The most powerful man in Britain received what was in essence a ten-page love letter to the SAS, in which his son boasted of his own courage while thanking the organisation for giving him 'the most exciting half-hour' of his life. Randolph's wife, Pamela, reported that Winston had been 'very pleased with your letter to him and terribly proud; in fact, I have rarely seen him so excited . . .'

Left to right: Randolph Churchill with his father Winston, sister Sarah and mother Clementine.

The prime minister was eager to meet Stirling. Once he had done so, he described him, quoting Byron, as 'the mildest manner'd man that ever scuttled ship or cut a throat'. Churchill, so prone to sudden enthusiasms, quickly became the SAS's most ardent supporter, as subsequent events would demonstrate.

As for David Stirling, it was clear that Churchill and Son were acting out the parts he had written for them. If he and his brother had sent Auchinleck a good sales pitch ten months earlier, he had now provided the prime minister with a better one – and he hadn't even had to deliver it himself.

19

THAT OTHER SAS

In May 1942, as the SAS and LRDG drove north-west from Siwa towards Benghazi, they encountered the Wire, a six-foot-tall, thirty-foot-wide barbed wire entanglement erected by the Italians to mark the border between Libya and Egypt. There were plenty of gaps in the Wire, and vehicles were able to pass through without difficulty. The enemy lines were about 130 miles further on, and once in Axis territory, the group travelled by night. During the day they laid up with vehicles camouflaged and a man on lookout.

One afternoon, as everybody tried to sleep in the searing heat, the lookout came running to say that he had spotted a vehicle moving in

Fitzroy Maclean.

A South African Survey unit at work.

the distance. Whatever this vehicle was, it was now speeding away, presumably to alert the enemy to their presence. David Stirling and Fitzroy Maclean leapt into the Blitz Buggy and roared off in pursuit. Stirling's manic driving soon brought them within distance, but the suspicious vehicle spotted them and tried to accelerate away. The Buggy was faster, though, and both cars soon ground to a sandy halt.

Two men in dirty khaki shirts and shorts climbed out of the other vehicle and walked over. When asked who they were, one of them replied, in a heavy accent, 'SAS'. This, thought Stirling and Maclean, was a clumsy attempt at a bluff. The SAS was now so well known that enemy soldiers were trying to pass themselves off as members to the organisation's own leader!

In fact, the men were not bluffing. But they were not soldiers. They were members of a South African Survey unit – *SAS* – whose job was to map the desert. They had simply been getting on with their work when, to their surprise, a Ford station wagon had suddenly come after them.

This odd little encounter occurred as 'L' Detachment was gaining an impressive reputation for originality and daring. Yet however innovative the unit might have seemed, however singular its exploits, it was not, evidently, the only SAS in the Western Desert. Caution against hubris, it seems, could appear in many forms.*

* To give a sense of the prevailing confusion in the desert, Stirling was never entirely convinced that the two men were not members of a German unit intended to emulate the Long Range Desert Group.

20

MALTA: A Call to Arms

The early summer of 1942 represents a key moment in the SAS's development. Rather than having to justify his next operation to the military authorities, Stirling received an invitation to the office of the director of military operations, where he was presented with a strategic problem and asked how 'L' Detachment could help.

The problem concerned Malta. Both sides understood that the future of the Mediterranean – and Egypt – depended on control of the island. The Allies held it, but it was under naval blockade and near-constant bombardment from Axis aircraft. Supplies were almost exhausted, and crucial convoys were about to be sent out from Alexandria and Gibraltar. What, Stirling was asked, could the SAS do to relieve attacks on these convoys?

An Axis bombing raid on Malta.

The answer, as formulated by Stirling and Paddy Mayne, was to launch a series of simultaneous raids on the airfields and aircraft most likely to be used against the convoys. Berka, Bernina, Barce, Derna and Martuba airfields were dotted around the hump of Cyrenaica. Heraklion was on Crete. The logistics of sending parties to so many areas, and finding the most suitable targets within them, was hugely complex. This was a classic SAS operation – but on a far more ambitious scale than anything attempted before.

The date set for the raids was the night of 13 June 1942, and the men involved would be a mix of old hands and new members. Most of the new men were Free French parachutists who had been sitting idle in Damascus until Stirling offered them an outlet for their energies. In the words of George Jellicoe, these Free Frenchmen were, 'very, very free and very, very French'.

Another, rather more unusual group would also be joining. It consisted of ten German Jews who had fled to Palestine before the war, two German

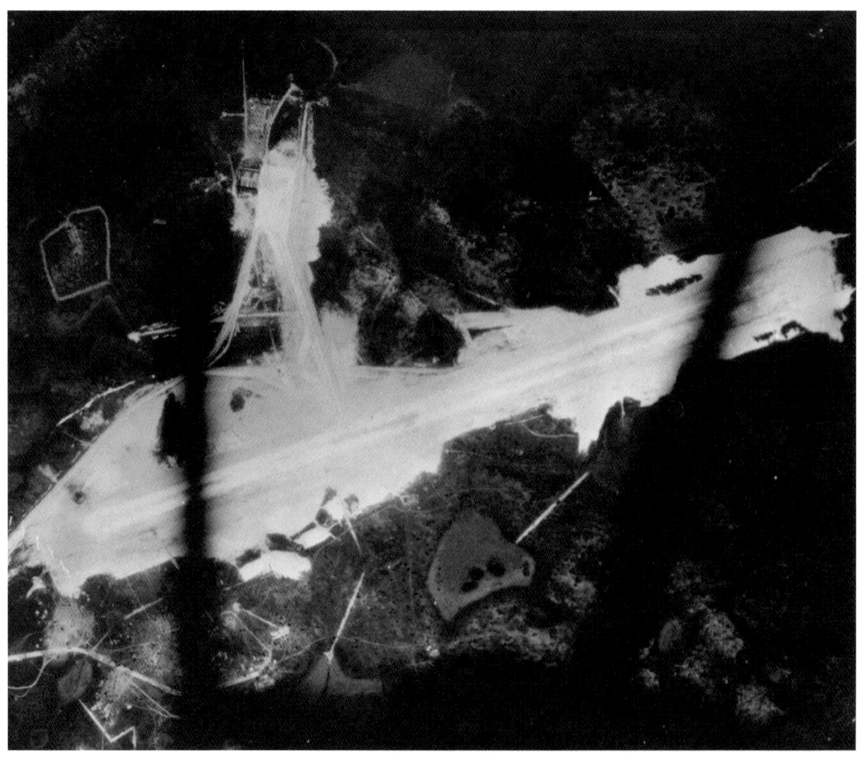

Below left: A reconnaissance photo of an enemy airfield in the desert.

Right: SIG members in 1942, including Maurice Tiefenbrunne (second right) and Walter Fassner (second left).

prisoners who had previously been French Foreign Legionnaires and a polyglot British officer named Herbert Buck. They were all members of a British unit known as the Special Interrogation Group, or SIG.

Consisting in total of about thirty men, SIG was modelled on the 'German Platoon' of the Palmach.* Formed and led by Captain Buck, its members did a job that was both daring and immensely dangerous. They moved around behind enemy lines, posing as German soldiers. They gathered information and carried out sabotage. They set up roadblocks, ate in German canteens and even drew pay from German cashiers. They were in absolutely no doubt as to their fate if captured. As one member, Ariyeh Shai, told historian Martin Sugarman:

> We received no promises. Captain Buck had warned that lives would depend on our ability to wear our disguises faultlessly, to learn to perfection the slang prevalent among the soldiers of the Afrika Korps, and to drill in accordance with all the German methods. 'If your true identity is found out,' said Buck, 'there is no hope for you.'

The men were visited by Isaac Levy, the Jewish chaplain to Eighth Army, who found them in a shed full of German uniforms and German army equipment. 'All the unit's activities,' writes Levy, 'were conducted in German, daily orders were published in that language and often in the

* The Palmach was the strike force of the underground Jewish army based in Palestine.

dead of night a man would be suddenly awakened and he had to speak in German. None must be caught by surprise.'

It was an indication of the SAS's remarkable expansion that it was about to send a group of Palestinian Jews, two recently captured German NCOs and a large party of Free French soldiers into enemy-held territory in Libya. 'L' Detachment had come a long way in a short time.

21

MALTA: The Old Rivals

Two of the raids around Benghazi were to be carried out by David Stirling and Paddy Mayne. Their rivalry was about to be rekindled as Stirling, Reg Seekings and Johnny Cooper raided Benina, the main aircraft repair base, while Mayne, Bob Lilley, Jimmy Storie and Arthur Warburton attacked the nearby Berka satellite airfield. Chauffeured as usual by the LRDG, the parties set off from Siwa for a rendezvous spot south of the Benghazi escarpment. There they spent an evening together before moving off to their respective targets.

Mayne's group reached their airfield just as a (mistaken) RAF bombing raid began. 'We felt very uncomfortable lying there in the middle,' says Lilley, who could not help noting 'how inefficient the RAF were compared with us when it came to destroying aircraft on the ground'.

Once the RAF had flown off, Lilley moved up to plant his first Lewes bomb – but, to his surprise, he found the aircraft guarded by a sentry. On this occasion, it seemed, the airfield was ready for the SAS. Lilley threw himself down as the sentry opened fire. Mayne, who was lurking behind Lilley, lobbed a grenade. The result was a pitched battle involving surprising numbers of enemy soldiers. The SAS men were able to crawl away as the defenders fired on each other in the darkness.

'Once off the airfield, our troubles really started,' remembers Lilley. Troops were waiting in the desert to cut the SAS men off. The evidence was mounting that, on this occasion, their arrival had been expected. 'It seemed impossible for us to get away,' Lilley continues, but 'then we spotted a bit of cover – a garden surrounded by a hedge.' Lilley and Warburton dived under the hedge but when soldiers started searching the garden Warburton panicked and leapt out. He was quickly spotted and taken prisoner.

Lying alone under the hedge as soldiers combed the area, Lilley seemed certain to be captured. As he awaited discovery, he somehow fell asleep, waking the next morning to the sound of sentries' voices. When the sentries moved away, a beautiful young woman in a summer dress appeared beside the hedge. 'Even in this situation,' he says, 'I couldn't help but admire her.' To complete the surreal picture, the woman had a dog which started to sniff Lilley out – so he punched it in the nose. It gave a yelp and moved on.

Trapped in enemy territory in broad daylight, under a flimsy bit of greenery, Lilley's options seemed limited. In the end, he simply stood up, leaving his kit behind, and started to walk.

Expecting to be stopped at any moment, he strolled through miles of enemy encampment, past countless men washing, shaving, milling around and queuing for food. Lost in the everyday, not a single person paid him the slightest attention until he reached a railway line outside Benghazi. There he was confronted by an Italian soldier who tried taking him prisoner. Both men were unarmed, so they began to wrestle. 'I got my hands round his throat,' says Lilley, 'and strangled him.'

Several miles further on, Lilley reached an encampment of friendly Senussi tribesmen. After two hours sitting inside a tent, pondering his next move, he received a welcome surprise: 'One of the Senussi told me there were two soldiers coming towards the tent. I looked out . . . and in the distance I could see Paddy Mayne and [Jimmy] Storie.'

United again, the little party remained with the Senussi until nightfall before returning to the LRDG rendezvous, where they met up with Stirling, Seekings and Cooper. Of the men who had set out, only Warburton was missing – but, for the first time, Mayne's party had failed to destroy any aircraft. Much now rested, it seemed, on how Stirling's party had fared.

The omens were not good. As he set out, Stirling had been in a troubled state of mind. According to Reg Seekings, 'His instructions were that if I was the only one left, I was to carry on 'til I was dead. Simple as that. That was the only time. Previously it had always been: "You save yourself!"'

This 'fight to the death' order reflected, in part, the unusual seriousness of the strategic situation and Stirling's own sense of personal responsibility. Middle East headquarters had, after all, explained to him the importance of the Malta convoys. If supplies did not reach the island, he was told, the island would be lost, with all that entailed for the future of the war. Stirling

Graham 'Johnny' Rose and Jimmy Storie.

had taken responsibility for destroying the aircraft that threatened the convoys, and he intended to live up to that responsibility. In his own mind, he could not afford to fail.

But the order also reflected Stirling's general physical and mental state. He was suffering terribly with fatigue, desert sores and the longer-standing effects of his parachuting accident. He had also quite possibly taken a large dose of Benzedrine (or 'speed'). In all these circumstances, an attitude of zero-sum desperation was hardly surprising.

In the event, on their arrival at Benina, Stirling, Seekings and Cooper spotted a large subterranean fuel dump. They were able to place several Lewes bombs into it straight away. They then found hangars full of aircraft under repair and crates containing brand-new engines. The enemy might have been anticipating an attack on the airfield at Berka, but they were clearly expecting nothing similar at the aircraft repair base nearby. The three men were able to choose targets at will.

Shortly after leaving the last hangar, Stirling acted out an oddly familiar scene. He opened the door to a guardhouse, politely said, 'Share this among you!' and tossed a grenade into a room full of sleeping sentries. The result was precisely the sort of carnage for which he had reprimanded Mayne six months before. One can almost feel the euphoric sense of rivalry playing out as Stirling finally emulated Mayne's success.

As the three men made their way off the airfield, the Lewes bombs began exploding, and Stirling came down with a terrible migraine. For a while he could barely walk and had to be helped along by Seekings and Cooper. A combination of constitutional and psychological factors were at play, but he rallied sufficiently, once he met up with Mayne's party, to revel in his success. So proud and pumped up was he that he 'half jokingly' suggested that he and Mayne should visit the site of his triumph. Mayne, every bit as competitive, agreed. He wanted to make sure, he said with a smile, that Stirling was not exaggerating his success. So Mayne, Stirling and four other adrenalised warriors, keen to keep the buzz going (and to outdo each other) set out once more in a borrowed LRDG truck. They were to return safely – though not before they had run a German roadblock and blown their own truck sky-high. Lilley remembers:

> I heard the click of a time pencil going off and smelt the safety fuse burning (the truck was full of boxes of bombs). I shouted and began to throw boxes of bombs overboard. The next second we had all left the truck in a hurry. There was a big explosion. What was left of the truck could be put into a small haversack. When we saw it we all burst out laughing.

If you had asked the men *why* they were laughing, Lilley notes, nobody could have explained. They took shelter in a Senussi camp until the LRDG arrived, as ever, to deliver them from trouble.

22

MALTA: A Cruel Betrayal

While Stirling and Mayne were engaged in their private battle, SIG members were posing as German soldiers on their way to Derna and Martuba airfields. Maurice Tiefenbrunner, originally from Wiesbaden, near Frankfurt, was one of them. He had arrived in Palestine on the refugee ship *Parita* in 1939, before joining the Pioneer Corps in December to help 'to destroy the German evil'.* Sent back to Europe, he had been one of the last men evacuated to Britain from St Malo in June 1940. When No. 51 (Middle East) Commando was created in October 1940, Tiefenbrunner had been a founder member, and in early 1942, he was approached by Herbert Buck to join SIG. 'Here, at last, was the opportunity I had been waiting for,' he told Martin Sugarman, 'to play a direct role in fighting the Germans.'

By the time of the airfield raids, Tiefenbrunner (who now went by the surname Tiffen†) had learned to think, act and speak as a German soldier. The plan called for him, and 12 other SIG members, to play the part of soldiers, while 15 Free French posed as their prisoners.

They would all travel together in a convoy through enemy territory, supposedly on their way to a prisoner-of-war camp. In reality, they were headed for a rendezvous, where they would split into three parties. One

* At this stage of the war, the British Army permitted Palestinian Jews to serve in non-combatant units only.

† The false name was accompanied by a false background. Maurice Tiffen was said to be a French-Canadian, born in Montreal. This, it was hoped, would give Tiefenbrunner a chance of survival were he to be taken prisoner.

would raid Derna, a second would raid Martuba, while the third would keep watch over the rendezvous point. They would then reconvene before heading back, as a single party, to Allied lines.

With the Palestinian Jewish SIG members were two German NCOs recruited from prisoner-of-war camps. Herbert Brückner and Walter Essner had both been members of the French Foreign Legion before the war. Since their capture at Tobruk, they had co-operated fully with the British and professed strong anti-Nazi sentiments. Tiefenbrunner describes Brückner as big and brash, in his twenties, while Essner was quiet and good-natured, and several years older than his less agreeable comrade.

The party was travelling in a convoy made up of two German trucks and a British staff car, which was designed to look as though it had been captured by the Afrika Korps. As it travelled through Axis-held territory, the convoy passed through two checkpoints. At the first, Buck and Brückner found themselves sharing a glass of wine in the guardroom with an Italian major. The major was convivial but obstinate: as nobody knew the current password, he could not let the vehicles pass. The problem was solved when Brückner began screaming convincingly at the major, 'You are holding us up! I'll report you to our superiors! Keep out of the way! Don't you see German soldiers are coming back from the desert?'

The major was so taken aback that he allowed the convoy to pass. At the second checkpoint, the vehicles were waved through by a rotund German corporal with a warning that British commandos might be about, even this far into Axis territory. The convoy passed the night as unobtrusively as possible in a nearby transit camp, where Ariyeh Shai joined the dinner queue to the amusement of the watching Free French 'prisoners'.

The following day, the group drove on to Derna, where they carried out a reconnaissance. To their delight they found two airfields – one full of Messerschmitt 110s, the other crowded with Stuka dive-bombers. They made their way to the rendezvous, halfway between Derna and Martuba, where they split into three parties as agreed. One, led by Buck and Essner, was heading for Martuba. The second, led by Augustin Jordan (the second-in-command of the SAS Free French squadron) and Brückner, was bound for Derna. The third, led by Tiefenbrunner in the staff car, was supposed to keep in touch with both raiding parties and make sure that everything was clear for a quick escape.

Maurice Tiefenbrunner.

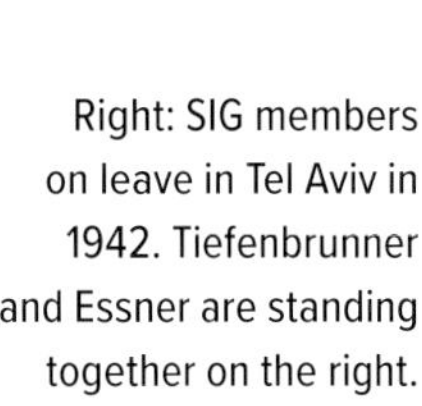

Right: SIG members on leave in Tel Aviv in 1942. Tiefenbrunner and Essner are standing together on the right.

After a while, Tiefenbrunner heard a series of loud explosions coming from the direction of Martuba. A message also arrived confirming that everything was going to plan with Buck and Essner's group. But there were no corresponding messages from Derna. After a while, Tiefenbrunner heard shouts coming from the darkness and, thinking he was about to be attacked, raised his machine gun. But the noise, it turned out, was coming from Augustin Jordan, who had struggled back from Derna on foot. His story, once he was in a state to speak, was devastating.

Herbert Brückner, the brash German NCO, had been driving the Derna-bound truck. Beside him in the cab was Petr Haas, a Palestinian SIG member. Behind them, in the truck bed, were Jordan, his fellow Free Frenchmen, and other Palestinians. The truck was apparently having engine trouble and Brückner kept stopping to look under the bonnet. Eventually, he told Haas that he needed tools, so he set off to get help from a nearby German post.

After an uncomfortable wait, Jordan, in the truck bed, suddenly heard German voices yelling '*Heraus*!' He peered out and was instantly grabbed by two soldiers. Seeing that the truck was surrounded by Germans, the Free French and Palestinians jumped out and began firing their machine guns. The Germans, superior in numbers, fired back. Haas, in the cab, took stock of the situation, and blew the truck – and himself – up. Jordan explained: '[Haas] had seen that he was hopelessly trapped, and while still in the lorry, had flung a grenade into a pile of ammunition in the back.'

In the chaos, Jordan managed to run clear, eventually reaching the rendezvous. No one else, it seemed, had survived (although evidence later came to light that Eliahu Gottlieb, a Palestinian SIG man, had escaped and found his way to a nearby hospital where he drew the suspicion of a doctor, thereby ensuring his murder).

As Jordan and Tiefenbrunner were speaking, Buck, Essner and the rest of the Martuba party arrived at the rendezvous. They were in high spirits, having destroyed 20 aircraft and suffered no casualties. They had done precisely what they had set out to do, and were profoundly shocked to hear of events at Derna.

What, though, of Brückner? It was clear to everybody that he had betrayed them – but the full story only arrived, later in the year, with the capture and interrogation of Friedrich Körner, a Messerschmitt 109 pilot based at Martuba. Körner revealed that Brückner had left the truck, marched directly to the Derna airfield office, and announced that he was a German soldier driving a lorry full of Allied troops in German uniform. He had agreed to drive the lorry, he said, 'as he felt it was the best way of getting back his freedom'. The airfield commander had initially doubted his story, but Brückner reacted so adamantly that soldiers were sent to surround the truck.

None of this detail was known by the surviving SIG and Free French as they made their way back to base, but their bitterness and fury were taken out on the blameless Walter Essner – who was now damned by association. Tiefenbrunner remembers: 'I took it upon myself to have my gun directed towards [Essner] just in case he should try any "funny business" . . . I made myself stay awake all the time, in order to be ready to kill [him], should he make a wrong move.'

The party reached Siwa safely, but Essner did not survive for much longer. He was shot 'trying to escape' while being escorted to POW camp. It seems, though, that his killing was premeditated, carried out by a fellow SIG member. As for Brückner, his epilogue comes from Jim Worden, a wartime member of the RAF, who met him after the war while they were both serving with the French Foreign Legion.

Brückner told Worden that he had personally received a gallantry award from Erwin Rommel for his action and then been posted to Tunisia. After the fall of Tunis, he had been taken prisoner by the Americans before eventually rejoining the Legion. But the fear had never left him, he told Worden, that 'the British might still be after me as a war criminal'.

Brückner never paid for his actions – but he was not forgotten by Maurice Tiefenbrunner and the other surviving members of SIG. Tiefenbrunner would become a permanent member of the SAS and was taken prisoner at the end of 1942. He survived captivity, as Maurice Tiffen from Montreal, despite making several unsuccessful escape attempts. He died in Jerusalem at the age of 97 in July 2013.

23

MALTA: The Broken Code

At around the time that Friedrich Körner revealed the details of Herbert Brückner's betrayal, another interrogation – of Messerschmitt 109 pilot Ernst Klager – disclosed a further detail. Klager, who was at Derna on the night of the attempted raid, said that 'a warning was issued in advance that a British raiding party would appear to carry out sabotage on the aerodrome that night'. It seems that *before* Brückner appeared in the Derna airfield office, the Germans had already been warned that an attack was coming.

This could explain why Paddy Mayne's party had encountered more problems than usual. Bob Lilley, after all, had found a guard on the very first aircraft he encountered, while soldiers had been posted in the desert to cut off the men's escape.

Who, then, might have given the enemy advance warning of the SAS raids? There was no truly effective German spy network in Cairo – and, even if there had been, how could a spy have got hold of such specific operational plans? Was there a traitor at Middle East headquarters? Within the SAS? Had the Germans made a lucky guess?

The answer was none of these. Though there *was* a leaky tap – or, rather, a faucet. The American military attaché in Cairo – Colonel Bonner Fellers – was inadvertently passing information directly to the Germans. So thorough was he that, by lunchtime each day, Rommel was reading the broad (and sometimes specific) details of British plans agreed the previous evening.

Bonner Fellers was an immensely sociable and well-connected man. When David Stirling met Hermione Ranfurly on the steps of Shepheard's Hotel in January, she was walking away from a lunch engagement with

Fellers, who had complained to her of the overconfidence of senior British officers. He may well have been right, but it was his own overconfidence that was about to be punished.

Since Fellers had arrived in Cairo, the British military authorities had been keen to feed him a rich diet of high-level information. He was known, after all, to be in favour of sending American troops to the Middle East, while the American president, Franklin Roosevelt, was understood to heed his advice. Fellers's telegraph messages to Washington were encrypted using a code which, in early 1942, was broken by the Germans. The British (who doubted the code's security) began insisting that Fellers obtain their approval before sending sensitive material. Fellers agreed in principle – but carried on as before.

Days before the SAS Malta raids, Fellers sent a message to Washington giving a succinct and accurate précis of the plan. He advised that parachutists, together with patrols of the Long Range Desert Group, intended to mount simultaneous attacks on aircraft on nine Axis airfields on the night of 12–13 June, using sticker bombs.

The message was duly picked up by the Germans, who retransmitted it on 11 June. This was deciphered, in turn, by the British, the resulting Ultra message being shown to Winston Churchill on 14 June. There can be no

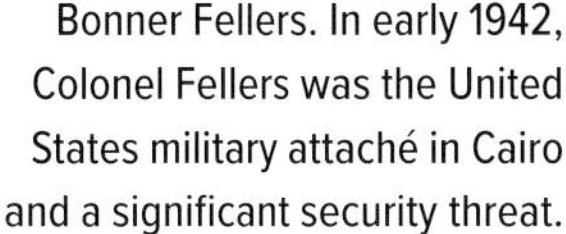

Bonner Fellers. In early 1942, Colonel Fellers was the United States military attaché in Cairo and a significant security threat.

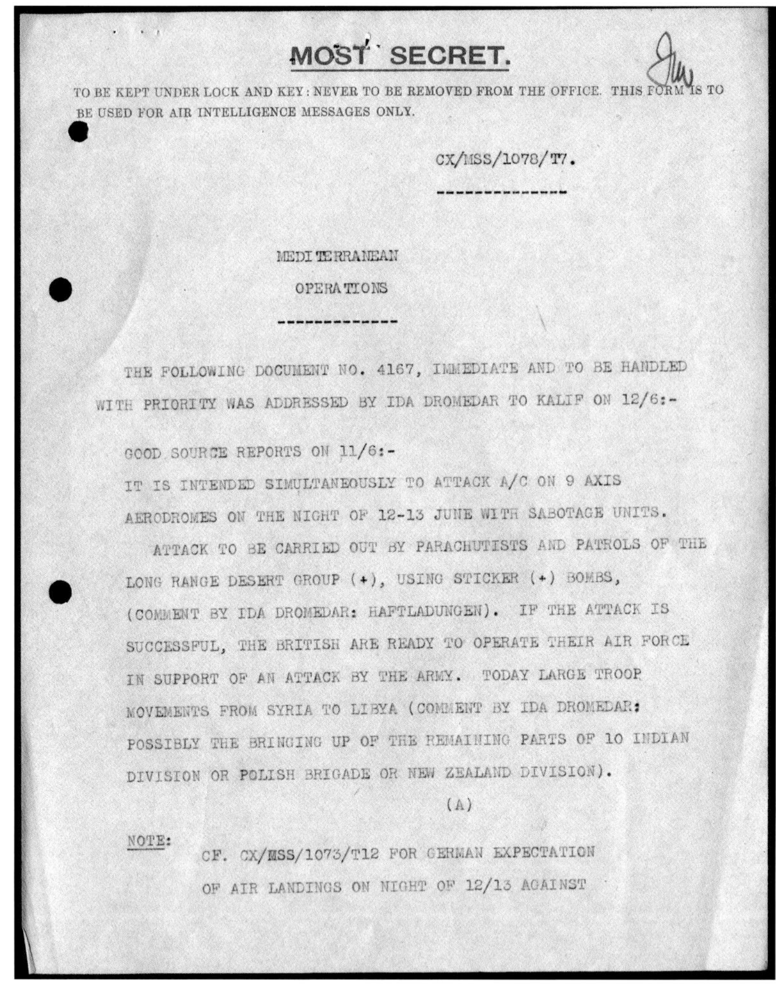

MOST SECRET.

TO BE KEPT UNDER LOCK AND KEY: NEVER TO BE REMOVED FROM THE OFFICE. THIS FORM IS TO BE USED FOR AIR INTELLIGENCE MESSAGES ONLY.

CX/MSS/1078/T7.

MEDITERRANEAN
OPERATIONS

THE FOLLOWING DOCUMENT NO. 4167, IMMEDIATE AND TO BE HANDLED WITH PRIORITY WAS ADDRESSED BY IDA DROMEDAR TO KALIF ON 12/6:-

GOOD SOURCE REPORTS ON 11/6:-
IT IS INTENDED SIMULTANEOUSLY TO ATTACK A/C ON 9 AXIS AERODROMES ON THE NIGHT OF 12-13 JUNE WITH SABOTAGE UNITS.
ATTACK TO BE CARRIED OUT BY PARACHUTISTS AND PATROLS OF THE LONG RANGE DESERT GROUP (+), USING STICKER (+) BOMBS, (COMMENT BY IDA DROMEDAR: HAFTLADUNGEN). IF THE ATTACK IS SUCCESSFUL, THE BRITISH ARE READY TO OPERATE THEIR AIR FORCE IN SUPPORT OF AN ATTACK BY THE ARMY. TODAY LARGE TROOP MOVEMENTS FROM SYRIA TO LIBYA (COMMENT BY IDA DROMEDAR: POSSIBLY THE BRINGING UP OF THE REMAINING PARTS OF 10 INDIAN DIVISION OR POLISH BRIGADE OR NEW ZEALAND DIVISION).

(A)

NOTE: CF. CX/MSS/1073/T12 FOR GERMAN EXPECTATION OF AIR LANDINGS ON NIGHT OF 12/13 AGAINST

The deciphered message shown to Winston Churchill on 14 June.

doubt that Bonner Fellers gave the enemy inadvertent and full warning of the Malta attacks.

The American code was changed in late June, finally depriving the Germans of their 'Good Source'. A German intelligence officer later wrote: 'We no longer had this incomparable source of authentic information, which had contributed so decisively during the first half of 1942 to our victories in North Africa.'

Bonner Fellers was sent home to Washington. His security breach was subsequently kept very quiet, and his name rarely mentioned. In November

1943, at a formal dinner, Hermione Ranfurly asked General Eisenhower whether he knew Fellers. 'Any friend of Bonner Fellers is no friend of mine,' snapped the Allied commander before turning away.

In spite of Fellers's forewarning and the unusually thorough preparations of the airfield defenders, the Malta raiders had been able to destroy a reasonable number of aircraft.* (It is open to question how many of these aircraft – those at Benina, for example – were intended to attack the Malta convoys.) In the end, though, the statistic that mattered was the number of ships that reached Malta to relieve the island. Of the 17 that set out from Alexandria and Gibraltar, only two arrived safely. The other 15, attacked by submarines as well as aircraft flown from Sicily and Italy, were sunk or forced to return to port. But the two successful ships managed to dock with sufficient supplies to keep Malta going until a larger convoy arrived.

In an interview with journalist and historian Gordon Stevens, David Stirling initially expressed his belief that all 17 ships would have been lost without the SAS raids. 'Therefore,' he said, 'we regard what we did on that raid as saving Malta.' But after giving the matter some thought, Stirling modulated his language: 'I suspect those two [ships] wouldn't have got through without us,' he said. 'I know we thought that at the time, but . . . we must be careful about that.'

What was beyond doubt, however, was that the war in the Mediterranean was turning sharply against the Allies in June 1942. Rommel had launched a desert advance that seemed likely to sweep British and Commonwealth forces out of Egypt. It certainly swept the SAS and LRDG out of Siwa, sending Stirling's men back to Kabrit. The iconic port of Tobruk fell ('No news has shocked us more since Dunkirk,' Hermione Ranfurly wrote in her diary) and Rommel's forces moved eastwards until they reached a little-used railway stop named El Alamein.

The enemy was only 60 miles from Alexandria and the Allied position was undoubtedly bleak – yet, for the SAS, there was light in the darkness. The longer Rommel's tail, after all, the greater the opportunity for a shapeless threat 'drifting about like a gas' somewhere out in the silent desert . . .

* The precise tally varies widely from 37 (as Stirling estimated) to over 70.

An SAS jeep before alterations . . . and after (below).

24

WILLYS BANTAMS

After the Malta raids, David Stirling travelled to Cairo where he managed to get his hands on a dozen tough little American cars. The Willys Bantam, or 'jeep', was a four-wheel-drive vehicle that Stirling and Mayne hoped would prove suitable for desert use once some changes had been made. Sun-compasses, water condensers and other Ralph Bagnold features were duly added, as were Vickers K machine guns fore and aft.

Before the jeeps could be put to use, however, a problem was encountered that surprised many of the officers. Almost none of the men knew how to drive. This fact reflected pre-war Britain, as Dave Kershaw explains:

> The majority of officers, at that time, had enjoyed ownership of a motor car . . . so taking for granted the fact anyone could and should be able to drive . . . and forgetting the fact that these men were more used to public transport, and, if lucky, the luxury of the borrowed pushbike.

Driving lessons were quickly organised and, once the jeeps were set to work, they quickly proved their worth. They were relatively simple to maintain, they could handle rough desert terrain over long distances, and, when they got stuck, they could be physically lifted clear. They had, as Mike Sadler remembers, another crucial desert advantage over larger vehicles:

> They were easy to camouflage because they were very low little vehicles, and you could make them lower still just by digging the wheels down a little bit. With the aid of a tarpaulin and a bit of netting, you could flatten them out so that there would be virtually no shadow.

Jeeps were worked so hard over such difficult ground that they could not be expected to survive for long, as Kershaw recalls: 'Once they'd gone beyond repair, we just blew them up. Because we always had spare bombs around.'

Perhaps the most distinctive component of the SAS jeeps were the twin Vickers K guns with their drum magazines and impressive rate of fire. Intended for use on aircraft, they took a shattering physical and psychological toll on the enemy when fired on the ground. They could unnerve gunners, too, as Sadler recalls:

> They were very difficult because they were on either side of a pillar. You tried to fire them at the same time, but often you didn't, and the one you fired first would pull round and shower bullets over the countryside. You had to get hold of it, and then you could do better.

The adoption of jeeps meant that 'L' Detachment would no longer have to rely on the Long Range Desert Group for transport. Raiding parties could stay out in the desert for longer periods without having to return at a designated time to be picked up. Like a young adult being entrusted with the car keys, the SAS was entering a new period of its life. 'That's when we really began to exercise our muscularity,' says Stirling.

But if the LRDG was no longer providing transport, neither could it offer its navigational expertise. Stirling's solution was to engage Mike

Sadler, who had previously been taking part in both LRDG and SAS operations, as 'L' Detachment's senior navigator. Yet he was never actually asked whether he wanted to join the SAS: 'All I knew was that David Stirling decided he wanted me, and somehow he got me. So I found myself spending time with the SAS instead of the LRDG. I didn't have much say in the matter.'

It is a measure of Sadler's standing that he was adopted in this fashion. When Stirling wanted something (or somebody), he usually went to great lengths to get it (or him). With its own transport and guides, and its freedom to decide on targets, Stirling's self-contained unit was truly turning itself into a private army.

Sadler was not purely a navigator, of course. One night, he and Stirling set out behind enemy lines 'looking for trouble'. This meant driving along the coast road, shooting at things coming the other way. And if there was nothing to shoot at, it could mean knocking down telephone wires and dragging them into the desert.

Above left: An SAS icon.

Right: The SAS icon in a modern-day South Wales amusement park.

On the way home, with Stirling driving, they passed a German camp to the side of the road. Stopping about a hundred yards away, Sadler climbed into the back of the jeep and, as Stirling drove slowly forward, he opened fire. He blasted away for five minutes, periodically reaching around the jeep for further ammo. After a while, he could see flashes and hear bullets cracking past. The enemy had started firing back. It was time to move on.

Despite being a relatively late addition to 'L' Detachment's desert compendium, the image of the jeep loaded with bearded warriors and machine guns has, for a modern audience, become the most instantly recognisable symbol of the wartime SAS.

Eighty years after the unit left the Western Desert, the jeep still shows up, with reference to the SAS, in unlikely scenarios. One child-sized example, labelled as 'the hero of many daring SAS missions', offers rides at a Barry Island (in South Wales) amusement arcade.

Jeeps were to change the working practices, and the image, of the SAS. And their adoption would give rise to an extraordinary and ferocious operation, so theatrical in its presentation that it might have been choreographed by Dudley Clarke himself.

25

FIRST DO NO HARM

In June 1942, an unlikely man joined the SAS. Malcolm Pleydell was a doctor, a general practitioner before the war, whose determination to live up to his colleagues occasionally masked, but more often revealed, a thoughtful and sensitive nature. He was, in his private letters, his diary and his published memoir, probably the most perceptive chronicler of life in the wartime SAS.

Pleydell arrived at 'L' Detachment from a Coldstream Guards battalion, where he had been nervous of demonstrating cowardice. He admitted to his diary that 'courage with me was flickering and evanescent, present one second, absent the next. Just a matter of trying to control fear, let alone panic and cowardice.'

This was probably true of most – but few expressed it so honestly and elegantly. Honesty, in fact, was a quality that Pleydell greatly admired, and one that he found in his new SAS colleagues. They were, he felt, straightforward and sincere. They did not seem to take life – or themselves – too seriously. Of Jim Chambers, an officer who would be dead of diphtheria by the end of the year, he writes, 'I never heard him say anything he did not mean, or even adopt a hypocritical attitude. That is high praise indeed.'

We have already witnessed Pleydell's first encounter with Paddy Mayne, during which he was awed by Mayne's hope that the coming raid would bring 'good killing'. Mayne was probably teasing Pleydell, even if his hope was genuine. One can almost see the smile on Mayne's face. But to Pleydell, it was no joke. He felt 'weak-minded and unwarlike' for his inability to enjoy killing. Continually questioning his own courage and character, Pleydell would ultimately shame himself into winning a Military Cross.

A reflective Malcolm Pleydell in the desert.

In fact, Pleydell's courage was demonstrated daily in his attitude to his work and his patients. And the work repaid him. Being medical officer in the SAS, in the desert, meant doing everything and being answerable to no one. He operated on troops in the field under anaesthetic, used plasma for transfusions, and when penicillin arrived in the Middle East in August 1942, he was among the very first to administer it, describing it in a letter as 'a very rare drug for injecting into abdominal wounds which, it is hoped, will save lives'. As he wrote to his fiancée: 'I am entirely responsible for the whole unit, post-operational treatment as well. It's rather wonderful, isn't it?'

So exhilarated was Pleydell by his extensive role and his ability to fulfil it, that he began to doubt that he could ever return to ordinary practice. He writes:

> Doctors, en masse, seem such a dull lot. They forget there is any excitement in life, any thrills. They just sit around on one end of a microscope and that's all there is in life for them . . . I do hope I don't find the post-war life too boring for words.

In fact the desert gave an unusual level of freedom to many soldiers – and doctors were no exception. But in this, as in other ways, Pleydell was unusually sensitive. He was already anticipating the difficulty that many would experience as they tried to settle down to a post-war world.

Pleydell's – and the jeep's – first major SAS operation came in July. The overall plan for the latest series of raids was worked out at the Cairo flat. With maps on the floor, confidential papers on chairs and tables, and people streaming in and out, it was decided to take a sizeable party through the Qattara Depression with supplies piled on jeeps, trucks and the Blitz Buggy. A base would be established behind the lines, from which raiding parties would set off for various coastal airfields stretching from Sidi Barrani in the west to El Daba in the east.

Sitting alongside a lorry driver, Pleydell set off from Kabrit in good spirits – but he soon experienced the realities of desert travel as a succession of problems arose. First, overloaded lorries started to bog down in the sand. To lighten their loads, several were sent back to Kabrit with unnecessary supplies. Then, a thick early-morning fog descended and Pleydell's lorry became lost in the gloom, the driver only finding his bearings when he took a compass bearing on a pair of arguing cockney voices. Listening to

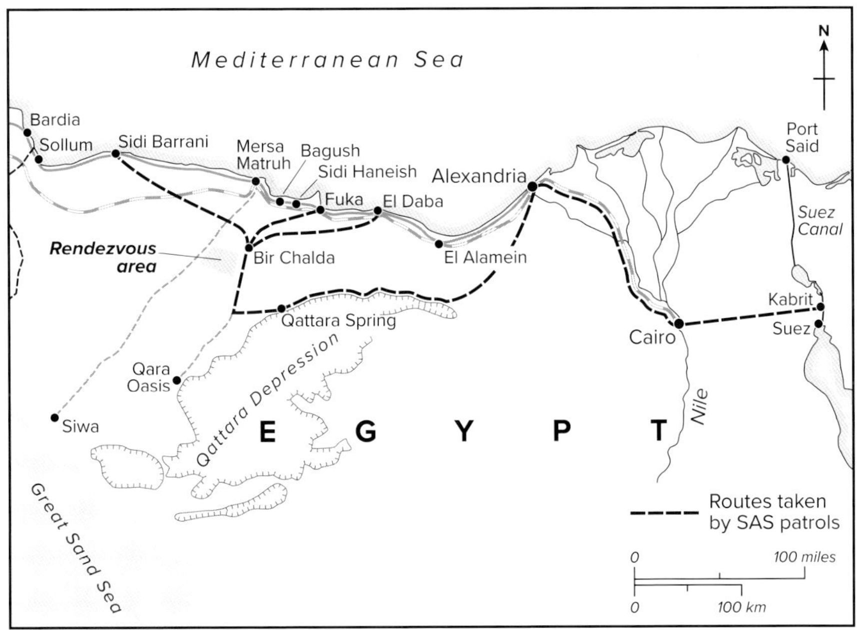

the banter that followed, Pleydell learned a lesson about army behaviour, and specifically SAS behaviour:

'Don't get all worried!'
'Who's worrying?'
'What you say?'
'I said who's worrying?'
'Nobody's worrying.'
'Oh yes they blinking is, see, 'cos you're worrying, see? That's half the blinking trouble! You worry too much, see?'

It was, realised Pleydell, a deadly insult to accuse somebody of worrying. Whatever a man's true feelings, he must appear calm and unconcerned. This was a code, of course, by which Pleydell was already living. He was not about to share his stray emotions with his new SAS friends.

As the fog cleared and the morning cold turned to heat, the party passed through Eighth Army positions, making rude signs to the men as they went. Hours and hours of lonely, barren driving followed, during which Pleydell's driver turned the lorry into whatever hint of a breeze might be blowing. Suddenly a lone human figure was sighted on the crest of a hill: 'I shall never forget that moment, and the quick catch of breath it gave me to see [him] standing up there like an Indian scout and watching our movements below.'

The scout was a Long Range Desert Group patrolman. Pleydell was immensely impressed and reassured by his calm presence. After camping for the night with the LRDG patrol, 70 miles south of Mersa Matruh, the party split up into smaller raiding groups. Bernard Schott and Peter Warr, both parachute instructors, were leading a raid on Sidi Barrani. Augustin Jordan and Bill Fraser were taking separate groups to the two airfields at Fuka. George Jellicoe was off to El Daba. Stirling and Mayne, meanwhile, were going together (for the first time) to Bagush.

Overall, the raids were not successful. Fraser was forced to call off his mission. Schott's party failed to destroy aircraft, although they did sabotage a water pipe flowing between Sidi Barrani and Mersa Matruh. Jellicoe received last-minute intelligence which prevented his party from attacking. But when that intelligence proved incorrect, his group (consisting of

Jellicoe himself, Carol Mather, Dave Kershaw, Bob Bennett and five others) went back several days later, in three jeeps, to the same airfield. They were no more successful this time. The experienced Kershaw and Bennett advised Jellicoe to avoid travelling during daylight hours, but their warning was ignored. The party ended up sheltering helplessly behind cactus plants while an Italian aircraft attacked and Bob Bennett sang 'St Louis Blues'. Two jeeps were destroyed but nobody was killed, and all nine members of the party returned on the remaining jeep, urinating by turns into the radiator to prevent the engine overheating.

Mayne and Stirling's raid was more successful, for unanticipated reasons. As Stirling mounted a roadblock, Mayne and four others (Bob Lilley, Jimmy Storie, Ted Badger and Derek Rawnsley) headed for Bagush airfield, where they planted Lewes bombs on every aircraft. But many of the bombs failed to explode due to damp fuses. As Mayne seethed with frustration, Stirling suggested that they should return to the airfield with a jeep and the Blitz Buggy, firing their Vickers K machine guns at the remaining aircraft. The guns were designed, after all, to destroy aeroplanes. Why not let them do it on the ground? The vehicles' immediate return came as a total surprise to the defenders, and the Vickers guns succeeded in blowing their targets apart in little more than five minutes. By the time they were

Bob Bennett.

finished, all 37 aircraft had been destroyed, either by bombs or bullets. Bill Fraser's tally, at Agedabia, had been equalled in innovative fashion.

Not too far away, meanwhile, Malcolm Pleydell and two SAS lorry drivers were waiting for the raiders' return. To pass the time, the middle-class doctor tried to get to know the working-class NCOs. This was a scene repeated countless times during the levelling-up years of the Second World War, but the novelty and awkwardness were rarely so clearly recorded. Pleydell learned of the Glasgow background of one, and the Brighton home life of the other. How one loved to take a boat down the Clyde and the other would paddle a canoe along the coast to Rottingdean. He described to them his own life, explaining that being a doctor 'wasn't much really – only a question of getting to know your job thoroughly'. As he spoke, he tried to persuade them – and himself – that he really was no better than they were.

The discussion was suddenly interrupted by the war. They heard machine-gun fire and saw long strings of red beads. There was a white flash and an explosion. From another direction came a terrific lightning flash – followed, a few beats later, by a heavy rumble. 'That,' said someone, 'is Major Stirling and Captain Mayne! You bet there's some fun over there!' For Malcolm Pleydell, the war had truly begun.

Over the course of the night, men began arriving back from their raids. The Free French showed up and theatrically let everyone know it. They were happy; they had blown up aircraft. Bill Fraser's party arrived. They were out of luck, though Fraser told of a split-second decision he had just made. Hiding behind a rise in the ground, he had watched a group of Italians pass in front of him. He gently removed a hand grenade from his pack, started fingering the pin, and was about to throw it when he suddenly stopped and put it back again. The young Italians would never know how close they came to death, how countless futures had been decided on a whim. We all like to think that our fate lies in our own hands – but, in truth, so much depends on chance, on the physics of a situation, on a momentary impulse like Bill Fraser's. In the hands of most members of 'L' Detachment, that grenade would have been thrown.

The following morning, the entire party moved north-east to another prearranged spot where they found more SAS men waiting. 'David Stirling was there,' writes Pleydell, 'welcoming us as if we had just come back from a game of golf.' Paddy Mayne was there too, 'giving us a sleepy grin as he lay in the shadow of his jeep reading a Penguin and flicking away an occasional fly'. Mayne said that he had destroyed about thirty planes, although he 'couldn't say how many for certain'. Pleydell, still nervous around the Ulsterman, could not think how to reply. 'Jolly good show,' he said, at last, for want of anything more profound.

The last group to return was George Jellicoe's. They had brought three prisoners with them, which initially annoyed Pleydell. It meant less food and water for everybody else. But as the days went by, and the doctor grew used to their presence, his attitude softened. One of the Germans was a gentle soul with chronic ear pain. 'Had he goose-stepped down the bedecked streets in the military parades of 1939?' Pleydell asked himself. 'I rather doubted it: for he was a simple countryman.' Pleydell took satisfaction from treating such a man.

He also began to derive enjoyment from the desert. He and his colleagues would linger over their evening meal, gazing at the red sun slipping beneath the flat horizon. They were 'waiting and watching, watching and waiting, until we felt that first touch of coolness in the air; the balm and solace of the wilderness'.

On one of these contented evenings, the men were allowed an extra jar of rum and a party atmosphere took hold. Men began to sing, at first

A fire at the end of the day.

self-consciously, then unashamedly. They sang traditional songs, bawdy rugby songs and their favourites – the sentimental jazz standards:

Come to me my melancholy baby,
Cuddle up and don't be blue.
All your fears are foolish fancy, maybe,
You know dear that I'm in love with you.

The Germans were bemused by the British soldiers' choice of songs. They had been raised, after all, to consider American jazz music degenerate. Pleydell started wondering why every other nation seemed to enjoy singing its national songs, while this bunch of young British men preferred to belt out Tommy Dorsey and Billie Holiday tunes. He turned to Paddy Mayne and asked why this was. 'Och, Malcolm,' said Mayne, 'there's nothing to worry about. They're happy. That's the main thing.'

After a while, the French joined in – and so did the Germans. They sang Bierkeller songs and a moving version of 'Lili Marlene', to the loud approval of the SAS. At some point, Pleydell realised just how much he was enjoying himself. Some people at home might not approve of their boys fraternising with the enemy – but what did that matter? This was *not* home. This was a patch of sand in the desert behind enemy lines. 'For most of us,' Pleydell writes, 'there was something especial about that night, something we would be remembering, something we would recall in later years when we spoke of the war . . .'

Malcolm Pleydell would leave the SAS in the early spring of 1943. By then, he had lost some of his closest friends and he was finding the medical work a strain. The unit's attraction had faded. But on that night in July 1942, with the rum, the music and the international camaraderie, he had found the straightforwardness, the honesty and the integrity that he valued above all else.

26

CHARIOTS OF FIRE

In mid-July 1942, Stirling led a patrol back to Kabrit to pick up supplies for the desert rendezvous, where Malcolm Pleydell, Jim Almonds and others remained. Pleydell and Almonds passed the time swapping paperbacks and searching in the desert for animals and historic artefacts. Pleydell had heard that so many Greek and Roman vases were being found in wadis and caves that the Cairo Museum had stopped accepting them – but he was excited when he found a Neolithic arrowhead.

When Stirling's relief party returned, with new jeeps and Vickers K guns as well as food, water, cigarettes and sweets, the rendezvous was increased in size, and the jeeps were placed inside a newly discovered cave where they could be hidden away and worked on. The cave, with its continuous hammering, clattering and singing, made Carol Mather think of the diamond mine from Disney's *Snow White and the Seven Dwarfs*, though who was Dopey he failed to record. (Doc was probably self-evident.)

There was a likely candidate for Grumpy, however. David Stirling had become deeply frustrated by headquarters' view of 'L' Detachment as a sabotage unit rather than a strategically effective force. He was looking for a way to change their view, and to demonstrate the SAS's versatility. Moreover, enemy airfields had started mounting more formidable defences. Raiding them was clearly about to become more difficult.

An answer to both problems, Stirling figured, might be a larger-scale recreation of the recent jeep attack on Bagush. If sufficient jeeps, each blasting four Vickers K guns, could take an airfield by surprise, then an enormous amount of damage could be done without a single man having to dismount. And if the airfield chosen was Landing Ground 21 at Sidi Haneish, with its large assembly of Junkers 52 transport aircraft, then

Sandy Scratchley.

Rommel's supply lines would be severely hampered. This, then, was Stirling's plan. A large squadron of modern chariots was about to descend on an unsuspecting enemy.

If the attack was to succeed, it would have to be very tightly choreographed. So many jeeps firing so many guns had the potential to wipe themselves out without any input from the enemy. The SAS men, most of whom were still ex-guardsmen, might not have done much drilling any more – but this operation would have to be carried out with parade-ground precision. The drivers had to stay in perfect formation, following the tracks of those in front. They had to form a line abreast and a line astern. They had to sit balanced and still; any lean, forwards or backwards, would place them in front of their own guns. The gunners had to restrict their fire accordingly to a rigid arc.

A dress rehearsal was held on the evening of 20 July, during which Pleydell found himself squeezed between the enormous Paddy Mayne and his driver. Everybody seemed to know their job, and before he fell asleep that night, Pleydell heard two officers – Jellicoe and Sandy Scratchley – laughing 'at the way we had held this rehearsal behind the enemy's own lines'. It undoubtedly demonstrated audacity – but it would count for little if the first night fell short.

Mike Sadler was responsible for leading the party of jeeps towards its target. He recalls:

> From base camp in the desert, we had to drive up to the coast and make our way to the airfield. We got to ten miles away. I then set up with the identifiable stars – and we ended up on a dirt track.

Sadler had always proved a reliable navigator. This was why Stirling had procured him from the Long Range Desert Group. But 17 jeeps and their adrenaline-pumped crews were relying on him, and he had led them up a barely visible path leading nowhere. After a while, Stirling stopped his jeep, jumped down and walked back. He did not disguise his frustration. 'Where's this bloody airfield, then, Sadler?'

Mike Sadler was, and remains to this day, an even-natured man. He did not panic. 'I think it's about a mile ahead,' he said. And at precisely that moment, landing lights appeared in front and a Junkers 52 came in to land. The airfield was exactly where Sadler thought it would be. 'It was perfect! It was wonderful!' Sadler remembers. For Jim Almonds, this was 'Mike Sadler's Finest Hour'. He had led the men to Sidi Haneish. Now he was sent to the south-east corner of the perimeter to wait until daylight 'for people who might have come unstuck and wanted somewhere to escape'. It was up to others now.

The first people to join Sadler were Almonds and his gunners, whose jeep fell into an anti-tank trap. The rest of the raiders accelerated towards the airfield, line abreast, as the noise from the aircraft drowned their own. Once they were close enough, all 68 Vickers Ks opened fire on the airfield defences. Before the landing lights could be switched off, the jeeps were on the airfield. Stirling fired his Verey light flare, casting an otherworldly green glow over the entire scene. The jeeps now merged into two columns, moving at fast walking pace, each keeping five yards from the car in front. 'One after another, the planes burst into flames,' writes Mather, who 'could see one or two figures running helplessly about'.

From his detached vantage point, Almonds watched 'brilliant flashes of exploding and blazing aircraft, murderous and continuous gunfire from the jeeps and the stabbing red lines of the tracer bullets'. He heard 'the deafening roar of thousands of rounds of ammunition being loosed off simultaneously, punctuated by intermittent explosions'.

One cannot imagine what it was to be caught on the ground in this Gehenna. An airman was seen lying between the wheels of his bomber, too terrified to move, unaware that flames were running along his fuselage towards the bomb racks. He hugged the earth as an explosion blew him and his aircraft to cinders.

At some point, a distant gun opened up. The gunners fired back, but a lucky shot struck one of the central jeeps. After that, there was sudden and shocking silence as the raiders stopped in the middle of the airfield and men began calling to each other. 'Anybody hurt?' 'Are you OK?' 'Any ammunition left?' Everyone started off again quickly – but as they were making their way from the airfield, Paddy Mayne, the maverick, jumped from his jeep and planted a Lewes bomb in the engine of a lone undamaged aircraft. Perhaps he was making a point.

The whole performance, from start to finish, had lasted less than 15 minutes, yet it took some of the jeeps three days to arrive safely back at the rendezvous once again. One man – John Robson, a 21-year-old from Gateshead – was killed and three jeeps were lost. Robson was buried the following day as the jeeps made their way through the desert. Stephen Hastings recalls:

> We got up and stood gathered round the grave while the body was lowered, sand and rock heaped upon it. There was no cross; some of the men were trying to make one from the scrub and a piece of old ration box, but it was not yet ready.

Soon after the end of the raid, Mike Sadler, still waiting at the perimeter, watched airfield personnel beginning to appear. Within ten minutes, he saw aircraft landing again, and before long, wrecked planes were being towed clear. The diligence and efficiency was startling. But the Germans were not quite so diligent as Sadler drove back to the rendezvous:

> I ran straight into a German column on the roadside. And there seemed to be no alternative but just to drive past them. They were all having cups of tea or coffee at the roadside, and, presumably, they were looking for us, but they obviously hadn't expected to see us arriving from behind. So I just drove right alongside them and came out the other end. A bit further on, I speeded up considerably!

The first man to arrive back at the rendezvous, in broad daylight, was Paddy Mayne. For security reasons, nobody was supposed to arrive at the rendezvous during the day, but, as he said to Pleydell, 'I got bored with waiting.' The doctor was not about to take issue. When other men started arriving, Pleydell overheard a comment about Mayne's use of a Lewes bomb. 'I reckon,' said an unnamed man, 'that's how we should've attacked. Now if we'd all gone in on foot we might've blown the whole place to blazes.' Most of the men, thought Pleydell, 'preferred to blow up planes with time bombs'.

Once everybody had arrived back, Stirling made a rare post-operation speech to his men. He spoke angrily:

> It's pretty plain that you think you have done jolly well. But if you want to know what I think – I'll tell you. It wasn't good enough! It wasn't nearly good enough! Some of you were firing at planes you could only just see – and a lot of you were firing wildly . . . And don't let me hear any of you say that you could have done better on foot. You couldn't! Get that quite clear in your minds . . .

Many years later, Stirling explained that he had in fact been very pleased with his men, but had not wanted them 'to become too blasé about the business'. There may well be some truth to this. He was regularly keen to ensure that his unit should not show complacency in its actions or attitudes.

But there is another possibility. Stirling had recently been gaining a reputation as 'The Phantom Major'. This soubriquet was coined by the Germans before being repeated by the British press. It evoked Great War attitudes to T.E. Lawrence – which, as a compliment, pleased Stirling greatly. But it also associated him closely with the desert war, just when he was trying to promote the SAS as a force with wider future potential.

Stirling had carried out the Sidi Haneish raid, in part at least, to demonstrate the SAS's potential and versatility to the military authorities, and to earn his unit an exciting future beyond Kabrit. So to hear his men harking back to the good old days of Lewes bombs was to hear his authority and ambition undermined. The great persuader would clearly have to do some persuading close to home.

27

RANDOLPH'S PAYOFF

At the start of August, the SAS returned to Kabrit from the desert. A new era was beginning in the Middle East. Auchinleck was about to be sacked by Churchill and replaced as theatre commander by Harold Alexander. Bernard Montgomery would take command of Eighth Army and begin planning a major offensive for late October.

A few days after David Stirling's return to Kabrit, Winston Churchill arrived in Cairo and invited him to dinner at the British Embassy. The prime minister was only in Egypt for a short time, on his way to Moscow to meet Stalin, but he insisted on an audience with the desert warrior with whom Randolph was so impressed. Stirling's plan – using the son to reach the father – was working well.

At dinner, Churchill, wearing his trademark siren suit topped with a bow tie, vied with his close friend Jan Smuts to see who could quote the most Shakespeare. Churchill won by inventing verse on the spot. After the meal, Churchill took Stirling and Fitzroy Maclean aside in the embassy garden.

Stirling had been warned not to reveal classified information to Churchill. (The PM had a reputation for indiscretion.) But the SAS leader was not a cautious man, and this was certainly not the moment for coyness. He revealed details of an SAS raid that was currently being planned and would take the unit back to Benghazi. He also laid down an important marker with Churchill: he said that, in his opinion, the SAS would have an important part to play in Europe later in the war. He was also careful to stress his unit's strategic potential over and above its sabotage abilities. Churchill was impressed; he sent a note the next day through his private secretary, asking Stirling what he could do to assist.

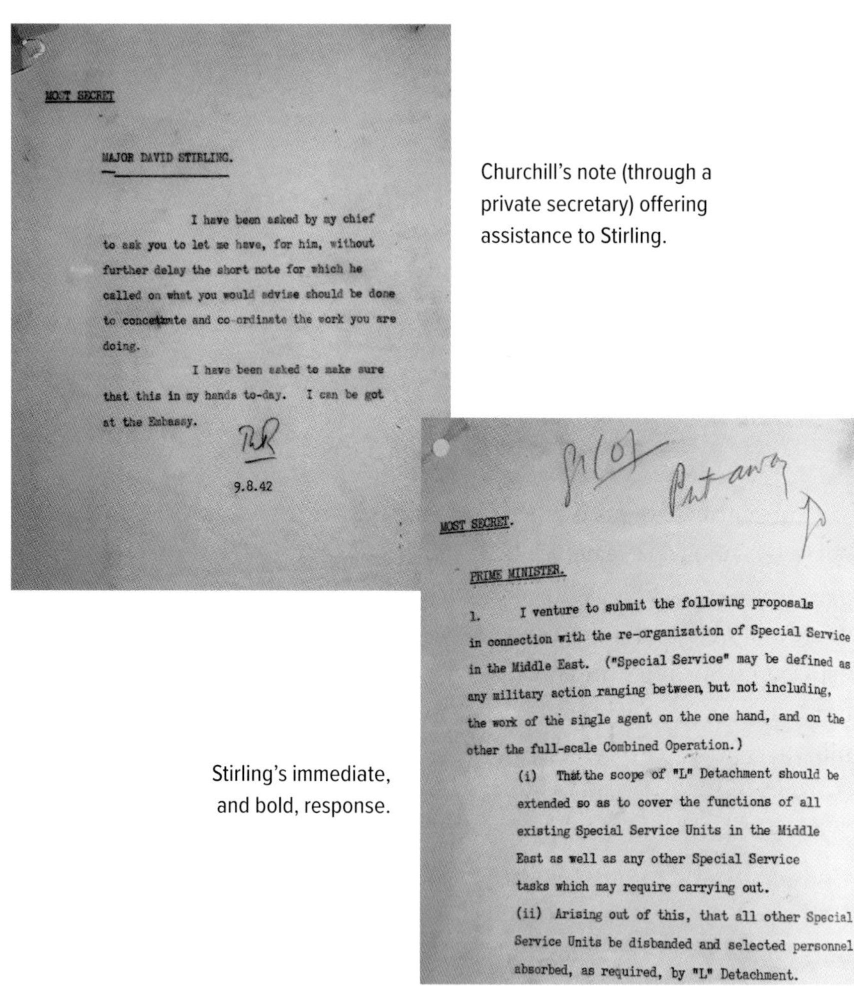

MOST SECRET

MAJOR DAVID STIRLING.

I have been asked by my chief to ask you to let me have, for him, without further delay the short note for which he called on what you would advise should be done to concentrate and co-ordinate the work you are doing.

I have been asked to make sure that this in my hands to-day. I can be got at the Embassy.

9.8.42

MOST SECRET.

PRIME MINISTER.

1. I venture to submit the following proposals in connection with the re-organization of Special Service in the Middle East. ("Special Service" may be defined as any military action ranging between, but not including, the work of the single agent on the one hand, and on the other the full-scale Combined Operation.)

(i) That the scope of "L" Detachment should be extended so as to cover the functions of all existing Special Service Units in the Middle East as well as any other Special Service tasks which may require carrying out.

(ii) Arising out of this, that all other Special Service Units be disbanded and selected personnel absorbed, as required, by "L" Detachment.

Churchill's note (through a private secretary) offering assistance to Stirling.

Stirling's immediate, and bold, response.

Stirling's answer came the same day. He requested 'that the scope of "L" Detachment should be extended so as to cover the functions of all existing Special Service Units in the Middle East [and] that all other . . . units be disbanded and selected personnel absorbed, as required by "L" Detachment'.

Stirling, in other words, was asking the prime minister to place him in charge of all irregular forces, with the power to decide on all operations. Churchill asked to meet Stirling again that evening – and Stirling hammered home his belief that his unit must last beyond the desert war. Churchill said little more, but the pair parted on good terms, with Stirling left to see what the future might hold.

28

BACK TO BENGHAZI: Keeping Shtum

Stirling's immediate problem, however, was the upcoming raid on Benghazi which he had just revealed to Churchill. This raid – a classic Layforce-style operation – was exactly the sort of job that Stirling had sworn the SAS would not carry out. Conceived by Middle East headquarters, and partly inspired by Stirling's previous visit to the town, it was to involve over two hundred men, half of whom belonged to other units, travelling a thousand miles each way in 80 vehicles, together with two tanks.

The raid – codenamed Bigamy – would attempt to destroy the Benghazi harbour facilities and as much of the town as possible. Italian ships would either be sunk or sailed to Allied ports by Royal Navy personnel. A prisoner-of-war camp would be liberated. And parallel attacks by other units would go in simultaneously at Tobruk, Jalo Oasis and Barce airfield.

Bill Cumper.

Not only was this raid contrary to SAS doctrine, it was also a great risk to take just as the unit seemed on the verge of an auspicious boost.

In Mike Sadler's eyes, the raid was poorly conceived. 'We disagreed with the whole thing,' he says. 'It was a very grandiose idea, much more on the lines of a Commando operation than an SAS one.' He points out that Fitzroy Maclean had talked the party's way into Benghazi on the last occasion; he was unlikely to do the same this time.

The raid was on such a large scale, with so many involved from so many units, that fears for its security existed. Shortly before its launch, 'L' Detachment engineering officer Bill Cumper and his driver, Jack 'Busty' Cooper, were standing in the Cairo YMCA when an ex-SAS member, who had carried out a raid but been sent back to his original unit, called over to Cooper:

> He shouted, 'Are you going up the desert again?' The place could have had spies in it. [David Stirling] knew it and told us all not to say anything to anyone. He came over to me and said, 'Where is it this time?' I looked at Bill and he turned his head. Bang! I downed him for opening his mouth. The place got in an uproar.

Once the fuss had died down and everybody was outside, Stirling walked up to Cooper, who was expecting to be placed on a charge. 'Well done, Busty!' he said. Back in their jeep, Bill Cumper added to the praise. 'You quietened him,' said Cumper, 'and he wanted it.'

29

BACK TO BENGHAZI: In Bagnold's Footsteps

The huge SAS convoy set off from Kabrit in late August. It headed first through Cairo and continued south alongside the Nile. One unlikely member of the group was Brian Scott-Garrett, a Royal Navy officer who, together with a number of other naval officers and ratings, had been given a few days' training at Kabrit and now found himself attached to the SAS. His job was to sail a captured ship to Alexandria (although he did not yet know this). For the time being, though, he was driving a jeep through Egyptian villages:

> All the kids would turn out and they would all be wearing long night-dress things called djellabas. And all the boys lifted them right up – so you could see they were boys! It was extraordinary! They all cheered!

For Jimmy Brough, one of the originals, the journey 'seemed more of a picnic than an operation'. There were plenty of new men involved, he acknowledged, 'but they were full of enthusiasm'. All the same, the movement of so many men and vehicles required discipline, and old hands like Reg Seekings were keen to see that the new men lived up to their standards. When a few started getting 'bolshie', Seekings found a way to motivate them: 'I went along and stuck my boot into one or two people's ribs. The only way to get them moving – just kicking the bloody men.'

Given the scale of the operation, mishaps occurred. A jeep collided with a bus on a dusty road in the Nile valley and ended up in a canal surrounded by water buffalo. And Brough was stung on the elbow by a scorpion. In terrible pain, he went to see (a not very sympathetic) Malcolm Pleydell, who asked him what colour the scorpion was. 'Yellow', said Brough. 'Those are harmless,' said the doctor, noting that 'the black ones could be quite serious'. Brough, not entirely sure of the creature's colour, waited two days for the pain to wear off.*

The convoy headed off the track at Asyut into the real desert. Scott-Garrett, who had spent many hours in ships' engine rooms, was enthralled by his new surroundings:

> We were about a week getting across to Kufra. The desert wasn't a flat place like a sandy beach. It was full of hills and mountains and gorges and plains. One time we were driving across this long flat plain covered in small boulders and every now and then you'd run your jeep over one and the sump was smashed and you lost all your oil.

Further west, the going became painfully slow. First one tank then the other became bogged down in the sand. Both were abandoned. Writes Brough: 'It was quite a sight to see hundreds of vehicles all milling about trying to ascend a sand dune, everyone concentrating on pushing and pulling one truck at a time, all head lamps blazing.'

Scott-Garrett was wary of 'razorback' sand dunes. 'You could drive up one side,' he says, 'and come to a razorback where the opposite side fell away in a precipice. We had quite a number of jeeps – particularly Free French – who just turned over and rolled down.' Scott-Garrett was discovering all sorts of surprises. He was amazed, for example, to see 'an enormous structure stretching up into the sky' several miles ahead. As he drove closer, it seemed to resemble the Leaning Tower of Pisa. Suddenly it disappeared, until, half a mile on, Scott-Garrett drove past a petrol can. The epic tower and the tiny can, it turned out, were the same object. The 'extraordinary mirage' left him bewildered.

With the pain of his scorpion sting subsiding, meanwhile, Brough was picturing himself 60 years back and 7,000 miles to the west:

* A member of the Israeli army, who was stung on bootcamp, has told the author that 'the black ones are bigger but less poisonous; the yellow ones do the damage.' The scorpion jury remains out.

> Kufra was alive with fires dotted all over the oasis. You could quite easily imagine yourself in Dodge City. Some of the inhabitants were not averse to trying out their weapons as the mood took them. We set up cans in the sand and used them as targets for our Colts or Smith & Wesson revolvers.

As the convoy moved north, cowboy fantasies gave way to the reality of modern war. Thermos bombs (small Italian anti-personnel mines resembling Thermos flasks) had started appearing along the track, and Bill Cumper took charge. As he prodded a stick from one side of the track to the other, he issued a warning in his broad cockney, unusual for an officer: 'No one moves off this track under any circumstances whatsoever – because I don't know where the mines are. And I'm getting you through!'

A few feet to the side of Cumper's beaten track stood an abandoned Daimler scout car in suspiciously good condition. One of the jeeps, containing Jim Webster and naval officer Richard Ardley, drove over the edge of the track to have a closer look at the Daimler – where it struck a mine. Ardley was sitting on top of the petrol tank when the mine exploded. Busty Cooper was about twenty yards away. 'What a bang it was!' he says:

> The jeep went up in flames. One of our sergeants jumped out of his jeep and ran towards the jeep that had struck the bomb. We pulled out [Ardley] . . . he was rolled in the sand to put the flames out. All his skin was burned off. I have seen some messes but this was the worst I have ever seen.

Ardley had come along as a friend of Stirling's. He was an experienced naval man with an Antarctic island named after him and a recent stint as Tobruk harbourmaster. Now, according to Jim Smith, who was first on the scene, he lay 'stripped like a snake shedding its skin with bare flesh'. He was given morphine and asked Smith a question:

> 'Corporal, could I have your revolver?'
> 'What do you want that for, sir?'
> 'I'd just like to hold a revolver.'
> 'No! You can't have my revolver!'

Richard Ardley. Tobruk harbourmaster and friend of David Stirling, he had recently been promoted to acting lieutenant-commander.

Ardley then lifted his hand to his head and said to Bill Cumper: 'Put a bullet through here.'

'I can't do it,' said Cumper.

Jim Webster, the jeep's driver, was also badly wounded. He had jumped out of the vehicle to help Ardley but had stepped on another mine which exploded, shattering his leg. 'I can picture him now,' says Cooper, 'writhing without screaming.'

Cumper set off to fetch Malcolm Pleydell, with the news that there was 'a job of work for the doc'. The relief when Pleydell arrived was palpable among the small group gathered by the wounded men. 'The burden of responsibility', as the doctor writes, was now transferred to him. He soon realised that he would have to amputate Webster's leg – no easy task in the desert. Ardley, meanwhile, was no longer asking to be shot; instead he was making jokes at his own expense. He briefly lost consciousness before waking to deliver a stream of delirious remarks: 'Hello boys! Where the hell are we? This is a fine kettle of fish! God! The pain in my eyes! It's my eyes!' At some point, David Stirling drove up, asking for a report on the patients. He agreed to leave a jeep and a lorry with the medical group as the remainder of the convoy moved on towards the rendezvous.

As Pleydell was finishing the amputation of Webster's leg (with the welcome assistance of an Australian pilot), the sergeant stopped breathing. For ten minutes the pair tried to revive him, pounding on his chest, but to no avail. Some time after they had given up, however, the pilot noticed Webster breathing faintly again. Jumping into action, Pleydell secured his skin flaps and transfused two pints of plasma.

Next the party set off towards the rendezvous. The injured men lay together in the lorry, followed by Pleydell in the jeep, as he explained in a letter to his fiancée:

> We had to hurry to catch up with the others, and driving behind the lorry, it was hell to watch three legs and one stump being flung up in the air and falling back each time the lorry hit a bump; so that we had to tie their legs down with a rope. And the dust was thrown up and fell all over them, so they quickly became yellow.

Ardley spent part of the journey singing his own composition – 'When I went into Benghazi Harbour' – to the tune of a navy drinking song, as he beat time with his bandaged hands. Webster, meanwhile, was suffering in silence. Eventually, after an agonising drive, the lorry reached the rendezvous at Wadi Gamra, where the medical party met up once again with the rest of the group. As Pleydell settled the injured men down for the night, Paddy Mayne revealed a side of his inscrutable dual nature, making hot sweet tea for the patients, gently supporting them as they drank, all the while displaying an inspiring level of care and empathy. Ardley was now much stronger, talking lucidly to his friends. His recovery was impressive. Webster, however, was growing weaker, and Pleydell doubted whether he would survive the night.

Woken in the middle of the night by his orderly, Pleydell learned that one of the men had just died. It was not Webster, however. It was Ardley, who had suddenly stopped breathing in his sleep. Over the next few days, Webster's condition improved. He became more cheerful and seemed rested. He began asking Pleydell about Ardley's condition. As Pleydell notes: 'I had noticed before how attached men became to one another when they had been wounded together.'

Pleydell now found himself telling Webster two white lies. The first was that Ardley had been moved further up the wadi to be with his naval friends. The second was to avoid any mention of his leg being amputated. That could wait, he felt, until Webster was stronger.

Ardley was buried the following day. The ground was so hard and stony that the grave had hardly any depth. 'We just lay down the body and piled stones over it,' says Brian Scott-Garrett. 'And it dampened our spirits a bit.'

By now, over two hundred men and a hundred vehicles had collected at Wadi Gamra, waiting to begin the raid. Only now were Scott-Garrett and the rest of his naval party told what they would be doing. A spanner was thrown in the works with the arrival of a local Arab spy with information that the coming attack was already common knowledge in Benghazi among inhabitants and defenders alike. Stirling sent a signal to Middle East headquarters asking whether the operation ought still to go ahead. After a few hours the answer arrived: no attention should be paid to bazaar gossip. The attack should go ahead as planned.

The main thrust of the assault would coincide with the end of an RAF bombing raid on the town. Instead of attacking at several points, Stirling now decided that a single attack would be launched, using the group's entire strength, on a toll gate to the south of the town. Once this roadblock had been breached, the group would split into smaller parties, each doing their assigned job. The first jeep in would contain Jim Almonds, his gunners, McGinn and Fletcher, and an Arab guide. Full of explosives and limpet mines, this group would drive to the harbourside, seize a destroyer, fill it with explosives and sink it across the mouth of the harbour. Dave Kershaw, in a following jeep, was to board a destroyer and sail it to Gibraltar. Reg Seekings, meanwhile, was simply to drive around the streets 'blasting up the town'.

There were a lot of variables to the raid, and a worrying number were out of the hands of the SAS.

30

BACK TO BENGHAZI: The Attack

Before the main party could assault Benghazi's southern toll gate, Fort Benito, an Italian fort guarding a pass above the town, had to be attacked and overcome. It contained a wireless post that risked revealing the raiders' arrival – assuming, of course, that it had not been revealed already.

The attack on the fort was to be led by Bob Mélot, a popular Belgian officer who had lived and worked closely with the local Arabs and was about to celebrate his forty-seventh birthday. With him were Jimmy Brough and ten others, including Chris Bailey, an officer who had managed a Cypriot hotel before the war.

Mélot and Brough initially approached the fort on foot, in broad daylight, without any visible weapons. As the fort's occupants came outside, they both delivered Nazi salutes and loud *Heil Hitler*s. Mélot said, in German, that they had come to relieve the post – but, just as it seemed their scam had worked, the Italians challenged them. Mélot's pistol jammed, but Brough managed to draw his revolver and shoot two of the enemy. As he began throwing grenades, the rest of his party arrived, firing Tommy guns. Brough recalls:

> It was all over very quickly. I went inside the fort with one of the corporals and the Italian sergeant was there dead with one knee pointing to the sky . . . In a corner of the fort was a little donkey munching away unharmed and happy. The wireless would never again send or receive any messages as we broke it into small pieces.

After the First World War, Belgian pilot Bob Mélot became an importer and desert explorer. His age disqualified him for service with Belgian forces at the outbreak of war, but he was readily accepted by the British Arab Force. After winning a Military Cross, he was posted to the SAS to take part in Operation Bigamy.

It might have been quick – but it could not be said with any certainty that the wireless had not already raised the alarm. To make matters worse, Bob Mélot and Chris Bailey had both been seriously wounded. Bailey was shot through the chest while Mélot was hurt in the shoulder, stomach and leg. This meant that Mélot would now be unable to guide the main party from the rendezvous into Benghazi. The job would have to be done instead by his Arab scout, who claimed to know an excellent route.

And so the main party of over two hundred men and fifty vehicles set off. The mood was initially good, with laughter and singing. The scout led the convoy down a steep path covered in boulders – which turned out to be the wrong route. After multiple corrections, the party was still making its way down as the Royal Air Force was raiding Benghazi. The timing was all wrong, and the convoy was forced to switch on headlights as they tried to reach the town before daylight.

When the roadblock was eventually reached, hours late, Jim Almonds's jeep was ushered forward by Stirling. He was, after all, to be the first man into the town. The road was lined on either side with barbed wire, and just as the jeep reached the barrier, the local guide sitting beside Almonds jumped out and ran back the way they had come. Stirling looked at Almonds, who said, 'I don't know Benghazi or where I'm going, but I'll give it a go.' Stirling gave a sign to Bill Cumper, who was standing across the road. Cumper gave a Nazi salute, shouted 'Let battle commence!' and raised the barrier to let the jeep through.

Before Almonds had moved far, a crescendo of fire came from the enemy. Says Brian Scott-Garrett: 'All hell broke out around us. We were surrounded in an ambush . . . and concealed in the ditches, were enemy soldiers.' The enemy began firing machine guns, mortars, even 20mm anti-aircraft guns at the SAS men. The road was narrow and restricted by barbed wire and ditches on either side, making it extremely difficult for the raiders to turn their vehicles around. Fortunately the enemy soldiers were some way behind the barrier. Had they been closer, 'L' Detachment might have been wiped out in a matter of minutes. As it was, a huge firefight developed.

Unable to retreat until others had turned, Mike Sadler sat back down in his jeep and fired the twin Vickers K guns at the flashes appearing in the ditches. However desperate the situation must have seemed, Sadler's reaction reveals his spirit:

> Surprisingly, in some way, I was a bit exhilarated! I suppose I was young and foolish. Frightened as well, of course, at the prospect of being shot up. But I think there was an element of exhilaration about succeeding and not being shot up.

The convoy somehow managed to reverse its way clear, and reached the escarpment by dawn. But it was pursued by aircraft including Messerschmitt 109s, Savoia bombers and little Italian CR42 biplanes. The biplanes may have seemed outdated, but they were particularly good at attacking sitting targets because, as Sadler recalls, they 'could turn on a sixpence and come back straight away whereas the Messerschmitts had to go several miles before they could come round again'. Jimmy Brough says that the men 'were like sitting ducks and the enemy sent anything that could fly over us'. Being hunted from the air for hours on end was 'altogether a horrible business', Sadler says. Men took cover from the aircraft as best they could. Brian Scott-Garrett hid with many others inside a cave, while Reg Seekings claims to have parked his jeep inside a Bedouin tent.

Back at Wadi Gamra, Malcolm Pleydell was in charge of wounded men. As well as Jim Webster with his amputated leg, Chris Bailey shot through the lung and Bob Mélot with his various wounds, there was a staff sergeant named Arthur Sque who had been thrown from a truck, and Anthony Drongin, who had been shot through the groin at the Benghazi barrier.*

When the time came to set out from Wadi Gamra on the long journey home, Stirling told Pleydell that there would be no room for stretcher cases on the transport. So many vehicles had been damaged or destroyed that there was, he said, barely enough room for the fit men. Of the wounded, Mélot could travel without a stretcher – but the others were not so lucky. Webster, Bailey and Sque needed immediate medical treatment while Sque, though not dangerously ill, could not move unassisted.

Pleydell worked out a plan. As the main convoy headed off from Wadi Gamra, a British medical man (either Pleydell or an assistant) and an Italian medical orderly would stay behind with the stretcher cases. The following morning, the British medic, guided by an Italian prisoner, should set out for Benghazi in an unarmed jeep to contact the hospital, bring an ambulance back, and then return to Benghazi with the wounded.

Pleydell offered to stay behind, but Stirling and Mayne made it clear that his duty lay with the fighting force. He would come with them. A coin was tossed and one of his orderlies was given the job of remaining. The wounded men, meanwhile, had no reason to suspect that they would be left behind. 'Perhaps the hardest part of the whole day,' writes Pleydell, 'consisted in informing [them] of the facts, and in bidding them farewell.' Drongin alone was too ill to notice, but the others were devastated to hear the news. Sque was in no pain at all, yet he was left behind. Even Webster, with his missing leg, was adamant that he was well enough to come along.

The men had good reason to be unnerved. There was a chance that they might perish before help arrived from Benghazi, or that it might never be sent. They might be actively mistreated by the Italians, who had a reputation for harsh behaviour towards prisoners in the desert. Or they might

* Anthony Drongin had come to the SAS via the Scots Guards and 8 Commando. He was a valued 'original' and friend to many. As he was being unloaded from a truck after being wounded, a newer officer had said to Bob Bennett, 'Right now! Come along there! Get *that man* off the truck!' The barely conscious Drongin managed to reply, 'That's Corporal Drongin to you, sir.'

simply receive inferior medical treatment. This was why Pleydell adds, 'It was as miserable a moment as I can recall . . . I could not help but feel as I was deserting them.'

It seems that after Pleydell had left with the main party, Reg Seekings arrived at the wadi with a vehicle full of fit men he had picked up. When he moved off again, he too left the wounded men behind, even though Sque was a close friend. He later called it 'the hardest thing I ever had to do in my life'.

Various members of the Benghazi party on their return, including (below) Seekings, Cooper, Stirling, Rose, assorted LRDG men and, possibly, Brian Scott-Garrett.

In fact, none of the men – Webster, Bailey, Drongin and Sque – would ever be seen or heard from again. Nor would the medical orderly who was left to care for them. It seems likely that they died before any of them reached Benghazi. How they died is a matter of pure conjecture.

The remainder of the party returned to Kabrit, aware that the operation had been a disaster.* They had, after all, failed even to enter the town of Benghazi. Over a quarter of them were killed, wounded or captured, while many more than half of their vehicles were disabled or destroyed. Almost all of those taking part were left with the firm impression that the plan had been somehow leaked, and the enemy had expected their arrival. Whether this was true or not, the plan had certainly not conformed to accepted SAS tactics, and it *was* too widely known about in advance. It is telling that, whenever Jim Almonds (who had been taken prisoner after the firefight at the barrier, only to escape from captivity months later) met up with David Stirling in their later years, Stirling would end up apologising for the events of that night.

Reg Seekings, though, has argued that the raid was a partial success, in that it forced the enemy to pull a lot of men from the front line back into Benghazi. Perhaps the only individual to derive much pleasure from Operation Bigamy was Brian Scott-Garrett, who had fallen in love with the desert and who later said:

> I had been hoping to seize an Italian destroyer and steam it back to Alexandria! That would have been a wonderful experience! It wasn't to be. But I'd taken part in something very interesting. It was an astonishing experience for someone who normally spent his time down in an engine room.

* The Tobruk raid that had been launched simultaneously turned into an even greater disaster. Almost all the troops involved were captured and two Royal Navy destroyers were lost.

31

ASSOCIATING WITH FAILURE

The consequences of the Benghazi raid were significant for 'L' Detachment and its leader, but not exactly predictable. The SAS was not censured or disciplined in any way. Instead, the unit received a huge promotion. On 28 September 1942, it ceased to be 'L' Detachment and became the Special Air Service Regiment. Having just lost so many personnel, its complement would now jump to 29 officers and 572 other ranks. David Stirling himself was promoted to lieutenant colonel.

In part, of course, this was due to Churchill's support (which was itself down to Stirling's clever politicking). But it can be seen, too, as Middle East headquarters' belated recognition of SAS success – achieved on the unit's own terms.

The regiment would also now benefit from the recent appointment to headquarters of John 'Shan' Hackett. Hackett's job was to sort out the various 'private armies' in the Middle East and to ensure that they conformed with the army's general aims. He and Stirling struck up an instant rapport, sharing the belief that the Middle East was a 'raiding paradise' and that the SAS was best placed to exploit its opportunities. To do so, both men agreed, the regiment had to be able to choose its own targets, as and when it wanted. Stirling could not have hoped for a better friend than Hackett.

Together they formulated a structure for the expanding regiment. It would absorb the Special Boat Section (soon to be known as the Special Boat Squadron). And it would divide itself into four squadrons, each made up of three troops. 'A' Squadron, led by Paddy Mayne with Bill Fraser as his number two, would consist mainly of existing members. 'B' Squadron, led by an officer named Vivian Street, would consist mainly of new recruits.

Bernard Montgomery watches his tanks move up to the front line, Second Battle of El-Alamein, November 1942.

'C' Squadron would comprise the Free French detachment. 'D' Squadron would be made up of the Special Boat Section, joined by a party of 21 Greek fighters, labelled the 'Sacred Squadron' in honour of 'The Sacred Band', a unit of lover-warriors from the ancient city of Thebes.

The ground was clearly being laid for the SAS's continuance beyond the desert. Stirling's ambition was to have regiments in all the coming theatres of war. To this end, he was already pushing for the creation of a second regiment. For now, however, 'A' Squadron would set up in the Great Sand Sea, attacking railway lines, convoys and generally causing as much nuisance as possible to Axis forces preparing for the coming battle. 'B' Squadron, meanwhile, would begin its training at Kabrit, aiming to be ready to begin operations by late November. Stirling, Sadler, Seekings and other key members would remain at Kabrit for the time being. But with so many vacancies to fill, who would be carrying out the operations?

In an effort to provide the answer, Stirling went with Shan Hackett to meet Montgomery in his front-line caravan. Stirling was used to warm receptions from the likes of Wavell, Auchinleck and Churchill. He was received in a different fashion by the awkward Monty, who asked him what he wanted. Realising that his usual charm had no currency with his commander, Stirling asked directly for 150 recruits, including officers and senior NCOs. Monty did not answer straight away. He stared, first at Hackett, then at Stirling. Finally he spoke: 'If my understanding of your brief is correct, you wish to take some of my men. You want only my best men. My most experienced and dependable men. I am very proud indeed of my men and I expect them to do great things in the very near future. What, Colonel Stirling, makes you assume that you can handle these men to greater advantage than myself?'

After further exchanges which failed to endear either man to the other, Monty concluded, 'My answer is no. No. I find your request arrogant in the extreme. It seems that you think you know the commander's duties better than I do. You failed in Benghazi and come here asking, no, demanding, the best of my men. In all honesty, Colonel Stirling, I'm not of a mind to associate myself with failure.'

Stirling's fury can be imagined. Not only was he going to have to look elsewhere for recruits, he had been patronised – humiliated, even – by the man whose support and assistance he most urgently needed.

The SAS had reached a decisive stage. Despite a recent failure, its future seemed secure. Indeed, it had earned regimental status and a considerable measure of prestige. But a warning shot had just been fired. The regiment could not always call on influential support, and it now had many vacancies to fill and great expectations to satisfy.

32

GROWING PAINS

So quickly was the SAS growing, according to John 'Nobby' Noble, 'that some people never volunteered and didn't even know they were members'. In this period of hurried growth, the regiment attracted some unusual individuals.

The explorer Wilfred Thesiger, for example. In November, Thesiger was told about David Stirling and the SAS – and, like so many others, he simply showed up at the anarchic Cairo flat. Stirling, who had never met him before, sent him off to Kabrit and telephoned ahead to warn of his arrival. Mike Sadler remembers: 'David liked people who were out of the normal run – and Wilfred certainly had plenty of features of his own. He just came out on a jolly. He wanted to come, and David thought he might be useful.'

Useful or not, Thesiger would, unlike many other 'B' Squadron officers, avoid capture. And, months later, he would take the surrender of an unhappy Italian prisoner who complained that 'for an hour I have been trying to surrender and everyone tells me to fuck off down the road. And, after all, I am an Italian general.'

Another unusual new member was Alec Le Vernoy, who joined around the turn of the year. As a member of the French army in Algeria in 1940, Le Vernoy had paddled a kayak to Gibraltar in an attempt to join the British. Told that he would be more useful to the Allies as an informant, he was sent back to Algeria – where he was arrested for desertion by the Vichy regime and sentenced to imprisonment with hard labour. After a series of adventures that saw him joining a spy network and rowing a small boat to Malta, he was sent to Cairo where he found himself recruited. The interviewing officer said: 'It's my opinion that to have gone from Algiers to Gibraltar in a kayak and then from Cape Bon to Malta in a rowboat . . . you must be completely crazy, perhaps barmy enough to deserve a commission in the SAS.' The officer further told him that the SAS had recently 'eased up on the requirements for new recruits'. And with that, Alec Le Vernoy was sent to begin his training in parachute jumping, hand-to-hand combat and desert warfare.

Le Vernoy's first battle, he says, was fought against high-handed fellow officers. He was either ignored completely or treated with contempt: 'After two days of being called a Frog and being openly baited, I had had enough.' In the mess, he banged a bottle down on the table, called the officers 'idiots', and shouted, 'I didn't come to this hellhole at the end of the world to fight the British! Dammit, we're supposed to be allies. It's not very sporting to condemn a man you don't even know. You can only find out what I am during battle, so until then lay off!'

The following night brought Le Vernoy's first raid. It was an attack on a munitions dump and fuel depot carried out by armed jeeps driving down three parallel alleys. In a planned manoeuvre, the SAS men fired their Vickers Ks and tossed grenades into stacks of munitions. At the end of one alley, a small group of 'crazed' Germans confronted the jeeps. They

Wilfred Thesiger wearing a keffiyeh (second left).

were shot 'in a murderous crossfire finished off by a last rain of grenades'. The raid destroyed its targets for the loss of two jeeps and several casualties. But Le Vernoy, singed and half deaf, now found himself accepted by his peers.

On his next raid, Le Vernoy's guns jammed as he drove towards an enemy petrol tanker. Dazed in the fever of battle, he drove straight towards it, only turning at the last moment to toss a pair of grenades. The resulting explosion was tremendous: 'My jeep was lifted high into the air, caught by a sheet of fire and smashed down far away by the blast. Bellowing, I was submerged in pain – in oblivion.' Le Vernoy woke up several days later in hospital. He was told that he had been rescued by fellow SAS members who had gone out of their way to save him. His brief but memorable sojourn in the SAS was over.

As recruitment increased, the regiment's fortunes became mixed. 'A' Squadron, under Paddy Mayne, did such excellent work in the build-up to Montgomery's victory at El Alamein that the previously sour Monty softened his attitude to the SAS. He had told Stirling that he did not associate with failure – but 'A' Squadron was now bringing him success.

The same could not be said for 'B' Squadron. When Reg Seekings was sent out with the squadron, he 'tried every possible way to get out of it'. In the end, he found its members 'only semi-trained' and 'not up to the proper standard'. In part, of course, this was because the squadron had been raised and prepared so quickly. Another factor, though, was a Royal Army Service Corps driver from north London with a foreign name and extreme views. Theodore Schurch, an 18-year-old bookkeeper from Wembley, had joined the British Army in July 1936 at the behest of an older Italian man who suggested that Schurch, already a keen fascist, could embed himself in the army and report back as an agent for the cause. In 1938 Schurch was posted to Palestine, where he began reporting details of British troop locations to a local Italian intelligence agent.

Once Italy had entered the war, Schurch wangled himself a posting to Tobruk, where his information took on a new importance. His unit was taken prisoner by the Germans in June 1942, at which point he declared himself as an Italian agent and came under the control of Mario Revetria, an intelligence colonel who began using him as a stool pigeon working with British prisoners-of-war. Posing as Captain John Richards, Schurch

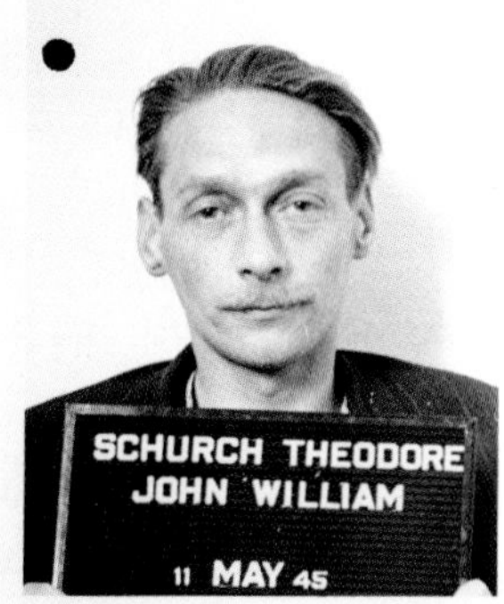

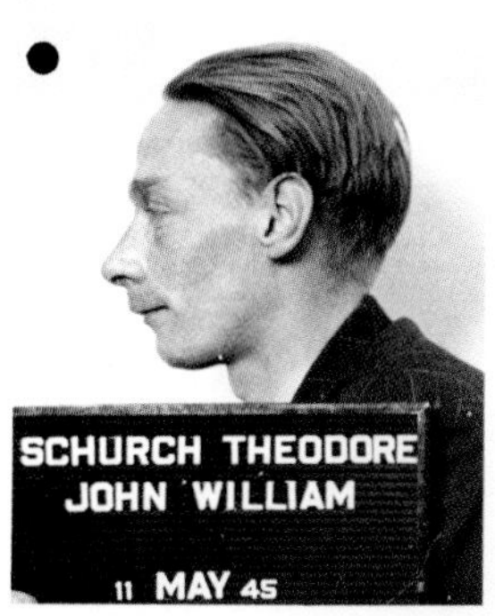

Theodore Schurch, aka John Richards.

was given a special job: to sit with SAS prisoners and coax information from them.

Derek 'Dusty' Miller of 'B' Squadron was one of the prisoners left in a cell with 'John Richards'. Miller did not initially doubt Richards' RAF dress, his accent, or his conversation. He only began to grow suspicious, he claims, when the officer spoke of his 'left-hand engine' being shot up. That, says Miller, 'didn't sound like an RAF pilot'. Then, when Richards brought an immaculate handkerchief out of his pocket, Miller grew alarmed. Nobody who had spent time in the desert, he thought, could possibly own a perfectly clean handkerchief. From that moment on, he says, 'I shut up and anything he asked me, I gave him whatever I thought was the wrong answer.'

Nevertheless, Schurch gathered enough information to compromise operations. When, in 1945, he came before a court martial on multiple charges of treachery and a single charge of desertion,* he told his accusers:

> I mixed with three officers and also other ranks of these captured patrols . . . and from information received in this manner and from documents captured we found where other patrols were located, and also their strength. From this information received we were able to capture two other patrols and acquired information as to the operations of other patrols in that area in the near future.

* In early January 1946, Schurch was hanged at Pentonville prison. He remains the last person to be executed in Britain for a crime other than murder.

returned to the Italians via the front line. I reported to Col. REVETRIA and a few days afterwards he again asked me to go through the lines at EL AGHELIA which I did again as a British private. At this time the lines were static at EL AGHELIA and Col. REVETRIA had his H.Q's at HOMS. During this time two or three patrols of the Special Air Service were captured and by this time Col. REVETRIA had made it my responsibility to get information from all prisoners of the Special Air Service. I mixed with three officers and also other ranks of these captured patrols again as Captain John RICHARDS and from information received in this manner and from documents captured we found where othe r aptrols were located, and also their strength. From this information received we were able to capture two other patrols and acquired information as to the operations of other patrols in that area in the near future. Also about this time a Major CHAPMAN of the ISLD was also captured, who was working behind Italian lines getting information re troop transports and lines of communication. Just after this, owing to the British advance, Col. REVETRIA changed his Headquarters to VILLAGIO BIANCHI and I went by Hospital Ship from TRIPOLI to NAPLES, and then to SIM. H.Q. is at ROME. This was at the end of January or the beginning of February 1943. I was then asked to try and locate a British wireless station operating in the VATICAN CITY, and for this purpose I operated in Civilian clothes without success. I was then sent to a special prisoners of war camp in ROME to get information from a British Colonel. I was put in with Colonel STIRLING, C.O. of the S.A.S. whom I found to be the Colonel referred to and whom I recognized from a description of his badges. I was posing as Capt. John RICHARDS of the R.A.S.C., and as all the necessary information respecting the S.A.S. had already been obtained, I was told only to obtain the name of Colonel STIRLING's successor. This I found out to be a Captain "PADDY" MAYNE. Later on, on Easter Sunday 1943, I again went to this Camp in ROME on behalf of the German Intelligence to whom I had been loaned, for the purpose of gaining information of all British submarine activities, etc in the Mediterranean from Lieut. BROMAGE of the Royal Navy Commander of the British submarine SAHIB and from Lieut. HARDY R.N.V.R. Navigational Officer of the British submarine SPLENDID, both thesex vessels habing been sunk. I again went as Capt. John RICHARDS of the R.A.S.C. and was dressed in British Battledress with Captains pips. From these two officers, unknown to themselves, I obtained information that "S" Squadron Submarines were operating from certain bases in the Mediterranean, the names of submarine commanders, and that the Squadron Commander, at that time was BEN BRYANT. About April 1943, I again went to this P.O.W. Camp to get information from three naval officers and one Army Officer of the Special Boat Service. One of the Naval Officers was Lieut. HART the Scottish Third Lanark footballer, and the Army Captain was a Captain Lee, who had been at one time a Sergeant in the Royal Engineers. I got the information and handed it to the Italians. For this purpose I was again Captain John RICHARDS of the R.A.S.C. About a month later, again as "Capt. RICHARDS", I got information from a Sergeant of the Special Boat Service, whom I learnt in peacetime was a Metropolitan Policeman. About September 1943 I was sent to PERUGIA in civilian clothes with my British Pay Book to get in touch with people who were supposed to be working for the British Intelligence, but owing to the Italian Armistice being signed, I was arrested by the German troops who believed me to be an escaped prisoner of war. Whilst in transit by rail, to Germany with other British P.O.W. I escaped with others and made my way to ROME where I was taken to Col. HELFRICH, Head of the Ober, by the German Military Police, to whom I had given my history. After being in Hospital for some time for injuries to my ankle sustained when escaping from the train, I was collected by Major SCHNEEWEIS, who was the Head of Colonel HELFRICH's Departments, and from that time I commenced to work for the Germans under the Ober and later the S.D. After this on several occasions I posed as a British escaped P.O.W. in civilian clothes, and also as a British Agent contacting Italian Agents working for the British Intelligence. This was to obtain information for the Germans. At the end of March 1945, I was detailed by General HASLER Chief of the German S.D. in Italy, and Senior Officers of Department 6 of the S.D. to come to ROME and the Vatican to get political information concerni

-2-

COMMITTING A CIVIL OFFENCE THAT IS TO SAY TREACHERY CONTRARY TO SECTION 1 OF THE TREACHERY ACT 1940.

in that he

at Homs, North Africa, in or about October or November 1942 with intent to help the enemy did an act designed or likely to give assistance to the naval, military or air operations of the enemy or to impede such operations of His Majesty's forces namely, having obtained information from members of His Majesty's forces who were prisoners of war in enemy hands relating to the Special Air Service, did communicate the said information to the enemy.

One of the treachery charges, moreover, related directly to information gathered from members of 'B' Squadron (see Schurch's statement, left).

'B' Squadron's commander, Vivian Street, was himself taken prisoner in December 1942. He was kept in a holding camp before being taken down to the docks at Misurata to board a submarine for transfer to Italy.

Street found the submarine uncomfortable to begin with – but even less pleasant after he and his 11 fellow prisoners were woken by a sudden crash that sent a shudder through the submarine and plunged the compartment into darkness. The engines shut off, the bulkhead slammed shut – and suddenly all was silent.

Several depth charges had been dropped, landing close by the submarine. The crew had acted quickly to shut off the bulkhead. This had sealed the two forward compartments, containing the prisoners, their four guards and two Italian officers, from the rest of the submarine.

Street and his companions now sat huddled together in one compartment. Lit by a single fading torch, none of them spoke. Street prayed silently to God, aware how little attention he had ever paid to religion. He concentrated on controlling his fear. Nobody must be allowed to see it. It was difficult to believe that this was really happening, that it was not a dream.

Left: Schurch's statement.

Below left: Schurch's court martial charge relating to the SAS.

Right: Vivian Street.

An American pilot broke the silence. 'I think this is it, major.' 'I'm afraid you are right,' said Street. The two men smiled at each other and the American sighed. An Italian started speaking in French, '*Dans un quart d'heure nous serons cuits*', and then repeated himself. There was no possible answer to this, thought Street.

After a few minutes, or hours, the torch gave out and Street became drowsy. He recalls that, by now:

> Nothing seemed real, nothing seemed to matter now that all hope had gone. The noise at the closed bulkhead beside me must be imagination. The shaft of light, which followed, could have no connection with me. A draught of air brought me back to reality and I saw that the bulkhead had been opened.

By an extraordinary stroke of fate, members of the crew, seeing that the enclosed compartments had not filled with water, had now returned to the bulkhead and opened it from the other side. The trapped men simply walked free. Some hurried, some took their time. Street and the American pilot both stopped to allow the other to go first – and then laughed. In fact, Street's problems were not yet over. Everybody was now left clinging to the sides of the submarine as it came under fire from a British destroyer, but he was eventually picked up by the same destroyer and returned to Cairo.

Against the odds, Vivian Street had survived. His squadron did not prove so enduring. Some familiar members of the regiment, though, were about to embark on an epic journey.

33

IN THE BAG

In late October and early November 1942, two great military events coincided on the continent of Africa. In the east, the British and Commonwealth Eighth Army triumphed at El Alamein. To the west an Anglo-American force invaded French-held territories. Two Allied armies now set out to meet in the centre to push Axis forces out of Africa.

All manner of consequences, great and small, flowed from these events. Church bells, for example, were rung in Britain for the first time since the threat of invasion had silenced them. Winston Churchill, with his usual pugnacious nuance, delivered a message which both raised and tempered Allied expectations: 'Now this is not the end. It is not even the beginning of the end. But it is, perhaps, the end of the beginning.' And Field Marshal Rommel, who had lost tens of thousands of men, killed, wounded or captured in battle, was forced to start retreating westwards.

Rommel's retreat presented exciting opportunities for David Stirling. He received permission from headquarters to harry Rommel's forces as they moved into Tunisia, and to investigate whether the field marshal was intending to make a stand at an old defensive works on the Tunisian border called the Mareth Line. If he was, then the regiment could discover a way for Eighth Army to manoeuvre around it.

As helpful as these tasks would prove to the overall Allied effort, Stirling had other reasons for wanting to involve the SAS. For one thing, he needed a practical sense of the unit's prospects in areas unlike the Western Desert. Tunisia would provide it. For another, he wanted to meet with his brother, Bill, who had begun raising a second regiment in Algeria.

Above all, though, Stirling wanted to advertise the SAS; he was determined to show that, far from being a localised sabotage unit, it deserved a

Freddie Taxis.

strategic role in all coming theatres of war. And he understood that if his men moved quickly, they could be the first to pass directly from one Allied force to the other. In blunt media terms, they would be the first Eighth Army Limeys to meet up with the Yanks.

None of this occurred to the recently commissioned Mike Sadler, however, as he set off from Cairo on an epic journey to Tunisia. It was not his business. 'We were,' he says, 'just thinking how we were going to survive the next bit.' Guiding a patrol containing Stirling, Johnny Cooper, Wilfred Thesiger and others, he headed west, keeping entirely to desert routes along the way. The patrol travelled by day, sinking into sand and digging themselves out as they went. Along the way they met up with a Free French SAS patrol making its way north from Chad. Reaching Ghadames, on the Tunisian border, a camp was set up; Thesiger was left in charge as Stirling decided to change his plan. Instead of outflanking the Mareth Line, his patrol would now head straight through the Gabès Gap, a narrow corridor between the sea and a series of salt lakes. This, as Stirling knew very well, was in breach of orders from headquarters. The corridor was crowded with Axis troops. It would not be a simple manoeuvre.

As the British and French SAS men conferred to the south of the Gap in the early morning light, a small German reconnaissance aircraft buzzed overhead. Little attention was paid, and the French patrol set off first. Stirling's group was to follow a different route. Sadler was in the leading jeep alongside Johnny Cooper and a 32-year-old Frenchman named Freddie Taxis. Another jeep containing Stirling would come behind.

At first, Sadler found himself driving through the middle of an unexpected German unit. The jeeps, fortunately, were ignored by the enemy soldiers. 'They were concerned with getting breakfast and lighting campfires,' says Sadler, 'but we were aware that we needed to get into cover before it was too late!' The navigator weighed up his options. Leading straight ahead was the coastal road. To the west was the almost impassable chain of salt lakes. 'I thought,' says Sadler, 'that if we split the angle between these two features we could get away as quickly as possible from the danger areas and into the hills further north.' Heading away from the road, the party drove towards an area of deep wadis where they should, in theory, have been able to hide. After passing a series of small dusty farms, they reached a wadi leading into the hills where they camouflaged their vehicles and settled down. Some of the men, including Sadler, went to sleep.

The next thing Sadler knew, he was being kicked in the back. He was lying, fully clothed and booted, in his sleeping bag. Looking up, he saw a German soldier with a machine gun looming over him. In a moment, he glanced across and saw Johnny Cooper looking back at him. A few yards further along, Freddie Taxis was making his own mental calculation. As the German moved away, the three men jumped out of their sleeping bags and ran. He says:

> It was quite difficult getting out of your sleeping bag in a hurry while wearing your boots! We hurried up the hill as fast as we could until we couldn't go any further. I had a lot of secret papers, with messages and things, which I tried to bury. We just had to lie there while they searched.

Sadler got away – but David Stirling had not been so lucky.* He was apprehended further down the wadi, and though he initially escaped from his captors, he was quickly recaptured and sent to Italy under heavy guard. His reputation preceded him.

* Stirling had made no official note of Sadler's recently awarded commission. He had just told his navigator to go down to the bazaar to get hold of some pips. After Stirling's capture, Sadler was called to headquarters and asked to explain why he was masquerading as an officer.

Sadler, Cooper and Taxis, meanwhile, waited until dark before moving off. They had nothing with them: no guns, water or food. Just assorted bits of battledress uniform and their suede desert boots. Over the coming days, they walked north-west in the hope of reaching the French Foreign Legion, who were thought to have taken the town of Tozeur. Fortunately for the two Englishmen, Taxis spoke some Arabic. 'He was able to ask for help,' says Sadler, 'if people showed signs of being friendly.'

Taxis suggested approaching a local encampment early in the morning. His advice was followed and the men were offered bread, dates and water by friendly tribesmen who clearly wanted them to stay longer. That afternoon, however, they met a group with very different intent. Sadler recalls Taxis acting as interpreter: 'He said, "They want our clothes otherwise they are going to kill us." One of them had an old shotgun – which I thought might be able to fire one shot.'

Cooper reluctantly handed over his jacket. This did not seem to appease the group and stones were thrown. One hit Cooper above the eye. As his wound streamed with blood, the men ran away. 'The Arabs had bare feet,' says Sadler, 'but we still had our boots so we didn't think they'd be able to follow.'

After many hours of further walking without food or water, the men reached the edge of Lake Djerid. Taxis, thinking the water was fresh, took a gulp. It was salty; he vomited and collapsed. The other two decided to keep walking. They would come back for their companion as soon as possible. They soon met a friendly local man who gave them dates and water – and then a French soldier appeared, who went off and brought back his sergeant, a grinning man with a huge ginger beard. A patrol was sent back to find Taxis. The three men had reached the Foreign Legion at Tozeur. They were finally safe after four epic days of walking. Cooper writes:

> When the patrol returned . . . we walked slowly along the track until it opened out on to the finest Beau Geste fort I had ever seen. The whole scenario reminded us of a film set: the palm trees, blue sky, strange uniforms and the brilliant white paint of the fort.

Once the men had been well fed and cared for, an American patrol arrived to take them away. The nearest Allied unit was far to the north, and the patrol members had never heard of the SAS. The men were taken to Gafsa, where they were handed to an American unit. It seems that Sadler, Cooper and Taxis of the SAS were, indeed, the first members of Eighth Army to make contact with the Americans.

Above left: German soldiers pose with David Stirling's jeep after his capture.

Right: A 'slightly dotty' Mike Sadler photographed after his desert trek.

A.J. 'Joe' Liebling, *New Yorker* journalist.

By chance, a journalist from the *New Yorker* magazine – A.J. Liebling – was with the American unit. He subsequently published an article describing the men and their adventure. They reminded him, he said, of Robinson Crusoe. Mike Sadler had particularly protuberant eyes and a beard 'giving him the air of an emaciated and slightly dotty Paul Verlaine'. These men, Liebling explained to his American readers,

> all belonged to an organization known as the SAS, which stood for Special Air Service. I asked [Mike Sadler] if it had anything to do with the RAF and he said no, it was an air service in a negative way. 'You see, when we were first formed, we used to specialize in destroying German airplanes on the ground,' he said. 'Get back of their lines, get onto an airfield at night – do in a sentry, you know . . . Quite a good idea. Colonel Stirling, the one we call Big Dave, really thought of it first. Bright chap.'

David Stirling's men had somehow made it through the Gabès Gap. They had been the first representatives of their army to meet up with the force coming from the west. They had been celebrated by the press. These were all outcomes that Stirling had hoped for. Unfortunately for him, he was not around to see it.

A REPORTER AT LARGE

GAFSA

I—THE EIGHTH ARMY FROM GABES

THE Anglo-American North African campaign, which has since spread to Europe, is sure to furnish a lot of historical controversy sooner or later, so there is no harm in correcting the record on one point immediately. The junction of the American Second Corps and the British Eighth Army, fighting its way north from Mareth, was copiously reported in newspapers in this country last April. Most of the reporters said that the meeting took place on the Gafsa-Gabès road. According to their stories, the historic moment came when an American motorized patrol met a British motorized patrol. Actually, the Eighth Army and the Second Corps joined up more than two months before the motorized incident, in the hall of the Hôtel de France, a two-story palace in Gafsa. I know, because I was there. In fact, I might say that I introduced them.

Gafsa, called Capsa by the Numidians, is a very ancient town on a very slight hill in south-central Tunisia. Warm springs gush from the foot of the hill, below a fifteenth-century Arab citadel, which was wrecked by our engineers during the fighting last February. The citadel was still intact when I first saw the place. The climate of Gafsa, even in late January, when an Associated Press correspondent named Noland Norgaard and I reached it, is warm and dry. There is an oasis around the town, which used to be an important knot in the web of caravan routes between the Sahara and the Mediterranean. Last winter Gafsa had, and by now probably has again, ten thousand inhabitants, of whom five or six hundred are Europeans, eight hundred are native Jews, and the rest Moslems who call themselves Arabs but are predominantly of Berber stock, like most North Africans. The Europeans are administrators or railroad workers. The Jews, whose ancestors came there not long after the Destruction of the Temple, are traders and traditionally middlemen between the Christians and the Moslems.

When Norgaard and I arrived in Gafsa, a battalion of American infantry was stationed there, together with several batteries of French seventy-fives, a battalion of Senegalese, and some Algerian *tirailleurs*. The Americans, who belonged to the First Division, were the only ground troops we had south of the town of Sbeitla, which was sixty miles away. They had been there for a month and were quite at home in the place, which, as almost every enlisted man you talked to was certain to say, looked like a set in a Beau Geste movie. Old Jews sold surprisingly good native pastries and Arabs peddled dates in the square in front of the American barracks. The soldiers had adopted Arab kids as mascots and clothed them in G.I. shirts and shoes. There was a great outdoor Roman swimming pool, filled by warm running water from the springs. The water contained a good deal of sulphur, but it was nevertheless pleasant to bathe in, and the Americans spent a lot of time swimming in it. The French soldiers preferred to dangle fishing lines in a nearby spring-fed stream and catch little, extremely voracious fish, which apparently were used to living in hot, sulphurous water.

There was also a clean Arab bath, in a narrow Arabian Nights alley, where the attendants would stretch you on the floor and twist your arms and legs out of joint and then pound you with a hot brick before allowing you to steam yourself in peace. I remember seeing, at the bath, an English captain I knew, a booby-trap expert, pink and jolly in the steam, wearing a towel around his loins. A couple of weeks later he accidentally blew himself up with an extremely special mine he had just devised. He simply vanished. Somehow I always think of him flying toward heaven draped in a towel and deeply embarrassed. Gafsa also had a bordello offering a dozen girls whom a friend of mine described as "sort of French" and a madam who was a de Gaulliste. When a British lieutenant general came to town for a look around, the much-junior American officer who was his host wanted to give him a touch of real luxury—sheets to sleep between. He borrowed a pair from the madam.

NORGAARD and I had gone to Gafsa because it was the American-held point nearest to Montgomery's advancing army and it seemed a likely place to witness the joining of the two forces. We expected the Americans either to hold on to the town until Montgomery arrived or else to launch an offensive from it in order to join him. The latter course presupposed heavy reinforcements, and we thought that we sensed their coming.

The Americans in Gafsa had carried out numerous raids against the Italian detachments that occasionally ap-

34

AN OLD FRIEND

Unsurprisingly, David Stirling did not take well to captivity. One man he soon met in prison was Theodore Schurch – or Captain John Richards, as the stool pigeon introduced himself. At his court martial, Schurch stated that he was 'told only to obtain the name of Colonel Stirling's successor. 'This I found out to be a Captain "Paddy" Mayne . . .'

And Mayne did, in effect, take over from Stirling. In March the regiment was divided into two arms. The Special Raiding Squadron (SRS), commanded by Mayne, would consist of about three hundred men (many of whom came from 'A' Squadron). The Special Boat Squadron, commanded by George Jellicoe, would contain about two hundred and fifty men. In addition, a second regiment was being raised in Algeria. It was to be commanded by David's brother, Bill, who had been such an influential figure in the unit's original creation.

Officially, the SAS now came under the control of Middle East Raiding Forces, but Mayne and Jellicoe had complete operational control of their respective arms. This meant that Mayne *was*, in practice, Stirling's successor. Theodore Schurch had been correctly informed.

It was clear from the start of his tenure, however, that Mayne would not be attempting to emulate his predecessor. Stirling's unit had destroyed well over three hundred aircraft. Its influence was acknowledged by Field Marshal Rommel, who wrote to his wife, on learning that Stirling had been captured, that the SAS 'had caused us more damage than any other unit of equal size'. Yet the war had now moved on and the SRS would have to comply with the new circumstances.

As American and British Commonwealth forces continued to squeeze the enemy in North Africa, the campaign had finally entered its drawn-out endgame. Allied focus would shortly switch to Sicily and Italy, where there would be no obvious scope for the SAS's trademark tactics. Instead the SRS would find itself playing a straightforward commando role at the forefront of a seaborne landing. Mayne had little choice in the matter. For the unit to retain its prestige and continue in its integral form, he would have to accept matters. But this, he insisted, was only a temporary arrangement. SRS members might play the part of commandos for a while, but they would not forget their roots. It might be argued that Mayne was showing impressive adaptability, which is, after all, a key component of leadership. The SBS under Jellicoe, meanwhile, would be heading to the Aegean, where its members could keep the torch burning by mounting traditional SAS-style raids from the sea.

The change in leadership and focus did not please everybody. 'There is no-one with [Stirling's] flair and gift for projecting schemes,' wrote Malcolm Pleydell to his fiancée. 'He ran the unit so now the ship is without a rudder.' Barney Waygood, speaking years later, says, 'the spirit went down after Stirling was captured and the administration was haphazard. Everything was falling apart.'

Right: Mick Gurmin in the fake SAS, 1941.

Below: Mick Gurmin in the real SAS, 1943.

In a sense, though, such feelings were inevitable. So many changes were occurring at once that the SAS would be forced to find its identity again. A lot of old faces were now gone. Others would have to adapt to new roles. (Mike Sadler, for example, would become an intelligence officer.) But, against all the odds, one extremely old face had returned. A face so old, in fact, that nobody recognised it.

Readers with long memories will remember that this book began with the story of Mick Gurmin, the young trooper who had played the central role in Dudley Clarke's SAS deception, and who might as a result be considered an original member of the SAS. Perhaps even *the* original member.

After Operation Abeam, Gurmin had received a commission into Middle East Commando. The unit was redesignated 1st Special Service Regiment in April 1942 before being disbanded in August in the wake of David Stirling's note to Winston Churchill. Mick Gurmin, along with other members such as John Tonkin and Peter Davis, then joined the SAS in October. Gurmin was far too discreet and professional to mention it to his new colleagues, but he had worn a pair of (fake) SAS wings long before Jock Lewes, David Stirling, Paddy Mayne or anybody else associated with the regiment.

Since joining the SAS, Gurmin and his colleagues in 'C' Squadron had journeyed deep into the desert and reached as far as the Mareth Line. Photographs were taken along the way (and a selection can be seen below and opposite).

The war in North Africa came to an official end on 12 May 1943. By this time, old and new SAS members were training hard for fresh challenges. The African adventure was over.

1091

PART THREE

EUROPE

Members of 'C' Squadron, 1st SAS at Nulut Oasis in Libya. Richard Lea is in sunglasses. John Tonkin stands beside him.

35

A NEW WAY OF FIGHTING

John Tonkin came to the SAS as the same time as Mick Gurmin. He, too, was an ex-member of Middle East Commando and 1st Special Service Regiment. He had arrived in the Middle East at the end of 1941 as a Royal Northumberland Fusilier, and was languishing in the depot, running up and down sand hills to stay fit, when he volunteered for the commandos. In October 1942, he joined 'C' Squadron, 1st SAS and began his training at Kabrit. After a journey into the desert, he arrived back at Kabrit in early 1943 and duly became a member of the Special Raiding Squadron.

The squadron was commanded by Paddy Mayne, whose second-in-command was Bob Mélot, now recovered from wounds sustained at Benghazi. There was also an artillery officer, Alec Muirhead, responsible for a detachment of 3-inch mortars.

The squadron was sent for training to Nahariya in Palestine, where they practised scaling cliffs and performing amphibious landings. They carried out a series of exercises using live ammunition; machine guns would fire a certain distance over the men's heads and they would have to estimate, from the sound of the crack, how high the bullets were flying, and whether it was safe to stand up.

Another exercise – which sounds more like a high-risk circus act – was intended to teach the men how to cross barbed wire. One man would throw himself, face down, onto the first row of wire, squashing it flat. A second man would come up behind, and stepping on the first man's backside, would throw himself down onto the second row of wire. The men following would step quickly over the now flattened wire. Once everybody was clear, the first two men would roll onto their backs and attempt to back-somersault over the wire to safety.

Dougie Eccles.

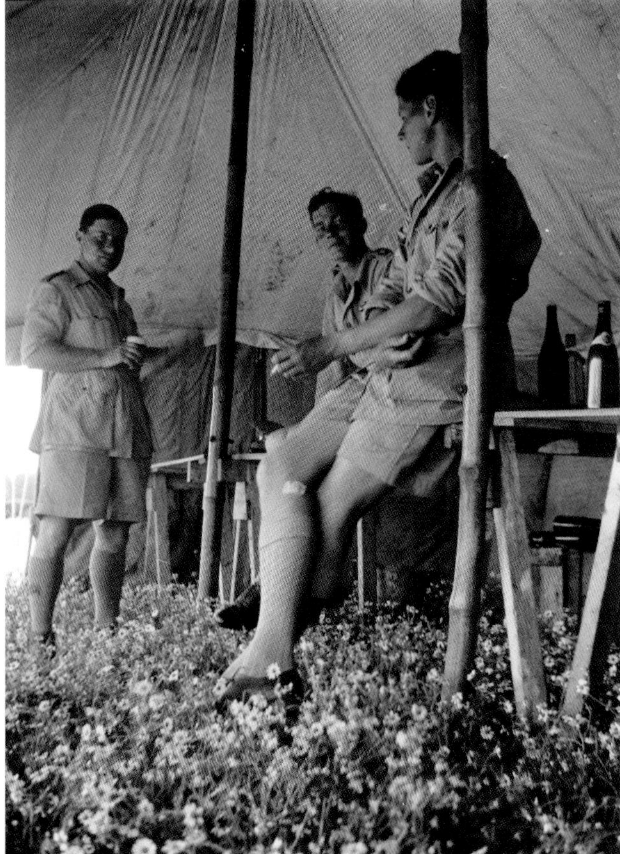

Left: Johnny Wiseman, Bill Fraser and John Tonkin in the flowery officers' mess at Nahariya.

From Nahariya, the men were sent to the Gulf of Aqaba at the northern end of the Red Sea, where they carried out assault training from landing craft.

While at the Red Sea an experiment was attempted with Benzedrine. The men carried out a practice landing and then marched all night, half of them having been given the drug. The drugged men initially performed better and stayed alert far longer. Peter Davis, who was *not* given the drug, says:

> All I know . . . is that on the way back we had to keep up a blistering pace . . . Paddy seemed to be everywhere, and like the Red Queen in Alice in Wonderland, kept on shouting 'Faster! Faster!' when we felt we were already putting up as fast a pace as we possibly could.

The men who had been given the drug were able to keep up with the pace more easily. But when, later in the day, an alarm sounded as everybody slept, those who had not taken Benzedrine rose from bed quickly, while those who had, stayed asleep and simply could not be roused. After that, says John 'Nobby' Noble: 'Nobody would take the damned stuff. That was the only time we were given anything, in training, and that was purely as an experiment. We all said, "No, we can do without it!"'

Early on the morning of 10 July 1943, the Special Raiding Squadron went into action for the first time. Two hundred and eighty-seven men would be assaulting Capo Murro di Porco on the south-east coast of Sicily. Their task was to knock out the artillery defences ahead of the arrival of the main invasion force. The invasion's success depended to a large degree on the SRS's ability to do its job.

As John Tonkin approached the shore, he saw gliders on the surface of the sea, and heard the cries of drowning paratroopers. These men were supposed to have landed ashore to assist the invasion but they had fallen short. The SRS men, sailing past them, were not supposed to stop to help. (Although a few drowning men, it seems, *were* rescued.) Derrick Harrison remembers his first moments on land:

> We clambered ashore, slipping and sliding in our rubber-soled boots on the spray-drenched boulders . . . In single file we began to scale the cliff. I could see neither foothold nor handhold . . . How long that climb took I do not know. It could have been ten minutes or ten years.

As Harrison reached the artillery positions, he noticed a slight movement on the ground a few feet away. He froze as he realised that he was staring directly down the barrel of a machine gun. 'I was too close to use a grenade and could pick off only one man at a time with my revolver,' he writes. Yet a moment later, the gun was lowered as three petrified Italians crawled out of their hole and surrendered to him.

While the job of No. 1 and No. 2 Troops was to attack the artillery defences, that of No. 3 Troop was to neutralise enemy soldiers stationed in a farmhouse. To do this, they fought their way down a row of stone walls.

The enemy guns were captured without a great deal of resistance and put out of action by the engineers. They opened the breeches and placed

Assault training in the Gulf of Aqaba. The *Ulster Monarch* lies in the background.

A landing craft tied to a jetty.

Inside a landing craft. Most of the men sit to the sides while the coxswain is in his armoured turret on the right.

Monty addresses the SRS on board the *Ulster Monarch*.

Men of No. 3 Troop fighting at Capo Murro di Porco. Dougie Eccles is firing over the stone wall.

SRS men sitting on the barrel of a captured gun.

charges across the hinges. Harrison heard their warning to 'stand clear' before one was blown. He lay down and waited. Then, 'there was a sharp concussion and flying pieces of metal whined eerily above our heads. As the sound of the explosion rolled away, from the signaller's set came the strain of "Land of Hope and Glory" as a broadcasting station crashed in on our frequency.'

Once the fighting was over and prisoners were being rounded up, a British naval cruiser spotted groups of Italians walking about onshore, unaware that they had already been captured. It fired two shots. Fortunately, a pair of naval officers attached to the assault party were able to flash a quick message – 'MQ MQ MQ'. This, says Tonkin, meant: 'You're shooting at the wrong bloody people!' Nobody was hurt and an apology was quickly flashed back.

Left and below: Italian prisoners milling around in the open. SRS men are attempting to round them up.

The scene outside a farmhouse after the fighting. Relieved civilians are emerging from the cellar. A medic treats a wounded Italian soldier under the large doorway to the left. SRS men in the foreground, meanwhile, smile at the camera.

The Capo Murro di Porco operation, a classic commando job, had gone according to plan. The only man killed was Geoff Caton, a veteran of various desert raids including Operation Bigamy. He had been shot in the groin while taking the surrender of a gun emplacement that was showing a white flag. According to Albert Youngman, Paddy Mayne held his hand as he died. His last words were, 'I'm ever so sorry to be such a nuisance, sir.'

The SRS had passed its first test. Eighteen large guns were captured or destroyed, as well as mortars, machine guns and range finders. More than five hundred prisoners were taken, for the loss of only Corporal Caton and two wounded men. Yet this attack clearly heralded a new existence for the SAS old-timers. It had been quite unlike any raid contemplated under David Stirling, and had involved scared civilians and false white flags. The desert war – 'war without hate' as it was described by Rommel – was truly over. And there was no time to rest. The SRS officers were told that a German division was strongly ensconced just south of a town named Augusta. Their next job was already waiting.

Termoli
Rome
Adriatic Sea
Cassino
Anzio
Bari
ITALY
Naples
Salerno
Taranto
Tyrrhenian Sea
Bagnara
Palermo
Messina
Cefalu
Ionian Sea
Mount Etna
Cannizzaro
Sicily
Catania
N
Augusta
Syracuse
Capo Murro di Porco
Pantelleria
0
100 miles
0
150 km

36

STIRLING AND STIRLING

On 13 May 1943, in advance of the assault on Sicily, a second SAS regiment was raised. It was commanded by David Stirling's brother, Bill. Little wonder that, to some, the initials SAS seemed to stand for 'Stirling and Stirling'.

Bill Stirling's contribution to the creation of the SAS is frequently overlooked. He had been the founder of the Lochailort irregular warfare school. He had helped his brother to develop Jock Lewes's ideas for a Middle East parachute unit. He had stressed the key concept of small parties carrying out strategic raids behind enemy lines. And just as he had helped his brother to draft a crucial memo in July 1941, so, almost two years later, he drafted a comparable document relating to his new unit.

In this document, Stirling accepted that certain unusual tasks might have to be carried out in support of the Sicily landings, but he stressed that the real job of the SAS was to perform vital activities behind enemy lines that could not be tackled by regular formations. 'The strongly guarded point is not, as a rule, the best objective,' he wrote pointedly.

Bill Stirling was making it very clear that while the SRS was being thrown, commando-style, at the enemy, he wanted to be able to send his own force, in small parties, to deal quietly with the enemy's supply lines. He wanted, in other words, to step into his brother's shoes.

The majority of 2nd SAS members were inherited from the Small Scale Raiding Force, a small unit that had been mounting raids on the Channel Islands and the French coast. One of these men was Harold 'Tanky' Challenor, who was immensely proud to be transferring to the SAS. 'I had heard many stories of the incredible exploits of the 1st SAS in the desert,' he remembers. Also joining was the experienced desert warrior

Dave Kershaw, who trained the new members in SAS tactics and weapons. 'Everything that Jock Lewes had taught us, I was teaching them,' he says.

In May, 2nd SAS began operations – but they were not immediately successful. Operation Snapdragon saw a ten-man team, led by Geoffrey Appleyard, sent to Pantellaria, an island lying between Tunisia and Sicily. Appleyard's brief was to find a suitable landing place for assault troops, to report back on the enemy's strength and to capture a prisoner. The party arrived off the coast in a submarine before climbing into inflatable dinghies. They landed and scaled a cliff. Appleyard's plan was to grab a sentry and bundle him down the cliff, and within minutes, a suitable candidate appeared, singing 'O Sole Mio' as he ambled along. Appleyard sprang for the man's throat but missed his hold, allowing him to let out a scream. Appleyard and three others jumped on him, but by now another sentry was running over. Ernest Herstell tried to tackle the sentry, but he opened fire, killing Herstell. A brief firefight began which led to the remaining SAS men scrambling back down the cliff trying to bring the captured sentry with them. They failed; he was dropped and killed. The survivors jumped into their dinghies and made their way back to the submarine.

Operation Marigold involved a landing of 11 men on Sardinia, again by submarine and dinghy. The plan was to simulate a large-scale reconnaissance (in an effort to persuade the enemy that a major attack was coming) and to take a prisoner. Tanky Challenor, perhaps adding his own spin to events, claims that, once the prisoner was taken, the plan was to 'wipe out' the entire garrison. 'As soon as we started for the beach things began to go wrong,' he writes. A member of the party dropped his gun in a rocky bluff with a loud clatter. This instantly attracted gunfire from all angles. Challenor wanted to charge the enemy guns, but, thankfully, wiser heads prevailed, and the party made its way back to the dinghies. As they paddled away from the beach the firing continued, with 'bullets putting up little spouts of water all round our very vulnerable dinghy'. The men paddled on, eventually reaching the submarine.

Operation Chestnut, meanwhile, was an important operation for Bill Stirling and 2nd SAS. Not only did it involve a raid on Sicily that would coincide with the SRS's operations on the island, but its plan most closely matched traditional SAS theory. Small groups were to carry out sabotage behind enemy lines before making their own way back to Allied-held territory. Most importantly, though, this was to be the first SAS parachute operation since the failure of Operation Squatter 18 months earlier. Parachute training had continued, and the men had carried on wearing wings – but the Special Air Service was finally returning to the air.

In advance of the parachute drop from an Armstrong Whitworth Albemarle, Dave Kershaw, who had taken part in Squatter, tried to set the scene:

> To get them into the fix of things, I dug out, in the sand, the exact bottom half of the fuselage of an Albemarle with a trap door. I had them all sitting round on the sand, explaining all the pros and cons. I said, 'Now you're beginning to feel a little bit of sweat on the top of your lip! Get ready! Red light on! Green light – go!' And all they had to do was get up off their arse and walk to the area marked out in the sand where they were supposed to jump out of!

When the time came, Kershaw flew with the men in one of the Albemarles. Sitting in the front with the pilot, he moved back to wish the men luck before they jumped – to find that they had all gone. They had mistakenly jumped ten minutes before the aircraft reached its dropping zone.

Robert Summers, jumping from a different Albemarle, made a good landing. He, and those who landed with him, decided to split into two,

An Armstrong Whitworth Albemarle.

one group setting off to cut an underwater telephone cable and the other intending to look for suitable targets to sabotage. Summers, a member of the second group, helped to mine a road and attempted to blow up a truck. After visiting a farmhouse and posing as a German soldier to beg some food, he and a colleague were very nearly captured by two civilian members of the Sicilian equivalent of the Home Guard.

Operation Chestnut finally ended for Summers and two colleagues with a nervous encounter, as he remembers:

> We saw some figures advancing towards us. At the same time I noticed a camouflaged but still very English looking 15 cwt truck. I tried to see with my glasses who the soldiers were who were approaching us. The mist on the lenses of the binoculars made it impossible to tell at first what sort of dress they were wearing. In my own mind I felt quite certain that they were British soldiers. The other two covered me as I went forward. I took off my beret and stuck it on the end of my carbine. As I got closer I shouted out, 'We are English!'. Just about then I could see that they were wearing British steel helmets. Someone shouted, 'Come on then!' We advanced with our hands well up in the air. We were told to drop our arms which we very promptly did. Our 'rescuers' were a platoon of the 2nd Seaforths.

Summers, and most of his Chestnut colleagues, made it back to Allied lines. A significant number did not, however, and very little effective sabotage was done. Telegraph poles were destroyed, wires and field cables were cut, booby traps were set, a number of trucks were destroyed and charges were laid on railway line near Cefalu. The post-operation report stated that 'few of the tasks were carried out and the value of the damage and disorganisation was not proportionate to the number of men'.

Nevertheless, the SAS was a parachute organisation once again, and it had learned lessons that would in time be put to use.

37

STREET FIGHTING MEN

At just about the same time as men of 2nd SAS jumped out of Albemarles over Sicily, their comrades in the SRS were heavily engaged nearby, attacking the east coast port of Augusta. The town was both strategically and symbolically important. In strategic terms, it was crucial for the Allies' northwards push. In symbolic terms, as Derrick Harrison notes, it was a major European naval base, and its capture would represent a significant notch on the tally stick. A challenge, however, was the immediate presence of members of the Hermann Göring Division. The SRS, it seemed, was in for a tough fight.

On the evening of 12 July, *Ulster Monarch* entered Augusta harbour, where the SRS men transferred to landing craft. As they did so, heavy shell fire opened up from the west. The naval ships responded by blasting the beach defences. Then, as the landing craft came close inshore, the SRS men could see splashes to the side of them from machine-gun bullets hitting the water. 'Everyone flattened down,' remembers John Tonkin, 'and we heard the rattle against the side of the armour as the bullets hit.'

The landing – in daylight – was being carried out against the advice of the navy. As the landing craft beached onto a causeway of boulders, the men hurried off. Two medics with 3 Troop, running alongside each other, were killed straight away by machine-gun fire, but the rest of the troop made its way into the town.

Third Troop split into two sections, each moving up one of two parallel streets. On each side of the street, two men took it in turns to move slowly forward. When the leading man reached a doorway, he kicked it in and dropped down, firing into the house from ground level as the other

HMS *Ulster Monarch* lying off Sicily.

Twin Vickers guns mounted on a landing craft.

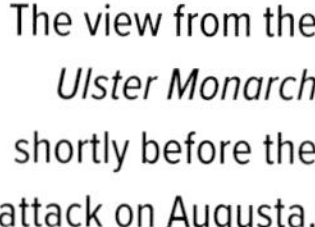

The view from the *Ulster Monarch* shortly before the attack on Augusta.

man covered him. The two were then overtaken by the men behind, who repeated the procedure. The final pair were walking backwards, scanning the area for activity from doors or windows behind them.

'It was a tense business,' writes Peter Davis. 'In that eerie half light we jumped at every shadow, expecting some sort of opposition from every corner, every doorway.' As he made his way through the quiet town, John Tonkin had a number of vivid experiences. First, just as he was about to kick a door open, a colleague screamed at him to stop. The man had noticed a booby trap stretched across the door.

Moments later, Tonkin opened fire on a man running down a connecting street – only to discover that the man was in fact his own sergeant, Dougie Eccles. Fortunately, Eccles was only hit in the leg, and he recovered quickly. 'He never held it against me, either,' says Tonkin.

A third incident occurred a while later. Tonkin's men had been sent forward to a crossroads, where they ran into heavy enemy fire. Suddenly, for no apparent reason, the firing stopped. A moment later, Tonkin remembers:

> We heard this shuffling . . . and this peasant woman appeared. She was very old, and she was just walking quietly, carrying some belongings, and she shuffled down the middle of the road. She just went by, not looking to one side or the other – and it was only after she had completely disappeared that the firing started up again.

The war had stopped for a little old lady to cross the road. This strange – but very human – moment affected John Tonkin deeply. He would never see anything like it again. Once the woman had passed by, the firing resumed so heavily that the troop was ordered to retreat. Yet, later that night, shortly after bringing tanks into action, the enemy suddenly withdrew. At a stroke the fighting was over and the SRS had taken the town.

The immediate result of the enemy withdrawal was a huge impromptu party enjoyed by most members of the unit. Some roamed around the empty town helping themselves to whatever they could find, wherever they could find it. Paddy Mayne even asked one of the unit's engineers to blow a safe open for him. When the men finally made their way back to *Ulster Monarch*, 'many of the more unscrupulous characters,' writes Peter

Davis, 'were pushing prams loaded with the junk that they had found lying about.'

It appears, meanwhile, that the Special Raiding Squadron had already gained a reputation for being at the forefront of events. The Special Intelligence Unit, a naval organisation responsible for rescuing enemy documents from newly captured areas, had arrived in Augusta immediately after the Axis withdrawal, ready to search through naval and air force installations. The unit's commander (and noted polar explorer) Quintin Riley prided himself on being first on any scene. The existence of the SRS, however, was making him nervous, and he grew anxious when he heard that Paddy Mayne's men had beaten him into the town. Fearing the worst, he sent parties directly into the most likely-looking buildings. Sure enough, he discovered, to his fury, that most of them already bore graffiti claiming 'CAPTURED BY THE SRS'.

3 Troop fought along this street. It was here that John Tonkin shot Dougie Eccles and was almost blown up by a booby trap.

38

MUSH MUSH

For some weeks, the SRS remained at Augusta. Operations were arranged and then cancelled, including a planned attempt to help Eighth Army to force its way past bitter resistance at Catania, and a proposal to capture road and rail bridges at Cannizzaro. In the meantime, between air raids, the men were able to enjoy themselves.

A difficult hazard to avoid during this period was Paddy Mayne's drinking bouts. Mayne, writes Peter Davis, did not like to drink alone:

> By 3am he would be really aroused and decide that he would like to make a party of it. So one of his henchmen would be dispatched to wake up all the officers and summon them . . . Woe betide any of us who were so foolish to revolt. If we locked our cabin door, it would be broken down and the first thing we would know about it would be to be borne triumphantly by a gang of toughs into Paddy's cabin . . .

Occasionally such nights would grow dark. A mess cook claimed to have identified Mayne's warning sign. If he started the evening singing a romantic ballad, 'Eileen Alannah' ('It seems years have lingered since last we did part, Eileen Alannah, the pride of my heart'), then the night would be relatively peaceful. But if he was singing the feistier 'Mush Mush' ('If you're in for a row or a ruction, just tread on the tail of my coat!') then the night might turn angry. One evening, Mayne took exception to the arrival of a group of English nurses from a local hospital. He sat brooding alone with a bottle of whisky until his mood was noted and the women were ushered away. 'Mush Mush' was duly sung, and at a key moment Mayne

Relaxing in a camp near the slopes of Mount Etna.

swept a row of glasses from the table. The senior mess officer tried to intervene – and pandemonium resulted, with a decanter thrown at one man's head, and another man lifted up and hurled across the room. As Davis writes: 'It was indeed an eloquent expression of the sway he held over us, and of the respect we had for him, that although there were thirteen of us, none of us dared to stand up to him . . .'

By the late summer of 1943, with Jock Lewes and David Stirling gone, Paddy Mayne entirely dominated the organisation. On the morning of 4 September, however, his brand of danger was replaced by another with the arrival of the SRS's next operation – an assault on Bagnara, a town near the tip of Italy's toe. The SRS was chosen for the job because of the attack's location: along a narrow strip of land unsuitable for access by a division. Once again, the town was successfully captured and Eighth Army's progress was secured.

Four days later came the announcement of Italy's surrender, quickly followed by the landing of Allied troops at Salerno in southern Italy. At the same time the Germans moved to occupy the country. Italy was swiftly turned into a battleground fought over by foreign powers.

39

TERMOLI

As British and American forces moved north through Italy, the Special Raiding Squadron was brought together with 3 Commando and 40 (Royal Marines) Commando to form a composite unit intended to prevent the Germans from establishing a defensive line. Once again, specially skilled SAS men were being used as commando shock troops. In the early hours of 3 October, over two hundred were landed by sea north-west of the coastal town of Termoli where they were to hold two bridges and a road junction. This would assist 78th Division's move northwards.

John Tonkin's section of 3 Troop was heading towards one of the bridges with orders to capture it and clear it of any enemy. Tonkin's men, at the head of the SRS advance, passed the town, and approached a farmhouse where a lot of activity was clearly taking place. Who was carrying out the activity was less clear. Tonkin had a quick decision to make. He says:

> We let fly with a hail of fire and it was Germans all right. They shot back and then skedaddled inland as hard as they could go. We pushed on up the ridge – and that was the first nasty surprise because we hadn't expected any German troops there.

Tonkin and his men soon found themselves pinned down by a solid wall of enemy fire. In small groups, they slipped down into a gulley which they believed led to the river. But it turned out to be blocked at the far end. Joe Fassam, an ex-member of 8 Commando, was killed by machine-gun fire as he tried to break out of the gulley. Tonkin recalls:

> This German officer came out very cautiously with a white flag. He was from the German 1st Parachute Division – who were bloody good troops – and he said, 'This is stupidity, we can kill you all, or you can honourably surrender. Your position is totally hopeless!' And it was perfectly true. So I said, 'All right, we'll come out.'

Tonkin was taken prisoner (with all but six of his men, who had managed to escape with three prisoners of their own) but his adventure was only just beginning. Other sections, coming up behind Tonkin's men, encountered similar resistance, and Bob Mélot, previously injured attacking Fort Benito at Benghazi, was again wounded. Nevertheless, by the end of the day, the town of Termoli had been taken and secured. The SRS was duly withdrawn to the Seminario Vescovile, a seminary near the waterfront.

The fighting was not yet over, however. A surprisingly fierce German counter-attack was mounted as Field Marshal Kesselring, commander of German forces in Italy, ordered 16th Panzer Division to retake the town. The SRS was duly sent back out to confront the Germans, and so, on 5 October, members of Johnny Wiseman's section found themselves sitting in a truck near the seminary, preparing to go into action. Seeing a messenger (probably Emrys Pocock of No. 3 Troop) approaching, Wiseman jumped down from the truck. As they began to speak, a shell landed on top of the truck. Wiseman recalls: 'I was talking to this fellow – and he disappeared into the telegraph wires above my head . . . There were only bits of him left. It was unbelievable . . . I wasn't scratched! Crazy!'

The shell wiped out Wiseman's entire section. Only one other man – Reg Seekings – escaped serious injury. 'I had a minute fracture in my fingernail,' remembers Seekings, who had been standing by the truck's tailboard when the shell landed. All around him was carnage. While fetching a jug of water from a nearby house to douse the burning body of Alex Skinner (a 23-year-old Geordie nicknamed 'Jesus'), Seekings spotted a young Italian boy whose 'guts were blown out like a huge balloon.' As the boy ran around screaming, Seekings shot him. 'There was absolutely no hope for him,' he says, 'and you couldn't let anybody suffer like that.' Seekings remembers speaking to two men – Jocky Henderson and Charles Grant – both with their hearts and lungs exposed. He went forward to the truck's cab where he found Bill McNinch (a likeable ex-member of Middle East

Commando who had joined the SAS at the same time as John Tonkin and Mick Gurmin) sitting in the driver's seat grinning. 'What the hell's wrong with you, Mac?' asked Seekings. 'Come on! Get out and give us a hand!' It was only when he jerked the door open that he realised McNinch was dead.

In all, 18 men were killed. Johnny Wiseman had to go to find Paddy Mayne to break the news. He says:

> Paddy asked 'What the devil are you doing here?' I said, 'I haven't got anyone under command anymore, sir!' The whole lot wiped out with one shell. We'd been together for months.

Despite the SRS's losses, the battle for Termoli grew fierce. For a while, that afternoon, it seemed as though a mini Dunkirk-style evacuation of British troops would have to be improvised. It was decided that about thirty fishing boats lying nearby could be brought into the harbour under a smokescreen to spirit men away. In the end, however, the SRS, armed with Bren and Tommy guns, was able to resist wave after wave of German tank, mortar and infantry attacks. A report compiled after the Germans had eventually withdrawn reveals the SRS's satisfaction – and surprise – at its own success:

> It is a good sign that, although the fighting of 5/6th was an all-out attempt to regain Termoli . . . and the enemy had ample forces and heavy support to smash the light force which was there, he was unable to do so, and it seemed as if their troops were without the morale to advance far . . . and the attack was abandoned when the threat to the town was greatest.

While the SRS was holding out against a Panzer division (and the odds), John Tonkin found himself having an unlikely meal with the division's commander, General Richard Heidrich. A while after his capture, Tonkin had been brought before the general – and asked if he would join him for dinner. Tonkin recalls: 'I didn't have any option . . . We ate quickly and after he realised he wasn't going to get any info, he was polite but he wasn't going to bother much.'

After dinner, Tonkin was questioned by a spectacularly inept intelligence officer, who began his interrogation by saying 'goodbye' instead of 'hello'. It was such a strange mistake that Tonkin began to laugh, and the officer was quickly removed. After his botched grilling, Tonkin was given a piece of information that he has never forgotten:

> This German parachute major came up to me and almost his exact words, his very precise words, were: 'I want you to listen very carefully to what I have to say. We now have orders which we cannot disobey that we must hand you over to the German Special Police and they are people that I will tell you, quite frankly, we do not like, and I must warn you that from now on the German army, to its shame, can no longer guarantee your life.'

Tonkin, it seems, was being warned he faced execution under Hitler's 'Commando Order'. This was Hitler's personal edict, issued in October 1942, that all British or Allied commandos, whether in uniform or civilian clothes, armed or unarmed, inserted behind the lines by any means, must be 'slaughtered to the last man'.

John Tonkin and Paddy Mayne in Bari.

At the time of Tonkin's capture, there was no Allied awareness of Hitler's order. Rommel had refused to enforce it in North Africa. Yet various members of 2nd SAS, including Bill Foster, Jim Shortall, Pat Dudgeon and Bernie Brunt (and probably also Dudgeon's fellow officer, Philip Pinckney), were executed in September and October 1943 after their capture in northern Italy while engaged on Operation Speedwell. Another 2nd SAS officer, Quentin Hughes, was fortunate to escape execution in January 1944 when he was captured after planting Lewes bombs on aircraft (in the traditional SAS manner) near Perugia as part of Operation Pomegranate. Hughes eventually escaped from captivity in April, at which point he revealed the existence of the order to British authorities. (A doctor had persuaded the Germans to delay Hughes's execution, giving him time to escape before it could be carried out.)

Yet a full six months before Hughes's revelation, John Tonkin had received a pointed warning. He must escape or be killed. And so, as he was being transported through Italy in the back of a truck, he prised a canvas canopy loose and bolted for freedom. As he attempted to make his way to Allied lines, he was helped by a succession of sympathetic Italian civilians. Eventually he reached Eighth Army positions, where he was offered a lift to Termoli by a British officer. Tonkin declined the offer as he wanted to find the SRS instead. It proved a very sensible decision – the officer had barely driven a hundred yards down the road before Tonkin heard a huge explosion. The officer had driven over a mine. His truck was destroyed and he was killed.

By mid-October, little more than a fortnight after his capture, Tonkin was back with his SRS colleagues in Bari.

From there he was sent to an assessment centre for returned prisoners-of-war, and finally dispatched back to Britain. He was ready for new challenges – as was the Special Raiding Squadron. It had served its time as a commando unit. Interesting times lay ahead.

40

THE BRIGADE

By the turn of 1944, the balance of the war had shifted entirely since those uncertain days when the first plans had been laid for the creation of 'L' Detachment. In the summer of 1941, a German invasion of Britain had still seemed a possibility. Now, the Allies – who included the Soviets and the Americans – were actively planning an invasion of France to be launched *from* Britain.

The SAS, too, had changed utterly since its first incarnation. The recent accomplishments of the SRS had enhanced its reputation; but 2nd SAS had not been noticeably successful trying to do things a more traditional way. There was no chance of the organisation's dissolution, but what form would it now take? And what exactly would it be doing?

The answer started coming in early January when Paddy Mayne received a promotion to lieutenant colonel and the unit became the SAS Brigade. The SRS was increased in size to become 1st SAS Regiment, commanded by Mayne; 2nd SAS remained under Bill Stirling; 3rd SAS and 4th SAS were now French regiments, while 5th SAS was a smaller Belgian detachment. Brigade headquarters were located near Darvel in Scotland, while tactical headquarters would be established at Moor Park, an estate in Hertfordshire.

Once again the SAS had to find members quickly. 'It suddenly swelled like nobody's business,' says Mike Sadler. Many new members came from the Auxiliary Units,* men already trained to wage war behind enemy lines. They seemed ideal recruits for the SAS. But there were many others.

* Had the Germans invaded Britain, these were the units that would have carried out acts of sabotage behind enemy lines. They were, in effect, the British Resistance.

Above: Ian Fenwick.

Left: Fenwick in France.

Justo Balerdi, from northern Spain, joined at this time. He had fought with the Republicans during the Spanish Civil War and the authorities now gave him the option of changing his name so as not to be identified as a Spanish republican if caught. The name he chose was 'Robert Bruce', while a colleague chose 'Francis Drake'. The victor of Bannockburn was considered acceptable by the War Office. The vice-admiral of the Elizabethan fleet was not.

Roy Close, then a member of the parachute regiment, was personally interviewed by Paddy Mayne. Standing in front of Mayne, Close was asked why he wanted to join. After giving an obviously prepared answer about the strategic value of guerrilla warfare, he made his pitch. He and his friends must all be accepted – or none. 'So it's giving the commanding officer an ultimatum already, is it?' said Mayne with a smile. Once the interview was over, the three men decided that they had gone too far. So Close knocked on the door. 'Another ultimatum?' asked Mayne. Close said that he and his friends had reconsidered. They would now be happy to join individually. 'Thank you,' said Mayne, 'I'll bear that in mind also.' Close admits, 'It was with surprise that a few days later we saw on the noticeboard in the Depot that we had all three been accepted.'

Not only was the SAS growing once again, it was placed within a convoluted new organisational structure. Administratively it came under the Army Air Corps. Operationally, it was under the command of 1st Airborne Corps. This had practical consequences. The sandy berets so valued by SAS men would now be replaced by red berets.* In fact, Frederick 'Boy' Browning, the commander of Airborne Forces, truly believed he was granting the SAS an honour by allowing its men to wear the red beret. SAS members, on the other hand, considered it a blatant attempt to rob them of their identity.

The spat revealed a major conflict of values. Paratroopers and SAS men were different kinds of soldiers. Roy Close is well placed to make a comparison: 'Coming straight from my Parachute Regiment training, I think when I got there I reeked a bit too much of bullshit for the relaxed yet quietly understood discipline of the SAS.'

The difference in values – and the mutual disapproval it caused – hinted at a potential problem. There was a risk that the SAS might find itself being used once again in an unsuitable manner, this time as shock troops dropped from the air.

If there were problems within the new hierarchy, there was also friction within the brigade itself: 1st SAS had a much larger proportion of original members than 2nd SAS, it had achieved more success, and its members were keen to remind others of these facts. There was even a pecking order inside the regiment. 'A' Squadron boasted Bill Fraser, Johnny Cooper, Jimmy Brough, Bob Tait and Reg Seekings, among other SAS royalty. As the living ghost of 'L' Detachment, it stood above the other squadrons. Seekings, in fact, had recently turned down a commission. So had Dave Kershaw, a proud working-class man who explains that accepting it 'would have meant acting the rest of my life – which I wasn't prepared to do'. Kershaw and Seekings make an interesting contrast with Bill Cumper, another proud working-class man who *did* accept a commission but never missed an opportunity to poke fun at his posh colleagues, and, by extension, at his own social isolation. He once said of Randolph Churchill: 'Christ! He's so stupid even the other officers notice it.'

* The sandy berets were introduced in 1942, replacing white ones that were often mocked by troops from other units as being ostentatious and effeminate.

RECKON WE LOOKS LIKE F**ING CHRISTMAS TREES IN THIS KIT!"

"*I don't care a damn, Maria, I'm going to tear them off and sun-bathe!*"

"*Nobby,*" *my old missus said,* "*if there was only two mines in all the blinking hatlantic you'd 'it 'em!*"

"*I want to be quite certain in my own mind before I volunteer for this Paratroop business!*"

"WELL TRY THIS ONE, SIR, ..."

Dave Kershaw and Ian Fenwick (far right).

Cumper (who, midway through his parachute training, cut a pair of SAS wings in half and wore them on his uniform) seems to have been adored by the people he ridiculed, which is perhaps another mark of the SAS's singularity. Certainly, in early 1944, it was still attracting exceptional personnel. One of these was Ian Fenwick, an ex-member of the Auxiliary Units. Fenwick, 33 years old when he joined in February, was a gifted artist who had already achieved fame as a cartoonist and illustrator. He designed book covers (including the latest P.G. Wodehouse editions) but it is his satirical cartoons, published in *Punch* and other magazines, which made his reputation. Not only are the cartoons still funny today, but they present a vivid snapshot of wartime conceits and concerns.

The cartoons' concerns are the period's concerns. These include shifts in attitudes to class, morality and social responsibility (as well as a laugh-out-loud gag about randy monks). As Fenwick's old friend David Niven writes in a book of his cartoons, published in 1944, Fenwick was 'a firm believer in the truth that the funniest stories are the shortest ones'.

Ian Fenwick was shot dead in a German ambush on 7 August 1944 near Chambon-la-Forêt in France. In that same book of his cartoons, published shortly after his death, the publisher's note observes perceptively that Fenwick 'would have played an important part in the post-war world'.*

* The publisher, Ian Collins, was also the liaison officer between the SAS and Supreme Allied Headquarters.

Monty inspects the Phantoms in April 1944.

41

PACKING FOR A TRIP

As the invasion of Normandy approached, the SAS Brigade received its operational instructions from Supreme Headquarters Allied Expeditionary Force (SHAEF). Given the influence of 1st Airborne Corps, there was at least a danger that the SAS would be offered an unwelcome role.

Sure enough, the order revealed that the SAS was not going to parachute behind enemy lines. Instead, 36 hours before the main invasion force reached the beaches, it would parachute *between* enemy lines. The men would establish a blocking line to prevent the Panzer tanks from reaching the beaches.

This plan had two observable problems. First, while it might fit parachute battalion doctrine, it was in no way appropriate for the SAS, whose members were currently being taught how to derail trains, liaise with the French resistance and use something known as a 'debollocker'.* Second, it would almost certainly result in the organisation's destruction.

Paddy Mayne took a back seat, allowing Bill Stirling to draft a letter to SHAEF in which he objected to the plan in the strongest terms. He proposed instead a version of 'L' Detachment's desert tactics, updated for a new theatre of war. Small groups should parachute behind enemy lines, where they would set up bases, travel around on foot or in jeeps, and strike at enemy lines of communication and other targets such as convoys and camps.

* A 'debollocker' was a six-inch hollow tube with a pointed end that was pushed into the ground, rather like a firework. Triggered by a man stepping on it, it would fire upwards into his testicles.

Aircrew of 620 Squadron in the doorway of a Short Stirling.

Before the letter was sent, however, Frederick Browning personally intervened by sending his own letter to the chief-of-staff of 21st Army Group with a similar proposal. Stirling sent his own, far more strongly worded letter anyway – and ended up resigning from the SAS, to be replaced as commander of 2nd SAS by Brian Franks. Another link with the early days was gone.

The immediate result, however, was that, on 28 May, revised operational instructions were issued. The SAS would be inserted behind the lines. It would attack communications and hinder the enemy in its efforts to move its forces towards the front. The unit would play the role for which it had been created.

Over the coming months, every SAS regiment would take part in the French fighting. As D-Day approached, however, three initial operations were planned. Operation Bulbasket would drop men of 'B' Squadron into the Viennes region near Poitiers. Operation Houndsworth, involving 'A' Squadron, would focus on the Morvan, near Dijon. A small 1st SAS party, meanwhile, would drop in Normandy to carry out a deception operation, codenamed Titanic.

These operations presented new challenges – and this meant the involvement of ancillary organisations. One of these was Phantom (GHQ Liaison Regiment), a signals unit with a similarly unorthodox outlook to the SAS. The original purpose of Phantom, according to member John Hislop, had been 'to obtain first-hand information of the most forward fighting and relay it straight back to GHQ'.

Phantom had been created to solve a particular wartime problem. News from the battlefield tended to be so delayed by long communication chains that it was often out of date by the time it reached headquarters. Phantom's specially trained members bypassed this communication chain and sent commanders an immediate and reliable picture of events. By early 1944, it had become clear that SAS parties in France would need a dependable wireless service to send and receive messages from headquarters. How else could supply drops be requested and organised? How could RAF air strikes be called up? How could information about German movements be passed on? And who better than Phantom to do the job?

A 620 Squadron Short Stirling at RAF Fairford.

Supply containers dropping from a Halifax.

From its earliest days, Phantom had encouraged its members to think and act independently. According to Hislop, they were trained to a high degree but were allowed a certain 'elasticity' in behaviour. When Phantom's 'F' Squadron, commanded by John 'Jakie' Astor, was attached to the SAS Brigade, Hislop immediately noted how similar the two organisations were in atmosphere. It made sense that they should work together.*

General Montgomery visited the SAS Brigade in late April, an occasion during which Hislop remembers a typically strange moment: 'When [Monty] reached my section of the line, Bill Stirling [still at this point commanding 2nd SAS Regiment] said: "This is the Phantom detachment," to which Monty's only reaction was to observe, "Don't use 'em!" and walk on.' Monty's advice was duly ignored and members of 'F' Squadron, including Hislop, accompanied the SAS to France.

Another organisation that now became crucial to the SAS was the Royal Air Force, which was to prove an even longer-range successor to the LRDG. Its role was to fly the SAS parties to their operational areas in France, and then, as the weeks and months passed, to maintain those

* By this time the commander of Phantom's 'A' Squadron was David Niven. It is striking how often Niven's name appears on the periphery of SAS activities.

parties with constant supply drops. Flying such missions was a highly specialised – and extremely dangerous – job.

Most SAS parties were flown from Fairford in Gloucestershire, where from March onwards, the Short Stirlings of 620 and 190 Squadrons (of 38 Group) were based. Indeed, there was a large wired-off area, known as 'The Cage', just beyond the airfield where SAS members were kept in isolation before their flights. Seventy-five miles to the south, Tarrant Rushton airfield was chiefly used for supply drops. The SAS also regularly employed 138 and 161 'Special Duties' squadrons, flying mainly Handley Page Halifax aircraft from Tempsford in Bedfordshire.

These flights were clouded in such secrecy that the airmen were not informed where they were flying to. Were they to be captured, after all, they must not be able to divulge any information leading to the capture of the SAS parties. Arthur Batten, an air gunner with 190 Squadron, remembers:

> These operations were all top secret and there were no names of villages or towns given in the briefing or on the navigator's charts. Just the rivers were shown – but there were no names to them. They were all blank.

The secrecy extended to the identities of the individuals being transported. And the crews never even discovered whether their supply drops had been successful. There were very aware, however, of the flak that was being thrown up at them over France. And they worked very hard. 620 Squadron was in such demand that operations were often flown without the benefit of moonlight, and SAS men sometimes had to be dropped 'blind' without reception signals or sight of the ground. As Flight Officer Thomas Higgins, of 620 Squadron, wrote in his diary: 'This Group is certainly operating like mad these days. Must be a war on . . . Personally I would like to do at least another 10 or 11 trips, but no more. Things are starting to get a bit too tough for that.'

Flight Engineer Malcolm Mitchell, of 190 Squadron, remembers a supply flight that went off as usual – until, climbing away from the dropping zone, his Stirling suddenly lost power and plummeted towards the ground, only righting itself at the last moment. It turned out that the pilot

– who normally flew alone – had fainted over the controls. By chance, however, an army glider pilot had come along for the ride and was sitting in the second pilot's seat. He had pushed the pilot aside and wrestled to regain control. 'We had never been closer to a crash,' says Mitchell, 'which would have remained unexplained.'

42

WAR OF HATE

Mike Sadler was, in the spring of 1944, the intelligence officer for 1st SAS Regiment. Not long before he had been an anti-tank gunner in the Rhodesian army. Now he was one of very few people in Britain with prior knowledge of the D-Day plans. Besides liaising with all manner of staff officers, Sadler was spending a great deal of time 'looking at maps and establishing where it might be suitable to establish bases, what the targets might be, and how they could be attacked'.

Another job was to see aircraft off from the various airfields and wait for their return in order to debrief the crew. But Sadler still had a taste for adventure – and for the egg-and-bacon breakfast served up on the crew's return. When he could, he would bag the second pilot's seat on these flights. As he says, 'I was very curious, intrigued to know what it was like doing these jobs. I got a rather good insight into the pleasures of flying at night in remote territories – and of being shot at from the ground.'

On one flight in a Stirling from RAF Keevil in Wiltshire, Sadler took the bomb-aimer's position. He felt a great deal of turbulence moments after a party of 12 SAS men had been released over the dropping zone 30 miles south of Paris. As the Stirling climbed away, a night fighter suddenly appeared. Sadler recalls, 'The attacking aircraft came in from the front and started shooting from half a mile away. You could hear the tracer coming in.'

The Stirling's pilot dived so quickly into cloud that the entire aircraft began shaking. It was an alarming experience for Sadler, but it did not bear comparison with what was happening on the ground. Instead of being met by members of the French Resistance, the SAS men were dropping into an enemy ambush. A mixed group of Germans and French traitors were waiting for them.

A firefight took place during which one man was killed, three managed to escape, and the majority were seized. The captured men were held in Gestapo headquarters in Paris for several weeks where they were interrogated and beaten before – astonishingly – being offered their freedom. They were told that if they changed out of their SAS uniforms into civilian clothes, they would be taken to Switzerland and exchanged for German prisoners held by the British. They were placed in a lorry and driven north out of Paris. One of the men later recalled: 'I realised that something was going to happen and I asked the SS sergeant in French if we were going to be shot. He laughed and said, "Of course you are going to be shot."'

The seven prisoners were lined up in a woodland clearing. A sentence was read in English condemning the men to death for collaborating with French terrorists and endangering the security of the German army. At that moment the men ran for their lives. Five were killed on the spot by machine-gun fire – but two managed to run to safety. They survived to give evidence to a war crimes tribunal.

Mike Sadler knew nothing of this, of course. Having dropped the men, his Stirling had evaded the night fighter and flown back to Wiltshire. Once the area had been liberated, however, Sadler returned to investigate the murders. He identified the body of a friend, Captain Patrick Garstin, and interviewed local people. His report, plus the testimony of the survivors, led to the capture of the perpetrators by an SAS War Crimes Investigation Team led by Major Eric 'Bill' Barkworth. As a result, six perpetrators were convicted of war crimes. Four of these men were sentenced to death; three were ultimately executed.

At the head of the chain of responsibility, of course, was Adolf Hitler. His Commando Order demanded the murder of 'sabotage troops', who were to be 'slaughtered to the last man'. As the men of the SAS prepared for their French adventure, they knew that they would be facing a dark and desperate enemy. But they did not know just how dark.

43

TITANIC DAYS

Towards the end of May 1944, the men who would be involved in the first parachute drops into France quietly disappeared from their units, leaving their colleagues and their possessions behind. They moved into 'The Cage' at Fairford, where they did their best to pass the hours as the time for action approached.

The very first men to land in France were part of a deception operation named, ominously, Titanic. The plan was to simulate a large-scale parachute drop in Normandy that would attract German forces away from the real dropping zones further north.

The operation was split into four parts. One part was cancelled and two others involved the dropping of dummy parachutists made from sandbags, known colloquially as 'ruperts'. Titanic IV, however, involved six members of 1st SAS, three each from 'A' and 'B' Squadrons. Dropped close to the invasion beaches just minutes after midnight on 6 June 1944, they were among the first uniformed soldiers to arrive in France on D-Day.

The officers and men – Poole, Fowles, Dawson, Saunders, Hurst and Merryweather – descended with a mass of ruperts, fitted with rifle and machine-gun simulators that would detonate for several minutes. Automatic flares were also dropped that would illuminate the ruperts in the air while simulating a reception party on the ground. The SAS men, meanwhile, were instructed to do all they could to attract attention to themselves.

According to John Tonkin, some of the more experienced SAS men at Fairford had been dismayed by the apparently suicidal nature of the operation. Keeping this to themselves, they tried to gee up Lieutenants 'Puddle' Poole and 'Chick' Fowles, telling them that it was a marvellous job. When

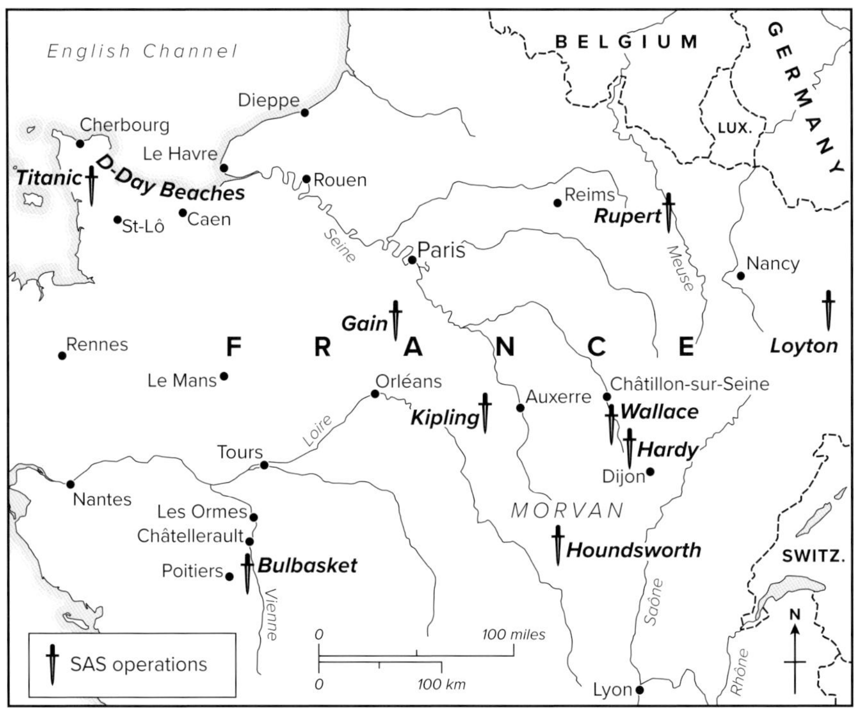

the operation was briefly called off, the old hands admitted their true feelings – only for it to be put back on again. At this point, the young subalterns appeared 'as white as sheets'. Paddy Mayne took them aside, telling them that they could pull out if they wished. But the pair insisted on going ahead.

In the event, the four troopers – Dawson, Saunders, Hurst and Merryweather – were initially forced to act on their own as they could not locate the officers. The next night they were rescued by a member of the local Resistance, Edouard Le Duc, who moved them to a safe hiding place. Le Duc then found Poole, who, it transpired, had tripped over his kitbag and knocked himself out on leaving the aircraft. Several days later, he also found Fowles, who had landed some way off and gone into hiding. For more than a month the group managed to avoid the Germans, until they were finally spotted by a pair of paratroopers who threw grenades, wounding Fowles, Hurst and Merryweather. The entire party was taken prisoner – although the three wounded men were released weeks later when their hospital was liberated by the Americans. Poole, Dawson and Saunders remained prisoners until the end of the war.

This odd little sideshow may have had some effect. General Max Pemsel, chief-of-staff to the Seventh Army commander, appears to have sent a brigade in search of the threat conjured up by the SAS men and their ruperts. And the subsequent discovery of such a large number of dummies may have influenced General Hans Speidel (who was in temporary charge of Army Group B while Field Marshal Rommel was in Germany) to doubt that an invasion was really underway.

It should be remembered, however, that Operation Titanic was running alongside other tactical deceptions (such as Taxable and Glimmer – the dropping of tinfoil strips from aircraft to fool German radar that an invasion fleet was approaching) and a large-scale strategic deception (whose undeniable success was achieved with double agents).* Titanic IV was a very small piece in a much larger jigsaw.

* As used to be said about rats and London, one is never very far from Dudley Clarke, the father of strategic deception, in the pages of this book.

44
BULBASKET

There was a good deal of confusion inside the Fairford Cage about who would be leaving for France and when. The overriding SHAEF directive had stipulated the creation of SAS bases – established in the Morvan, near Dijon, by Operation Houndsworth, and in the Vienne, near Poitiers, by Operation Bulbasket* – from which the movement of German forces towards Normandy could be impeded.

On 29 May, John Tonkin, now commander of 13 Squadron, 1st SAS, was told that Bulbasket was going ahead. He was to be dropped with a party of four officers, 40 men and five Phantoms. Two days later, the plan was changed: he would now be dropped the following morning with 20-year-old Richard Crisp, formerly an Old Vic drama student. They were to constitute the Bulbasket advance party. This plan too was changed. Tonkin and Crisp ended up being driven to London with Mike Sadler and the equivalent Houndsworth advance party.

In London the parties were split up. The Houndsworth group went one way, while Tonkin and Crisp went another – and they were pumped full of information. The bitter politics of the French Resistance, also known as the Maquis, was explained to them. They were told that the Maquis consisted of two groups, one communist, the other loyal to General de Gaulle, neither of which communicated with the other.

They were then shown photographs of the Special Operations Executive (SOE) agent who would meet them on arrival in France. The SOE

* The curious name 'Bulbasket' had a double meaning. On the one hand, it referred to the baby Moses, left in a basket among the bulrushes. On the other, it abbreviated John Tonkin's nickname within the SAS: 'Bullshitting Basket'.

had been formed in July 1940 after the British Army's evacuation from continental Europe, its role being to carry out sabotage and espionage in Nazi-controlled areas. In Churchill's pithy words, they were to 'set Europe ablaze.' In practice this meant organising and supplying local resistance groups. The agent whose picture was now placed in front of Tonkin and Crisp was Amédée Maingard, a French-Mauritian codenamed Samuel. He was to be greeted with the words, '*Est-ce qu'il y a une maison dans le bois*?' If they did not receive the immediate reply, '*Oui, mais il n'est pas tres bon*', they should open fire instantly and start to run.

Next, they were introduced to a member of the Maquis who had been in France since the Germans' arrival in May 1940, but had recently come to England. This man had been living as a hunted animal under German

John Tonkin in France.

occupation. His knowledge was hard-earned and Tonkin listened carefully to all he said. He advised, for example, that when help was needed from the French population, Tonkin and his men should always go to the poorer areas. The rich were likely to try to maintain their position by assisting the Germans. The poor, on the other hand, had less to lose by helping the Allies. If help was needed in the countryside, meanwhile, they should go to a small farm and wait for an old woman on her way back from the outhouse. Old, because she could remember the previous war (and perhaps even the Franco-Prussian War) and would almost certainly hate the Germans. A woman, because women are more sympathetic than men. And on her way back from the outhouse, because she would be in a far better mood coming back from the toilet than if she was on her way . . .

The Frenchman had plenty more advice. A brothel, he said, was a good place to hide because the women, who had often been brutally treated by the Germans, were keen to gain their revenge. He stressed that the Bulbasket party should always have a reserve base that was known to everybody; the existence of the main base might be compromised at any moment – and there would not be sufficient time to organise a new one. Finally, the man gave Tonkin a piece of advice that flatly contradicted something he had just been told: he should never assume that the latest password had got through to the reception committee. Tonkin should not, in other words, be too quick to shoot Maingard if his challenge was met by a blank stare. 'Don't shoot,' said the Frenchman, 'until you're quite sure that you're shooting at the right guy.'

After two days in London, Tonkin and Crisp were taken to Hazells Hall, near Tempsford airfield in Bedfordshire. This stately home was in constant use by the SOE, whose agents would stay there before missions. Tonkin remembers solving jigsaw puzzles with the courageous young SOE agent Violette Szabo, who was about to parachute into France for the second time. Szabo, according to another SOE agent, sat chatting on the lawn happily, and played the Mills Brothers' recent hit 'Paper Doll' continuously on the gramophone. She would be murdered in Ravensbrück concentration camp eight months later.

On 5 June, Paddy Mayne paid a visit to Hazells Hall to wish the men luck (and to offer the Titanic team a last-minute reprieve). Later that night, at 1.37 a.m., dropping blind, Tonkin and Crisp jumped out of their Halifax

Violette Szabo.

and into France.* Tonkin's landing was gentle, and as soon as he was down, he was approached by a young man.

As instructed, Tonkin gave the challenge: *'Est-ce qu'il y a une maison dans le bois?'* The man simply ignored the question and carried on talking. Tonkin did not follow instructions and open fire. He trusted, as the Maquis member had warned might happen, that the password had simply failed to get through – and he was proved right.

Tonkin and Crisp spent the night in the young man's family farmhouse. The next morning, with the Normandy invasion well underway, they were introduced to Amédée Maingard. Several hours later, the Germans made a sweep of the area. They raided the farmhouse – but by then the SAS men had gone.

* Jumping with Tonkin and Crisp from the Halifax was a 'Jedburgh' party. This was a three-man SOE team, usually made up of one British member, one American member and one member from the country it was dropping into. The team would parachute into an enemy-held area, where it would work closely with the local resistance, helping to co-ordinate and supply its members, and generally creating trouble for the Germans. The SAS and the Jedburghs usually co-operated but there was often an overlap of responsibility – and tensions sometime arose. The Jedburgh team jumping with Tonkin and Crisp was led by William Crawshay. His attitude to the SAS can be probably be gauged from a remark made many years later to an interviewer: 'The SAS force was added on at the last moment. It had nothing to do with our instructions. All we had to do was hand them over to a Frenchman and get the hell out of it.'

Maingard, meanwhile, had found a possible SAS base, which he showed to Tonkin. It was clearly suitable, and using the Jedburgh team's wireless set, Tonkin sent its map reference to Moor Park headquarters. By return, he received a message that a further nine men, one of whom was a signals operator, would be sent that night from Fairford, together with nine containers of supplies including weapons, explosives and other equipment. This presented an urgent problem. How could such a weight of material be transported from the dropping zone to the base without discovery?

Once again, Maingard provided a solution. He had adapted a number of petrol-driven trucks into 'gasogene' vehicles, running on wood gas. The drop was successful – and everything (and everybody) was loaded onto the trucks and driven along quiet roads away from prying German and French eyes.

Now that men, weapons and explosives were arriving, the Bulbasket team was looking to plan operations. A meeting was held with local Maquis chiefs to discuss the unifying of tactics. But another important question arose. With uniformed British soldiers roaming the area, how would the team's existence be kept a secret? Between them, Tonkin and Maingard came up with the solution. Quite simply, it would not. Tonkin remembers:

> We made a conscious decision that we would broadcast as widely as possible the fact that we were there. It would become known to the Germans anyway. But the sensible thing to do was to make sure the French also knew about it.

Once the team's existence was known, Tonkin and Maingard hoped to start receiving specific information about enemy activities and movements. It was a calculated risk as it clearly left Bulbasket vulnerable to spies and informers. But the immediate result was an unexpected visit from an extremely nervous local railway worker who

> turned up on the morning of 10th June with a report that there were eleven railway sidings just south-west of Châtellerault filled with petrol tankers for the German army. They were heavily guarded by German troops. From our base that was fifty-two kilometres north-west. My problem was what the heck I could do about it.

Amédée Maingard's gasogene trucks crowded with SAS men and supplies.

Tomos 'Twm' Stephens, dressed as a Frenchman, about to cycle to Châtellerault to find the railway petrol tankers.

Stephens, sitting in front, as he was usually dressed. Richard Crisp is second left.

'Twm' Stephens with Maquis members and the car used to attack a road bridge.

Above: Bulbasket members on 17 June.

Right: Surprised in their sleeping bags.

The first thing Tonkin could do was to check that the report was accurate. He dressed a recently arrived officer, Tomos 'Twm' Stephens, in civilian clothes and sent him off on a bicycle, in company with the railway worker and a maquisard, to find the railway tankers.

The following day, Stephens and his companions returned. The lieutenant confirmed the existence of the tankers in marshalling yards spread out over several hundred metres. He also confirmed that they were too heavily guarded for the Bulbasket team to attempt to destroy them. He had, however, noted their exact position, which was sent as a map reference to Moor Park.

The following evening, 12 de Havilland Mosquitos, exceptionally strong and quick fighter-bombers, were sent from three squadrons to attack the marshalling yards. The petrol tankers, intended to fuel the vehicles of 2nd SS Panzer Division 'Das Reich', were obliterated with extraordinary accuracy by bombs and cannon fire. Within days of arriving, Bulbasket had held up a fanatical Panzer division as it moved north towards Normandy, and struck hard at the French railway network.

Two days later, 'Twm' Stephens and three maquisards blew up a road bridge over a railway line. Tonkin took a photo of Stephens with Maquis members and the car used in the attack.

Despite this success, the bulk of Tonkin's men, and his vital supplies, were proving slow to arrive. On the night of 10 June, a 620 Squadron Stirling carrying the main operational party had been forced to turn back to Fairford after the crew could see no reception lights at the dropping zone. Tonkin, who was on the ground at the time, had seen no aircraft. The following night, two 190 Squadron Stirlings made another attempt. Once again, Tonkin was waiting on the ground. He had almost thirty people with him, and ten bullock carts, to haul much-needed supplies from the dropping zone to the gasogene trucks. He recalls:

> We were out on the dropping zone by dusk and we prepared three bonfires to be lit in a line running parallel to the road. The fires are a guide to the pilots as to where to drop. We were expecting the planes at around 1am on the 12th June. At about ten to one the first vehicles of the motorised column appeared and there was just a steady stream of headlights. They kept on and on and on, towards Poitiers.

The headlights belonged to the vehicles of the Das Reich Division, which had just slaughtered 643 French civilians in the nearby village of Oradour-sur-Glane and was probably now on its way to refuel its vehicles at the Châtellerault marshalling yards. If the supply drop went ahead, Tonkin worried, the bonfires might well be seen from the road. As he was deciding whether to cancel the drop, the sky suddenly lit up: 'We saw a great fire ball rising from over the horizon in the direction of Châtellerault.'

This, Tonkin realised, was the Mosquito raid on the marshalling yard. With a new burst of energy, he decided to proceed with the drop, and as the Nazi division headed past, lights blazing, he heard the drone of two aircraft arriving overhead. Looking up, he saw an extraordinary sight:

> The sky seemed to be full of multi-coloured lights, green, blue, white, red, you name it. There were forty-five of them swinging below parachutes. Almost immediately all the German convoy lights went out and we could no longer hear their engines. We expected an attack at any moment.

The multi-coloured lights were a new idea intended to make supplies easier to find. Bulbs had been attached to each container. They were supposed to light up as they hit the ground – but they had malfunctioned, switching on, instead, as the parachutes opened. Every man on the ground began frantically smashing the bulbs and trying to collect up supplies. 'Those bullocks had never been driven so fast,' says Tonkin. But the expected attack did not come. The fearsome Das Reich regiment had seen the lights, stopped their vehicles and taken shelter by the side of the road. They believed they were coming under aerial attack. Their mistake gave Tonkin's men sufficient time to get away with the new reinforcements and supplies.

As June progressed, the mood in camp remained good. Roads were regularly mined and railway lines successfully cut. Four jeeps with Vickers K guns were dropped, allowing the men to roam more widely and experiment with new tactics. Richard Crisp became a road-mining expert. One of his schemes was to spread dirt across a road. This mimicked a recently laid mine – and caused any approaching enemy vehicles to stop. Their

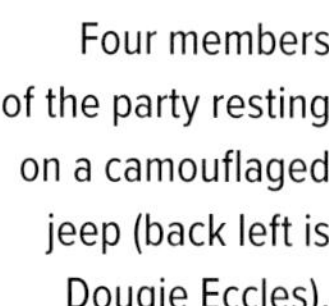

Four members of the party resting on a camouflaged jeep (back left is Dougie Eccles).

Tonkin (far right) at a meeting with Maquis leaders. Beside him is Amédée Maingard.

A relaxed atmosphere in the Forêt de Verrières camp. This calm would very soon be shattered.

occupants would climb out to begin sweeping the road. As they did so, the drama school student would open fire with his Vickers K guns.

As the end of the month approached, the enemy's presence seemed to increase and the party found itself changing bases with annoying regularity. Supply drops began to fail, which became a particular worry as the group was growing larger. Some of these newcomers were SAS men, while others were maquisards who had simply taken up residence in the camp. On 25 June, Tonkin, nervous of the base being discovered, moved to a new spot in the Forêt de Verrières, only 15 miles from the strongly German-held city of Poitiers.

Three days later, Dougie Eccles (the sergeant whom Tonkin had accidentally shot in Sicily) and Ken Bateman set off to sabotage a railway line at Saint-Benoît. A jeep driver dropped them off and waited – but they failed to return. The railway line was adjacent to the headquarters of the German 80th Corps; Eccles and Bateman were quickly spotted and captured. They

A supply drop from a Stirling.

Lieutenants Morris and Weaver making cigarettes from pipe tobacco and toilet paper in the Forêt de Verrières. Their table is made from the end of a supply container.

refused to reveal any information under questioning from Erich Schönig, the intelligence officer of 80th Corps, but they were subsequently handed over to the SD (the Nazi Party's intelligence service). Once in SD hands, they would undoubtedly have been tortured for information.

Security at the new camp, meanwhile, was becoming lax. For one thing, the men, most of whom were not involved in sabotage operations, were growing bored. For another, it was commonly understood that the Germans were in retreat. A number of soldiers, who had lived so much of their young lives in a state of constant alert, were starting to relax their focus. A few had begun wandering into the nearby village to chat up girls and drink in the bar. Some of the girls had tried to find the camp. The existence of Operation Bulbasket was becoming far too well known. Tonkin realised that the party would have to move on again straight away.

The evening before the planned move, a motorcycle and sidecar containing three men stopped a mile away from the camp. The SAS man on sentry duty brought the men inside where they were questioned by the Maquis. The men explained who they were and what they were doing – and they were released. And the following morning, the camp moved to a new location in the Bois des Cartes. Tonkin remembers:

> We'd done a recce of it and there was a well in the middle of it – but the water supply just wouldn't stand the numbers of people. The moment we tried to draw on it, it just faded out. And that was when they'd had their worst drought for many years in that central part of France. So we moved back again into the Forêt de Verrières, back to our old campsite on the afternoon of the 2nd July.

Dougie Eccles and Ken Bateman, meanwhile, were still in the clutches of the SD. They had said nothing for several days, assuming that the Bulbasket party would have moved camp in the intervening period. But, as Erich Schönig reveals, the SD started to prise information from one or both of them. According to Schönig it was learned that 'these two belonged to a group of parachutists who were encamped in a wood near Poitiers. There was a group of twenty to thirty-five men who were in touch with the Maquis.'

An operation to cut a railway line in mid-July.

Preparing the landing strip for Bulbasket's return.

Unfortunately, on the morning of 3 July, the group had returned to that camp. Schönig continues:

> The SD was interested in capturing this group and requested military reinforcements . . . The SD sent a French confidential agent to the vicinity of the camp to find out whether the camp was still used. This was the case. Consequently the action against the camp was decided upon . . .

Clearly the men on the motorcycle and sidecar had been enemy spies. This was how it came about that, early on the morning of 3 July 1944, members of the SAS and Maquis,* lying asleep at their Bulbasket base, were woken by gunfire. The camp came under attack by hundreds of troops, mostly members of the 17th SS Panzergrenadier Division. Men tried to

* As well as an American pilot, Lincoln Bundy, who had taken refuge in the camp.

run to safety. Most went downhill towards a valley and were eventually captured. Eight others, including John Tonkin, ran the other way, into the woods. These men eventually assembled safely at a farm named La Roche that was known to all Bulbasket members; it was the reserve base advised by the Maquis member Tonkin had met in England.

One SAS member – Tomos 'Twm' Stephens, the young Welsh officer who had cycled to Châtellerault – was killed immediately on capture. Already wounded, he was beaten with rifle butts and shot in the head. Seven maquisards were executed in the forest. Meanwhile, 30 captured SAS men, as well as a medical orderly and the American airman, were sent to a military prison in Poitiers. Three of them – Joe Ogg, Sam Pascoe and Reggie Williams – who had been wounded in the attack, were transferred to hospital.

On the night of 6 July, the unwounded prisoners were joined by Dougie Eccles and Ken Bateman. They were all placed in trucks and driven south to a quiet spot in the Bois de Guron. Richard Crisp, the 20-year-old who had dropped with Tonkin exactly a month earlier, was the senior officer present. He listened as an order of execution was read by a translator. It was followed by a statement from Erich Schönig, who expressed his shame at having to carry out Hitler's Commando Order. But Schönig's words made no difference to the outcome. The men shook hands with each other and hugged. And then they were shot dead. Two days later, the three wounded men, Ogg, Pascoe and Williams, were removed from hospital, returned to prison, and executed by lethal injection.

On 14 July, Mosquito fighter-bombers were called into action again, carrying out a revenge attack on the SS troops who had raided the Bulbasket party. The 'wooden wonders' struck their camp with pinpoint precision as they were sitting down to their evening meal. Casualty figures vary, but it is likely that over a hundred SS men were killed or wounded.

Operation Bulbasket did not end in early July. John Tonkin, unsinkable in his resolution, continued to lead his remaining men on reconnaissance jobs and attacks on railway lines. The party was boosted by the arrival of several American pilots – but its smaller size, more in line with the self-supporting desert parties of the David Stirling era, was arguably helpful to its operations. There were certainly fewer men to become bored, and far less chance of leakages or betrayal.

'Twm' Stephens's wartime grave with SAS cap badge and wings attached to the cross. The photograph was given to John Tonkin at the end of 1944.

Tonkin with ex-Maquis members at the Saint-Sauvant Memorial, erected in 1973 at the site of the murders.

Unsurprisingly, Tonkin was now immensely vigilant. Together with Amédée Maingard, he questioned a man claiming to be a Canadian soldier. He recalls:

> This fellow was standing in a slouch in Canadian army uniform. The moment I entered, he just looked at me in a casual fashion, and [Maingard] barked at him 'Stand to attention in front of an officer', and the fellow jerked to attention and stood there rigid. [Maingard] instantly pointed at his hands and he said 'You're a German!'

Maingard had set a trap which the unfortunate man had just failed. He had stood to attention in a German manner with his hands open – whereas British and Canadian soldiers would tighten their hands into a fist, with only the thumb pointing down. The man was immediately taken out and shot. Tonkin describes the incident as though justice was undoubtedly served. Throughout France, however, this was a period of paranoia and summary judgment. Many people were unfairly labelled. This man may have been one of them. Or he may not.

At the end of July, Tonkin received an order from Paddy Mayne to cease operations. He and his men would be returning to Britain, and they would be brought home by aircraft. Several days later, they began preparing a landing strip, 1,100 yards long and 220 yards wide. Hedges were cut down, a road was levelled, and a harrow, towed by a jeep, was employed to smooth out the surface of an amenable farmer's field.

Two 161 Squadron Hudsons duly landed to bring home the remainder of the Bulbasket party. At 5 a.m. on 7 August 1944, two months and a day after he had left, John Tonkin landed back at Tempsford airfield.

45

WHAT DAYS ARE FOR

What are days for?
Days are where we live.
They come, they wake us
Time and time over.
They are to be happy in:
Where can we live but days?

Ah, solving that question
Brings the priest and the doctor
In their long coats
Running over the fields.

'Days', Philip Larkin

The SAS did not just consist of fighters. Some of its most popular members were cherished *because* they did other things. They possessed the skills that kept the fighters safe and enabled them to do their jobs. They were unlike others in the brigade – and were valued for it.

We have encountered some of these men already. Mike Sadler, for example. Sadler actually did a good deal of fighting – but without his navigational skills, as David Stirling quickly realised, the SAS would have been left wandering the desert like mechanised nomads. Sadler was a gentle man but the toughest members of the unit depended on him for their lives – and their appreciation has been expressed many times over the years. Something similar might be said of Malcolm Pleydell. A gifted doctor at war with his fears, his presence reassured the kind of men who barely seemed to need reassurance.*

Another man who would earn devotion, without ever carrying a gun, was Fraser McLuskey, chaplain to the SAS Brigade. Like Sadler and Pleydell, McLuskey's presence offered the men an increased chance of survival. Descending into France as a member of Operation Houndsworth, he brought with him a sense of normality and purpose. He taught the SAS, as Larkin might have observed, what days were for.

Operation Houndsworth, made up of members of 'A' Squadron, 1st SAS, was sent into the Morvan near Dijon. Led by Bill Fraser, its aims were similar to those of Bulbasket. It would impede the movement of German troops towards Normandy by attacking roads, bridges and railway lines, and by calling in RAF air strikes. It would work closely with local Maquis groups. It would carry out reconnaissance. And it would look out for any viable opportunity to damage the German war machine.

Its experience would prove different to Bulbasket's, however. It was not threatened by encroaching German forces to the same degree, and it remained in the field for a full three months, causing at least 220 German casualties for the loss of only two men killed and seven wounded. It achieved considerable operational success. Almost two dozen railway lines were cut, six trains were derailed, numerous air strikes were called in and a synthetic oil factory was twice attacked – on the second occasion, in August, with mortars and Vickers K guns. It was supplied with 6-pounder guns and jeeps; a rewarding tactic involved driving the jeeps along minor roads and strafing enemy vehicles on parallel major roads with the Vickers Ks.

Houndsworth was never struck with disaster as Bulbasket was – not, at least, on the ground. Early on the morning of 17 June, one officer, Leslie Cairns, and 15 men died while flying to the Houndsworth dropping zone when their Stirling disappeared over the Channel. Forty-five years later, Cairns's wife wrote of her husband of six months: 'He was too happy, too buoyant, too loving of life. He had a sort of "fatality" about him.'

* The same could certainly be said of Pleydell's successor as medical officer, Major Philip Gunn MC, about whom McLuskey writes, 'No medical officer was more beloved.'

Members of the Houndsworth party – including Fraser McLuskey – in front of their aircraft shortly before take off.

On the same night, Fraser McLuskey was on board another Stirling heading for France, but his aircraft was forced to turn back due to bad weather. Five nights later he tried again. This time, the Stirling managed to locate the dropping zone and McLuskey jumped – although, as a crew member notes in his diary: 'We damn near ran into a mountain after the final run-up. Well that's all for now, bed calls.'

McLuskey landed upside down in a tree, hanging by one leg from a branch. In a great deal of pain, he pulled out a knife and tried to cut his harness away. Suddenly he was falling: 'My last recollection is of crashing head first through innumerable branches. I knew no more until I wakened on a soft, grassy bank at the foot of the tree being violently and noisily sick.'

In the morning light, he could see that he had fallen from 40 feet. McLuskey's SAS career had very nearly ended on arrival. But with his entrance out of the way, a serious problem remained. What was the conceivable role of a chaplain with a small group of saboteurs behind enemy lines? Paddy Mayne had clearly wondered as much when he had first met McLuskey. As the padre recalls: 'If he didn't actually ask who the devil I was and what the devil I was doing there, I gathered at least that was at the back of his mind.'

Fortunately, McLuskey had quickly taken to both the atmosphere and the men of the SAS. Even more fortunately, they seemed to have taken to him. He noted, like so many others, that these men displayed little discipline in the traditional sense, but a huge amount of loyalty to the unit and to each other. They did not seem particularly interested in religion – but he decided that he would arrive prepared in France. He landed in his tree with an oak cross, a silk altar cloth, communion vessels, and as many hymn books and New Testaments as he could carry.

Arriving in France on a Thursday, McLuskey quietly wondered whether anybody would want a service on the Sunday. He joined about thirty other men at Bill Fraser's campsite in a wood near the village of Châleaux where

The Reverend Fraser McLuskey.

McLuskey officiates at one of his hugely popular services in the Morvan.

tents were improvised from parachutes hung from trees. And when Sunday arrived, everybody came to McLuskey's service. More importantly, everybody seemed to *want* to come. He remembers: 'Few of them, in different circumstances, would have gone of their own accord to worship God. [But] in this forest glade they were finding the activity of worship the most natural thing in the world.'

McLuskey noted that everybody was to some degree homesick and afraid. Nobody knew what lay in store. The concerns of 'civilised' life were disappearing, to be replaced by more fundamental needs and desires. These included the need for meaning and protection. This made McLuskey's presence, and God's, welcome. With normal life out of the picture, McLuskey found that worship became the most normal thing in the world.

For a padre, this was an exciting observation. He had been worried that the unusual circumstances of Houndsworth would limit opportunities for worship, or that his presence would appear an unnecessary luxury. On the contrary, he had parachuted into the most fertile religious soil he had ever known. The communal sense of uncertainty stripped away pretensions, bringing each man closer to the next. Hymn singing, he found, fostered the sense of community. And the biggest lesson he was learning was not that war made people afraid, but that peace made them too little afraid, too secure, too closed off to the challenges of ordinary, everyday life, and too resistant to selfless acts and comradeship. As he said to Reg Seekings at the time, 'These last few days, I've seen religion lived. Men helping one another. No thought of reward or anything, they just go and they help and do all they can to help.'

In a sense, what McLuskey was discovering in a French forest camp was not very different from what British city dwellers had discovered in underground shelters and ARP posts in 1940 and 1941.

It is arguable that his experience might have been different had he parachuted into Bulbasket rather than Houndsworth. What is not arguable, however, is that McLuskey's presence had a positive – and unexpected – effect on the morale of the men. Particularly when they saw how keen he was to assist both with their personal problems and with the practical issue of conducting a war. On the evening after his first service, hearing the sound of nearby gunfire, he pitched camp with the medical officer, collected stretchers and a first aid kit, and set up as a Regimental Aid Post.

At first only one casualty – Reg Seekings – was brought in. The almost indestructible sergeant major had been struck by a bullet in the head. As the doctor attempted to remove it, McLuskey assisted. Another wounded man arrived, as gunfire continued all night. The following morning, the Aid Post was moved deeper into the forest, which also meant moving the wounded men. That night they moved once again, this time to a new base camp. 'It meant a longish trek with our two casualties; but somehow or other we managed it.' Seekings, meanwhile, has unusually high praise for McLuskey: 'This is where the padre, I maintain, saved my life, because by this time I'd seized up . . . But the padre carried my kit as well . . . McLuskey really nursed me, really looked after me.'

Seekings remembers that McLuskey gave him a shave – and the pair discussed their favourite reading material. For Seekings it was a series of popular detective novels. For McLuskey it was the New Testament. But before long, McLuskey had been spotted reading detective fiction and using phrases like, 'I'm just gumshoeing around . . .'

As McLuskey settled into a routine, he began making regular rounds of his 'guerrilla' parish. He would give services at each camp, tend to his parishioners and visit the wounded. In one camp he even offered confirmation classes. He would travel sometimes on foot, but usually in a small Renault saloon that was requisitioned early on, or in jeeps, once they had arrived.

Given the nature of the parish, there was always the possibility of a funeral to conduct. One night, two aircraft, a British Halifax and an American Liberator, collided directly above Bill Fraser's camp. Every man on both aircraft was killed. McLuskey was woken by the explosion, and through the black silk of his parachute tent he watched a ball of fire shooting across the sky. The men spent the following day working through the wreckage of the Liberator until, as McLuskey remembers, 'we were tired and grimy, and we smelt of death'. Graves were dug, and McLuskey read the burial service, his thoughts reflecting Churchill's words immediately after the Dunkirk evacuation. This Liberator crew, after all, had been the embodiment of 'the New World, with all its power and might, [stepping] forth to the rescue and liberation of the old.'

The wreckage of the Halifax, meanwhile, was discovered by the Germans and buried separately. Days later, McLuskey and a party of Houndsworth men showed up at the cemetery and held a service attended by men, women and children from the local village. Gunfire could be heard nearby, but the ceremony went ahead as a long line of villagers filed past the graves to lay flowers.

In camp, McLuskey started to become a pastoral handyman, serving as driver, interpreter and ambulanceman among other roles. During an alert, when it was feared that the Germans were about to attack, he was placed on guard duty outside the camp: 'What an eternity these two-hour watches seemed at first, until, like all else, they quickly fitted into the pattern of our outlaw state.'

It would have seemed wrong, of course, for the padre, a full member of the camp, to refuse such an important defensive duty. Yet, as a non-combatant under the Geneva Conventions, he, unlike every other member of camp, was unarmed. So he could not defend himself – or others – if the Germans attacked. This begs the question, *should* he have been armed? McLuskey, it seems, might have been willing to carry a gun. He considered the matter at length and concluded that he should not, explaining that the men 'liked to see their padre without the weapons they had to carry'. He was an important symbol that they were only carrying weapons in the cause of peace. His non-military presence, in other words, was a reminder of 'what days are for'. To serve his purpose, he must remain unarmed.

McLuskey was not in fact the first successful serving member of the SAS not to bear arms. In early 1943, as the SAS was looking to expand quickly, a conscientious objector – Keith Killby – had joined as a medical orderly. Not only was Killby an avowed pacifist, he had just published a booklet entitled *Peace – What Then?*, which espoused his views. One might have expected Killby to be quickly discarded, or at least ostracised, by his colleagues – but he seems to have been a popular and valued member of the unit. One of his first jobs was to bandage Paddy Mayne's hands after a fight in a Cairo shop. Mayne, perhaps surprisingly, did not object to his pacifism. 'He accepted it,' says Killby, 'but he couldn't understand it.'

Killby trained with the Special Boat Squadron, taking part in exercises which threatened to blur his principles. He learned to plant bombs, for example, as live bullets were fired over his head. In June 1943, he took part in

Left: Keith Killby: a conscientious objector in the SAS.

Below right: James Hutchison (centre) wearing his new face.

Operation Hawthorn, a series of SBS raids on Sardinia led by John Verney. He was captured and escaped several times, eventually being imprisoned in Stalag VIII-B in Silesia. Killby's trials did not seem to weaken his views. On promotion to sergeant after his release, he still refused to bear arms. His courage, though, was never doubted.

Fraser McLuskey was, of course, in a very different situation to Keith Killby. He was a man of peace but not a pacifist. Yet he was sufficiently detached from tactical and military decisions to appreciate the absurdities of his unusual life. He took pleasure, for example, in the eccentrics he was meeting. James Hutchison was one.

Hutchison, a hugely energetic 51-year-old, was an SOE Jedburgh who had been dropped into the Morvan to co-ordinate the local Maquis groups. Known to Bill Fraser and the party team as 'Colonel Hastings', he enjoyed good relations with the SAS, liaising closely and sometimes sharing his wireless set. But he had gone to quite extraordinary lengths to prepare for his mission.

Hutchison had already been known to the Germans before he dropped. This made his use as an agent extremely unwise – unless he was somehow able to disguise himself. He made an appointment with a Harley Street plastic surgeon, asking whether he could be given a new face. The surgeon considered the matter.

'It can be managed,' he said, 'but I'm going to give you a good doing.'
'The more thorough the better,' I agreed.

The following day the operation took place at the London Clinic. The prominent bridge on Hutchison's nose was removed. The tops of his ears were chopped off. And some bone from his pelvis was extracted and added to his chin. Once the scars healed and his new features settled down, Hutchison found shaving a challenge, used as he was to the contours of his old face. The real test came, however, when he saw Peter, his seven-year old son. He writes:

> [I] rang the bell. Peter came and opened the door. 'Hullo, Peter. Is Mummy in?' I asked. He looked at me with the serious unrecognizing look of a child and then, leaving the door open, dashed off. I heard his young feet hurrying and then his voice: 'Mummy, there's a man at the door to see you.'

The Germans did not recognise Hutchison either. He survived his time in France to become the post-war member of parliament for Glasgow Central.

Fraser McLuskey's (and Operation Houndsworth's) lengthy stay in France coincided with, and indeed contributed to, the turning of the tide of the war. 'The Germans could see the writing on the wall,' McLuskey writes, 'they wanted to get out of the country as quickly as possible.' The joy of the French people at the imminent departure of their oppressors, even if they were sometimes premature with their celebrations, was unrestrained. A great deal of gratitude was showered on the SAS. When the various Houndsworth camps combined to enter the village of Anost, the inhabitants gave them a wonderful reception, despite the existence of a nearby German garrison. Most gratifying, perhaps, was the welcome given to the most deserving of recipients, 'A' Squadron's commander, Bill Fraser – who had entered the village wearing his kilt. His appearance caused a stir, and he was asked to make a speech in the town square. McLuskey recalls:

> Bill was a man of few words, even in his own language, and when it came to French, almost inarticulate. But his appearance on the balcony of the Hotel de Ville, complete with kilt and glengarry [a traditional Scottish cap], rendered any speaking quite superfluous.

As Fraser tried to speak, his words were drowned by a carnival of deafening cheers. The hero of Agedabia had, says, McLuskey, conquered the hearts of the people of Anost.

46

LA LIBÉRATION

The liberation of France was characterised by the related extremes of joy and agony. SAS men from all five regiments would experience the full range of drama.

Operation Kipling was dropped into France in mid-August with the intention of extending the Houndsworth area of operations to the north. Derrick Harrison, previously on Sicily with the SRS, was in charge of an advance party. On 23 August, two jeeps, containing Harrison and three others, were on their way to contact the local Maquis when the men spotted burning buildings and heard gunfire coming from the village of Les Ormes.

A woman cycling past Harrison told him that two or three hundred Germans were inside the village. 'Save yourselves!' she said, urging the SAS men to drive away. Instead they drove into the village, where they found a crowd of SS troops in front of the church. Against a wall, 20 civilians had been lined up for execution.

At the moment the Kipling jeeps arrived, two of the civilians had already been shot. In the firefight that ensued, the others ran to safety. The effect of the jeeps' Vickers K guns was instant, as Harrison writes: 'The crowd of SS men stampeded for cover. Many of them died in those first few seconds in front of the church, lit by the flickering flames of the burning vehicles.'

The two jeeps caused between fifty and sixty SS casualties. Harrison's jeep was eventually disabled under heavy fire, killing James 'Curly' Hall, a veteran of Sidi Haneish and Operation Bigamy. Marcel Friedmann, a French interpreter with 1st SAS, managed to drag Hall's body to the working jeep, and the three survivors drove back to the Kipling camp.

Above: James 'Curly' Hall.
Left: Derrick Harrison.

Below right: Liberation day in the town of Châtillon-sur-Seine in the late summer of 1944.

Charlie Radford, meanwhile, was a member of Operation Rupert, a 2nd SAS operation intended to attack targets near Nancy in eastern France. As the Germans moved out of the area and the Americans moved in the danger receded but the intensity remained. One evening Radford was invited to dinner with a member of the Maquis, where he met the man's teenage daughter. 'There was plenty of wine, and it loosened our British inhibitions,' writes Radford. Over the next few weeks, Radford was billeted in a barn in the village. His romance with his French girlfriend 'matured rapidly and reached its consummation one hot, lazy afternoon'. Far too soon, orders came to leave the village. Radford writes that his last night 'was one of mixed emotions. I felt rather like one of the *Bounty*'s mutineers when they had to leave Tahiti.'

Radford's young girlfriend was particularly upset because her family was watching her closely. She was not able to sneak out to meet up with Radford on his last evening. And the pair did not see each other again for half a century. Then, while on holiday in France, Radford decided to look her up. He found her address and knocked on her door. 'She did not know me from Adam,' he writes, 'until I produced a photo of her and another of me, taken in 1944.' She was delighted to see him, and they shared a bottle of champagne as they remembered a time of intensity that had brought so many people together in so many different ways.

Two of the first British soldiers into Paris after its liberation were Mike Sadler and Paddy Mayne. They had parachuted into Houndsworth in early August before moving on to Operation Gain – where they discovered that Ian Fenwick had been killed. Not long afterwards, they drove to the recently liberated French capital. 'We were giving ourselves a holiday in Paris,' says Sadler. They each had their own car, Sadler a Ford coupe, Mayne a Delage, and they found the city almost entirely shut down at night. 'There were not many people out on the streets and there were just bicycle taxis to take you around,' says Sadler, who remembers:

> Going to a restaurant, you had to knock on the back door and they would let you in. You'd have this lovely food which had been brought in by chaps on bicycles from the country.

The pair stayed a few days in the glorious George V hotel. 'It was sort of half-open,' says Sadler, 'they were very much cut down but that didn't prevent us having a nice bedroom and ensuite. So we had rather a decent time!'

The pair also 'went to various places where there were charming ladies to entertain us with glasses of this and that. I don't think Paddy enjoyed them as much as anyone else, if I could put it that way. But he was enjoying it.'

While in Paris, Paddy Mayne played a practical joke with a hand grenade that has grown into a key part of his personal legend. Sadler, though, was witness to what really happened. He and Mayne had been taken to a club near the Champs-Élysées where they were sitting with a group of local people when Mayne suddenly produced a grenade from his pocket. Sadler recalls: 'He pulled the pin out and stuck it in the middle of the table. It started to smoke. I knew it would have a seven second fuse. It was very disturbing.'

Some people dived under the table. Others shrank back against the wall. Sadler had to make a snap decision. Was this a joke or had Paddy gone mad? Should he stay in his seat or run like hell? He decided to stay. 'I knew Paddy well enough to think it was only a joke. I certainly hoped he was only joking. I sat there solemnly watching until it got down to the end of the fuse. It didn't go off so we were able to laugh.'

Mayne, it turned out, had previously cut the detonator from the fuse. It had been a very carefully prepared joke – although, in this period of emotion and intensity, anyone seemed capable of anything. Not least Paddy Mayne.

Mike Sadler at the wheel of a jeep in recently liberated France. Paddy Mayne is probably nearby.

47

THE BELLY OF THE BEAST

In March 1945, two squadrons each from 1st and 2nd SAS Regiments came together for a joint operation codenamed Archway. The SAS was going to have to reinvent itself once again. Over the last three and a half years, it had both been and not been a parachute unit. It had constituted a shapeless threat in the desert, a straightforward commando unit, and a sabotage franchise with branches across France. But always it had been the focused hunter, either ambushing its prey or meeting it head on in set-piece encounters.

Now, as the European war entered its final stage, the SAS was setting out to defeat a desperate enemy on its own territory. It would do so by pressing into Germany, carrying out reconnaissance, clearing a path and shooting up whatever it could find. It would, in effect, be skirmishing – and this would make it vulnerable, for the first time, to ambush by soldiers who did not fear dying for their cause. Some very bloody fighting lay ahead.

The plan was for almost three hundred SAS men to cross the Rhine in support of British and American parachute landings before pushing deeper into Germany. They would be driving beefed-up versions of the jeeps that had arrived in the desert in 1942. They still had their Vickers Ks, but they now also had bulletproof windscreens, bazookas, and even smoke flares that could shield the jeep in a large cloud.

SAS men were no longer wearing either sand-coloured or red berets. Now that Hitler's Commando Order was fully acknowledged, they were wearing the black berets of the Tank Corps. In fact, they were ordered to remove all SAS insignia, and even to remove references to the SAS from their paybooks. The SAS was now in effect an undercover unit. Its

Two pictures of John Tonkin with his jeep. Note the black tank corps berets and the bullet-proofed windscreens. Also the strand of white tape (top) marking out an uncleared minefield.

job, according to John Tonkin, was 'to stir up trouble, to probe, to force German formations to declare their positions and to constantly feed back information'.

With an end in sight, there were plenty of men more nervous than usual of going into battle. Alex 'Sandy' Davidson, a sergeant who had won the Military Medal in the desert, almost went AWOL before the start of Archway, only arriving back at the last moment. When asked by his officer, Roy Close, what had happened, he said, 'I didn't know whether to come back for this one or not. I don't fancy it.' Not everybody felt this way, of course. Harold 'Tanky' Challenor writes, 'I personally experienced a sense of elation at standing on the home soil of those who had killed so many of my pals.' And Reg Seekings relished the SAS's new role. For the first time since the desert, he felt that 'we were fighting a war which I liked, which made sense to me.' The prospect of driving hard through enemy lines before turning back and shooting them up in the rear, a role that combined

Members of 2nd SAS, including Harold 'Tanky' Challenor (sitting on right).

Above: A 'buffalo' crossing the Rhine (top) and the view from inside a 'buffalo'.

Left: Freddie Oakes.

commando and sabotage elements, appealed to him. As did the knowledge that the SAS would be carving the opening from which the ordinary army would break through.

The operation began with the crossing of the Rhine in armoured amphibious craft known as 'buffaloes' on 25 March. From the banks of the river, Freddie Oakes, a 2nd SAS signaller, drove into a marshalling area in a wood, where he discovered a German signaller dead at the control of his wireless set. It was, he writes, 'a sobering sight'. The following day, as he set off to carry out reconnaissance for the 6th Airborne Division, he found 'numerous burnt out gliders with charred skeletons still sitting in the remains of jeeps inside the fuselage'. This was clearly going to be a bitter fight.

Joe Patterson, 2nd SAS Medical Officer, had a close escape from a mortar attack at a road junction. Six mortars fell in quick succession, the second hitting a tiled roof beside him; it 'must have divided the splinters outwards and downwards, leaving me in a clear arc. Otherwise it would have landed five feet from my right ear and would certainly have killed me.'

From the earliest encounters, it was clear to all that the Germans were going to resist fiercely. Even Tanky Challenor, himself a ruthless fighter, notes his amazement at 'the fanaticism with which so many Germans fought; it seemed as if they still clung to the vague hope that the Führer would perform some last minute miracle and turn the tables'.

And it was not just the seasoned soldiers who resisted. 'The kids, that was the big trouble,' recalls Reg Seekings. 'They were fanatical, no two ways about it.' At one point, Seekings found himself in a stand-off with a 14 or 15-year-old boy. The boy stood poised with two grenades – which he dropped just as Seekings was about to shoot him. A moment later, a party of camouflaged German paratroopers stepped out and surrendered. If Seekings had shot the boy, he was told, the paratroopers would have fought to the death.

Roy Close, meanwhile, drove into an attempted ambush by a group of boys hidden in ditches on either side of the road. With his firepower he was able to outgun them, killing several and wounding one, who then approached with his hands up. Close took the wounded boy to a nearby cottage – where a female occupant began shouting in English that Close

The SAS about to enter an apparently ordinary military camp.
This, however, was Belsen.

was a coward for shooting the boy as he surrendered. Close pointed out that the boy was wounded in the back. How could he have been surrendering? Another woman started shouting and threatened Close with a saucepan, at which point he left to continue fighting the war.

Everywhere, the Germans were fighting desperately and brutally. Seekings witnessed the SS forcing civilians to hold up a white flag before moving into position to fire on British troops who came to take their surrender. 'At this place I'm talking about they wiped out the entire farmer's family . . . killed their own people because young kids wouldn't take rifles and fire. These nine or ten-year-old kids weren't even big enough to hold a rifle.'

Joe Patterson entered another farmhouse to find an extraordinary sight: the body of a German soldier was lying in a barn on some straw. Its head was split open – and a pig was eating the brains. The farmer had dragged the corpse into the barn to feed to his animals. Patterson simply stared at the pig, 'up to its eyebrows in gore'.

Freddie Oakes and his colleagues entered another village where they found SS troops asleep in a barn. The men were woken, handed shovels, and told to dig a large hole. As they were doing this, 'the CO appeared and, on finding out what was being planned, gave orders that they were not to be shot. Having had a burst of Vickers fire over their heads they were led away into normal captivity.'

These SS men were luckier than many. Such was the SAS's fury at the Commando Order that prisoners were not always taken. Tanky Challenor was standing beside a Russian SAS member when an unarmed German ran out of a house with his hands up. The Russian's first bullet hit the soldier in the stomach, dropping him to his knees. The second struck him in the head. The Russian smiled. Yet when Challenor shot a badly burned cat that had run out of a burning house, to put it out of its misery, the Russian began to cry. 'I'll never understand you, you bastard,' said Challenor. This was not quite true. Challenor was soon checking his gun and 'looking for more Germans to kill'.

Bill Fraser, meanwhile, had been absent from the action since 27 March. His squadron had gone to the aid of Canadian paratroopers in a wood. He had been trying to outflank an enemy force when he was hit by a bullet in the hand. It was a minor wound – but after so many successful actions, Fraser's war was finally over. Those moving further into Germany, however, were about to reach a town named Celle. And a sight that they would never forget.

48

CELLE AND BELSEN

The 2nd SAS reached Celle on 12 April. In the town Joe Patterson was approached by a German civilian who told him that there were some bad casualties in a 'concentration camp' in the town. The words had no particular significance to Patterson, but he duly drove to a large barracks and into the square. There he was confronted by a sight that, after years of bitter war, he could not possibly have imagined. He and other members of the SAS were, over the next few days, to experience a horror beyond description or understanding. At first, Patterson found 'two fantastic figures, like filthy animated skeletons in dirty striped, grey and black trousers and jackets

like pyjamas. These creatures were very weak and hardly recognisable as human beings.'

Patterson was led out to a stable where, buried in a heap of manure, were living people:

> The horrible stench from the rotting wounds in the manure, and the staring eyes gleaming out of those slatey skeleton faces in the filth made an impression it is impossible to describe. It was difficult to imagine that these had once been men.

Patterson went into another shack, where he found 'about 100 creatures who once were human':

> They were utterly filthy, starved to a degree hardly credible, and at least half were severely wounded, and all wounds were vilely infected. To a man they were covered with septic sores, and the stink was choking. At first they did not realise who I was, but as soon as they did I was overwhelmed by them, screaming and shouting and weeping with joy. I did not know what to do.

Patterson spent the day moving as many of these people as possible into the hospital in Celle. When he had finished he covered himself with disinfectant. He then made a point of showing local worthies, such as a countess with whom he was billeted, around the camp. One of them stared at a human skeleton and said, 'I don't think we should treat anyone like that, even though he is a Russian.'

Unbelievably, this was not the worst of it. Three days later, 1st SAS reached another camp. This was Belsen. The first to arrive were probably John Randall and his driver. Others who followed were John Tonkin, Duncan Ridler, Reg Seekings and Johnny Cooper. Tonkin was taking pictures. From the outside it seemed like an ordinary military camp.

One of the guards was smiling. Tonkin says that he was probably smiling as well. He had no idea what he was about to find.

Cooper remembers being greeted by an SS officer who introduced himself as Kramer. He was pleasant but said that he was not responsible for the inmates' condition.

Right: A German guard outside Belsen. John Tonkin, who took the photo, had no idea what he was about to find.

Left: Josef Kramer, the Beast of Belsen. As commandant, he welcomed the SAS into the camp.

Above right: Kramer under guard with Irma Grese, the sadistic warden of the camp's women's section. They were both executed in December 1945 for war crimes.

Cooper would never forget his first sight of the inmates. They seemed barely human. Some of them summoned the energy to approach the barbed wire – and impaled themselves without giving any indication of pain or distress. John Tonkin remembers the huge open pits in which bodies were piled up. It took him a while to realise that some were still alive. 'People don't believe it,' he says. 'But that's how terrible it was.'

Tough SAS men, who had seen and done things that most would find unendurable, were unable to comprehend what they were seeing. They could not understand how such behaviour was possible. Cooper watched as a female prisoner reached under the wire for a rotten turnip – and a camp guard, knowing he was being observed, simply shot her dead. According to Tonkin:

> The place was guarded by Romanian Nazi troops and while we were there, they were still just shooting prisoners. We got hold of all these

> officers and we lined them up and I said, 'Unless that shooting stops immediately you are all going to die very horribly.' And the shooting stopped. That was the only way to deal with it.

Little wonder, given what was found at the camps, that SAS attitudes to German civilians hardened. Joe Patterson recalls an elderly German woman approaching Eric 'Bill' Barkworth, 2nd SAS's intelligence officer, and asking him to shoot her as she was alone with nobody to care for her. Barkworth told her 'to apply to Himmler as he was rather good at that sort of thing'.

49

PRISONERS

As the end of the war approached, the most notable SAS prisoner to be released was David Stirling. He was released from Colditz, arriving back in London on 15 April with a number of other prisoners. They were told that they would not be allowed to return home immediately; they would first have to be examined by a psychoanalyst. 'Next morning,' remembers Stirling, 'there wasn't a single individual left in the camp. We'd all escaped in the night. Twelve o'clock that evening I was in a night club. By 2am I was having my first roger for years.'

Other SAS prisoners were being released from other camps. John Cochrane, captured during Operation Hawthorn, had kept an illustrated diary at Oflag 79.

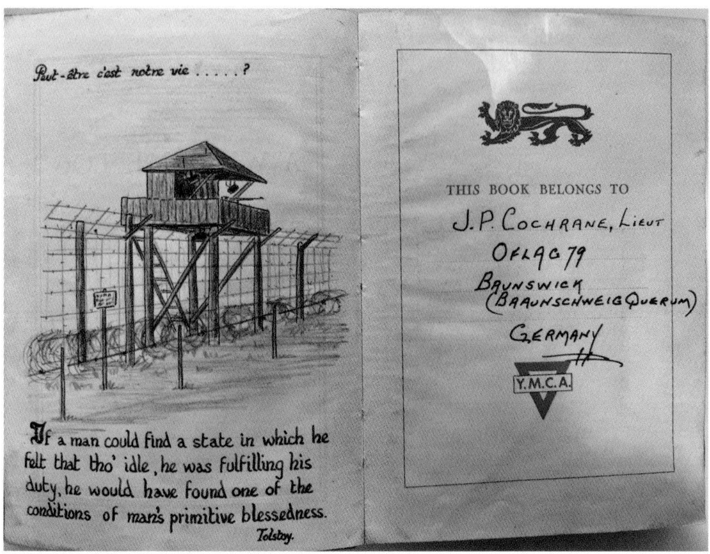

Cochrane's entries for April, as the Americans approached the camp, make tense reading:

> 6 April – Reports that our own troops are less than fifty miles away. There's certainly a very marked tightening of tension throughout our ranks – and the burning question is: Will they try to move us on? If they do try it, where will they send us and how? If by cattle trucks I shall certainly try to make a break before I get locked into one.
>
> 7 April – The excitement and suspense is mounting daily.
>
> 8 April – Had a touch of 'prisonitis' all of a sudden about four – could have cut my throat or drowned myself in one of our bomb-water filled holes – but when I heard our troops are only 10 miles away my spirits went sky-high . . .

The diary continues in a similar vein until, on 12 April, an entry announces: 'WE'RE FREE MEN'.

April 12th 1945

WE'RE FREE MEN!!!

AT SIXTEEN MINUTES PAST NINE TROOPS OF THE 15? U.S. RECCE REGT DROVE INTO THE CAMP AND GAVE US ALL BACK THE MOST PRECIOUS THING IN THE WORLD

OUR FREEDOM!!!

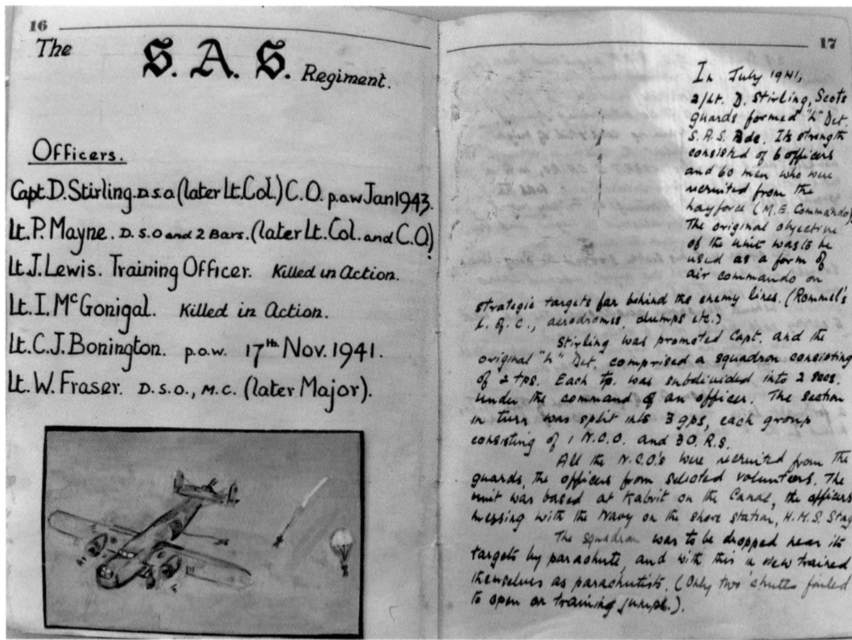

16

The S.A.S. Regiment.

Officers.

Capt.D.Stirling.D.S.O.(later Lt.Col.)C.O. p.o.w.Jan1943.
Lt.P.Mayne. D.S.O. and 2 Bars.(later Lt.Col. and C.O.)
Lt.J.Lewis. Training Officer. Killed in Action.
Lt.I.McGonigal. Killed in Action.
Lt.C.J.Bonington. p.o.w. 17th Nov.1941.
Lt.W.Fraser. D.S.O., M.C. (later Major).

17

In July 1941, 2/Lt. D. Stirling, Scots Guards formed "L" Det. S.A.S. Bde. Its strength consisted of 6 officers and 60 men who were recruited from the Layforce (M.E. Commando). The original objective of the unit was to be used as a form of air commando on strategic targets far behind the enemy lines. (Rommel's L. of C., aerodromes, dumps etc.)

Stirling was promoted Capt. and the original "L" Det. comprised a squadron consisting of 2 tps. Each tp. was subdivided into 2 secs. under the command of an officer. The section in turn was split into 3 gps, each group consisting of 1 N.C.O. and 3 O.R.s.

All the N.C.O.'s were recruited from the guards, the officers from selected volunteers. The unit was based at Kabrit on the Canal, the officers messing with the Navy on the shore station, H.M.S. Stag.

The squadron was to be dropped near its targets by parachute, and with this in view trained themselves as parachutists. (Only two 'chutes failed to open on training jumps.)

A notable SAS men who was liberated from Oflag 79 on the same day was Charles Bonington. Captured after Operation Squatter, Bonington had been one of the very first officers to join 'L' Detachment. He wrote an illustrated history of the SAS while a prisoner.

The other SAS man liberated from Oflag 79 on 12 April 1945 was Mick Gurmin, the star of Dudley Clarke's SAS deception who rejoined the SAS in October 1942.

Lichtbild

Größe	Haarfarbe
171	dkl. [illegible]

Fingerabdruck des rechten! Zeigefingers

Above: Pages from Charles Bonington's illustrated history.

Left: Mick Gurmin's POW registration card.

50

AMERICA

As David Stirling and Mick Gurmin were being liberated from their respective POW camps, Mike Sadler was experiencing a very different kind of adventure. He, together with fellow SAS members Bob Tait, Graham 'Johnny' Rose and Oswald 'Mickey' Rooney, was enjoying a publicity tour of the United States.

THE DETROIT TIMES C—15
June 1945

BRITISH HEROES HERE

Times Photo

Four crack British paratroop commandos drinking a toast to Detroit war workers from their room in the Book-Cadillac Hotel after making a goodwill tour of war plants here. All veterans of the bitterest scraps in Africa, Italy and Germany—and all bound for the Pacific—they are (from left) Sgt. Maj. R. D. Tait, Sgt. Maj. Graham Rose, Maj. O. B. Rooney and Maj. W. M. Sadler. With them is a CIO relief committeeman, who acted as guide.

The four men travelled around the United States by train visiting local dignitaries, British consuls, Red Cross canteens, aeroplane factories and shipyards. They gave speeches and made radio appearances. They spent time in Hollywood where they were shown around by starlet Martha Vickers. They were described in the American press as 'crack paratroop commandos', 'jumpers', 'heroes' and 'veterans of the bitterest scraps'. 'And there was a great deal of drinking,' remembers Sadler.

Left: Having fought a long, bitter and exacting war, a few members of the SAS received some welcome American hospitality.

Right: Martha Vickers – now best remembered for a scene-stealing performance in *The Big Sleep*, and a brief marriage to Mickey Rooney.

Below: Mike Sadler and others in Hollywood.

51

THE END: Germany

As the war in Europe was drawing to its close, German soldiers, who had been fighting so bitterly, surrendered in large numbers. An entire German division tried to surrender to John Tonkin. 'There were about eight thousand of them,' says Tonkin who initially told the commander to go away. The commander was so persistent, however, that Tonkin eventually gave him a signed piece of paper formally accepting surrender and told him to park his men off the road.

Moving through the country, Reg Seekings was meeting German civilians and reaching some sharp conclusions. Older people, he discovered, would not admit to being Nazis. Their children, however, were another matter. Stopping at a farmhouse for a rest, he began chatting to the owners who seemed pleasant. But when their young daughter came into the room and saw British soldiers, 'she struck her mother and father, she kicked and

spat, she screamed her bloody head off'. The parents explained that their daughter would be perfectly willing to report them and have them sent to a concentration camp. 'They were bad little buggers,' Seekings says of the youngsters.

In another house, Seekings heard a knock late at night at his bedroom window. It was a German soldier paying a nocturnal visit on the daughter of the house whose room he had borrowed. Seekings reached for his gun and fired. 'I was laughing so much I missed him,' he remembers. 'I bet he never came back to see his girlfriend!'

Seekings and his party were eating with a friendly family in yet another house – when the father suddenly stood up and said, in German, 'Please shoot me!' He went on:

> Be honest, you are trying to trick me, then you'll shoot me! You are not English! You look like a German! You speak like a German! You act like a German!

The man's daughters had a hard job persuading him that the SAS men were not members of the Gestapo or SS trying to deceive him into an act of collaboration. 'There was a lot of fear there, no two ways about it,' recalls Seekings, who was aware that significant pockets of resistance remained.

In fact, just days before Germany's unconditional surrender, SAS men were still being killed. On 29 April, Dayrell Morris and Bob Boxall of

Left: A German division that surrendered to John Tonkin and followed his instruction to park off the road.

Dayrell Morris and Bob Boxall (far right).

2nd SAS died as they attempted to cross the Elbe. A bomb landed behind Boxall's jeep on the Allied side of the river while Morris was shot on the other side as he took the surrender of a party of Hitler Youth. A young boy, who had dropped his Schmeisser sub-machine gun, picked it up again and opened fire. 'Dayrell was a very good chap,' writes Wallace Rennie-Roberts, a member of his troop, admitting that 'we were getting a little blasé as the war was all but over.'

Another man who died shortly before the war in Europe ended was Alex 'Sandy' Davidson, the sergeant who had almost gone AWOL in order to avoid Operation Archway. Davidson, a member of Layforce before joining the SAS in 1942, was badly hurt when his jeep was blown up by a mine on 14 April. Roy Close ran over to him and hurriedly put field dressings on his wounds. Davidson was taken to hospital but did not survive. 'The tragedy of his premonition,' writes Close, 'has haunted me ever since.'

Close remembered his section's final act of the war. 'It was the most carefully conducted patrol of the campaign,' he writes. 'Our fieldcraft was perfect.' Once it was over, he had expected to feel elated. But he and his men simply lit cigarettes, relieved that they had survived. Otherwise, they felt rather flat.

A stroke of serendipity, meanwhile, found Reg Seekings marking the surrender at Poperinghe in Flanders where his father had fought during the previous war. Drinking with his mates and running frequently to the toilet, Seekings overheard an old woman saying, 'They're just like their fathers. Drink, drink, drink. Piss, piss, piss.' History, it seems, was repeating itself.

52

THE END: Norway

Adolf Hitler had long considered Scandinavia to be his 'zone of destiny'. After his invasion of Norway in 1940, the region provided the Nazi war machine with much-needed metals and minerals and was defended by hundreds of thousands of German troops. These soldiers had to be disarmed after the surrender and their return to Germany supervised. This job – known as Operation Apostle – fell to members of 1st and 2nd SAS.

Freddie Oakes of 2nd SAS was one of these men. On 15 May, he flew to Stavanger in Norway. From Stavanger he sailed north to Bergen where he began living 'the life of Reilly'. He says of his time there:

> We were invited to many parties and the Norwegian girls were not only pretty but most spoke good English. This upset their menfolk many of whom were in a para-military organisation and dressed in grey uniforms.

John Tonkin, meanwhile, had been appointed area commander of Odda, south-east of Bergen. Here, too, 'the women were absolutely superb and the men didn't like our presence at all.'

Tensions between the SAS and the local men grew in Odda after a football match was organised between an SAS team and a team of Norwegians. The match was played on a pitch beside a makeshift prisoner-of-war camp housing German soldiers. The Germans, watching from behind the wire, cheered loudly for the SAS – who beat the Norwegians 2–1. 'It caused great embarrassment,' says Tonkin who did his best to appease local feelings.

Local women on a picnic with SAS members.

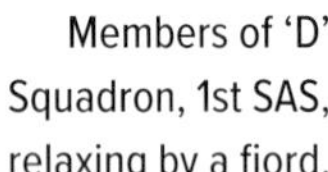

Members of 'D' Squadron, 1st SAS, relaxing by a fjord.

An international football match in Odda, 1945: SAS 2–1 Norway.

Eighty miles away, meanwhile, Freddie Oakes was taking part in the 'Battle of Bergen'. This, he claims, began when some Norwegians picked a fight with a pair of SAS men on their way back from a night out. 'We had spent five or more years leading a hectic and stressful life,' he writes, 'and there was no way we were going to accept anyone beating up our chaps.' The result was a large-scale affray involving both officers and men. 'There were no local repercussions,' says Oakes, although a 'dim view' was taken by the War Office.

The actual work of processing German soldiers did not begin for several weeks. The first stage was a medical check which, it was hoped, would reveal members of the SS trying to pass themselves off as members of the Wehrmacht. (SS personnel were required to have their blood group tattooed on the underside of their left arm.) Any men caught were handed on to intelligence staff.

Next the Germans' kit was searched and, finally, they were marched down to the docks and placed on ships bound for Germany. 'In one part of Bergen,' says Oakes, the SAS 'would receive some verbal abuse from the locals' as they shepherded the Germans towards their ships. But this was not his biggest surprise. That came when a pornographic photograph found on a German soldier clearly featured a serving member of the SAS. The SAS man, it transpired, was a Belgian who had posed for the camera in 1940 to make some money after the German invasion.*

While his comrades were in Norway, Johnny Wiseman was placed in charge of SAS Headquarters at Hylands House in Essex. When they returned to Britain in late August, Wiseman, who had been living off base with his wife, received a note telling him to return quickly to camp as Paddy Mayne was on his way. Wiseman, who had been working closely with Mayne for several years (and had once received an unwelcome shave) did not make it back in time. He recalls that Mayne asked him where he had been. Wiseman replied he had been staying outside the camp. Mayne wasn't happy. 'It's not good enough! You're sacked!'

And so Johnny Wiseman, veteran of the desert, the Termoli truck explosion and Operation Houndsworth, was 'sacked from the SAS just

* While carrying out these searches, Oakes claims to have discovered that German soldiers possessed far more pornography than their British counterparts.

like that'. But, he claims, 'it didn't really matter to me. I'd had enough of the SAS by then.'

In fact, the organisation did not last much longer than Wiseman. Discussions had been underway about sending men to fight in the Far East but the dropping of the atomic bombs and the subsequent surrender of Japan ended that prospect. Instead, on its return, the SAS Brigade simply began to break up. The Belgian and French regiments were transferred to their own armies. Then, after a final parade at Hylands Hall in front of brigade commander Mike Calvert, the SAS received disbandment orders. Stirling's mob was demobbed.

Or not quite. An SAS War Crimes Investigation Team, under Major Eric 'Bill' Barkworth, had been created in May to investigate the murders of SAS men in France, while a series of SAS Mobile Teams were subsequently sent into Greece to examine the roles of local people in the rescue of Allied servicemen. These unofficial SAS teams were still in existence in 1947 when the 'SAS' name (and idea) was revived with the creation of 21st SAS Regiment, a unit of the newly reformed Territorial Army.

Reports of the SAS's death in 1945 were, perhaps, an exaggeration.

53

AFTERLIFE

John Hislop, the Phantom who was attached to the SAS in France, was both nervous and excited about leaving the army at the end of the war. This kind of military life had, after all, suited him. He had greatly enjoyed its variety, companionship, travel, excitement, limited responsibility and ordered routine. He had, he understood, been through experiences that he could never forget, both good and bad. Life would probably never be as interesting again.

War, Hislop believed, had brought him both tolerance and cynicism, harshness and sympathy. It had revealed human inconsequence, and the simplicity of basic human needs. But it had also given him a nomadic restlessness.

Several years of life stripped to the essentials of existence had left him philosophical rather than ambitious. He was relieved at having survived rather than desperate to improve his situation. He had little feeling of hatred for the Germans, no recrimination or bitterness – although he wanted justice for those murdered in France.

Socially, he now found himself more comfortable with men than women. In character he had become more self-centred, more introverted, and less responsible than he might otherwise have been for a man of his age. And less familiar with the ways of civilian life. In some ways he had grown wiser; in many others he was a child.

In the short term, however, the end of the war allowed Hislop to approach the future with little thought and little concern. He was alive, life was good and tomorrow could take care of itself.

Christopher Sykes of 2nd SAS, who had served with Hislop in France, emerged from the war with greater empathy and an understanding that humanity comes in all forms. He had dropped into France with the very English belief that true courage was unassuming and understated. Yet the bravest man he ever met, he recalls, was a member of the Maquis who boasted endlessly about his own courage.

John Tonkin's daughter Jane recalls her father describing a consequence of his wartime experiences:

> Dad's family were religious but he wasn't in the end. He told me he lost his faith when one of his fellow soldiers had his stomach blown open by an explosion and he was trying to stuff the contents back in. The man said he didn't understand why God had done this to him. That seemed to change Dad's beliefs.

Tonkin's respect for the SAS padre, Fraser McLuskey, never faltered, nor did the men's close friendship, but Tonkin's perception of life had changed forever.

An SBS man, an Irishman fighting in the Aegean, experienced greater doubts than Tonkin. He fired questions at a sympathetic officer:

> What are we all doing here? Killing a few German, bein' killed ourselves and gettin' hundreds of Greek people shot for helpin' us? What's it all for, sorr? What are we doin' here?

Perhaps an answer as good as any was provided when the SAS liberated the camps at Celle and Belsen. But for a particularly thoughtful man such as Bill Fraser, the wider picture could never allay the daily struggle. The gentle Scotsman responsible for the classic SAS raid of the war (on the airfield at Agedabia) and a remarkable act of humanity (in sparing a group of Italians at Fuka) had never expected to survive the war. But he did survive – and the ensuing years proved even more challenging. After a 1946 court-martial for drunkenness, he left the army. During the 1950s he was sent to prison for a long string of burglaries. He died in 1975, destitute, aged just 58.

Mike Sadler, the SAS's most popular navigator, was also a sensitive man but he emerged from the war mentally unscathed. In fact, he had thoroughly enjoyed the excitement of life in the SAS. 'There was a lot of freedom about serving in the SAS,' he says, 'even compared with civilian life where people were constrained by having to work and earn a living and look after their families and all that sort of thing.' In order to keep the freedom and excitement alive, Sadler jumped at an opportunity that landed on his desk as he waited to be demobbed:

> We got a letter from the colonial office asking if anyone would be interested in going to the Antarctic with the Falkland Islands Dependencies Survey. I took the letter in to Paddy Mayne and said, 'I'm the first volunteer!' Paddy just said, 'I think I'll come too.' So we were two volunteers and we got one more: John Tonkin.

Sadler, Tonkin and Mayne soon found themselves living a wild and dangerous existence in the Antarctic. They caught seals, drove teams of dogs and camped out in brutal conditions. The first to leave was Mayne, whose ongoing back injury (probably acquired during Operation Squatter) was causing him difficulty. Sadler stayed for 13 months, while Tonkin remained in the Antarctic for 2 full years. At one point, in August 1946, he was very nearly killed falling down a crevasse. He found himself wedged upright with both legs dangling free. Another man was carefully lowered down the crevasse to try to pull him free. Tonkin's diary records the incident:

> I got pretty desperate. I was scared stiff that I wouldn't be able to hold out much longer and that would have finished everything.

Sadler and Tonkin in Antarctica.

> I determined I'd make my shoulder muscles hold out longer. We tried a pull with everything they had. At first there was just nothing doing and then suddenly I moved. Was I pleased? I shot up the fifty odd feet to the top like a lift.

Not only did Tonkin survive, but he met his future wife – a third generation Falkland Islander – while on the expedition. He subsequently worked for Shell Oil and moved to Australia in the 1950s where he became the general manager of a uranium mine near Darwin. He died in 1995 having been awarded an Order of Australia Medal for his services to the Aboriginal peoples.

Paddy Mayne, the rugby international, frustrated writer and wartime recipient of four Distinguished Service Orders (but, controversially, no Victoria Cross), seems to have found life without war less than fulfilling. A pre-war solicitor, he became Secretary of the Law Society of Northern Ireland, but he drank prodigiously and, according to Sadler, 'found it very difficult getting back to ordinary life.' It was a shock to many – but not a huge surprise – when Mayne was killed, in December 1955, drunk-

enly driving his sports car into a stationary lorry. He was 40 years old. His funeral service was conducted by Fraser McLuskey, and one of the pall bearers was Bob Bennett, who once said that he felt 'immune to danger and untouchable' when working by Mayne.

David Stirling, the frustrated artist and founder of the SAS, did not attend Mayne's funeral. After the war, he moved to Rhodesia where he founded the Capricorn Society, a relatively progressive organisation aimed at bringing Africans and Europeans together to 'integrate the region into the world economy.' When this venture failed, he embarked on a series of more controversial security ventures in Africa, the Middle East and Britain. He died in 1991. At his memorial service at the Guards Chapel in London, Fitzroy Maclean, a man with whom Stirling entered Benghazi and chased the South African Survey, said in his address:

> There are people who pride themselves on showing a proper appreciation of the art of the possible. David was a specialist, if ever there was one, in the art of the impossible. Another thing that David did was to make it all fun.

Left: Paddy Mayne's funeral procession.

Right: Jamie Coreth's portrait of David Stirling hanging in White's Club.

Bringing his story full circle, a portrait of Stirling by the artist Jamie Coreth now hangs in White's Club, Stirling's lifelong haunt and the establishment where Robert Laycock began recruiting his well-connected friends – including Stirling – into 8 Commando.

A man whose name has never before been associated with the SAS is Mick Gurmin, leading figure of Operation Abeam who 'rejoined' the SAS in 1942. After the war, Gurmin moved into the steel industry. He became chief executive of a large company – and never revealed his remarkable wartime story to anybody. He died suddenly at the age of just 58 in January 1978.

The memories of Mike Sadler run through this book like a spine. After the SAS and his Antarctic expedition, he was employed in government service for many years. His navigational skills were employed in later life as he sailed around the Mediterranean. At the time of writing, Mike is 103 years old and enjoying good health. And, as the pictures opposite show, he is unmistakably the same man who survived an epic desert trek in 1943.

Mike Sadler, then and now.

ACKNOWLEDGMENTS AND NOTE ON SOURCES

There had been a great deal written and said about the wartime SAS over the last seventy-eight years. Aware of this fact, I have searched for new material, fresh stories and previously obscured angles – and I have been very generously assisted, above all by the Special Air Service Regimental Association. The unfailing hospitality – and advice – of John Allcock, Tracy Hawkins and Terri Hesmer has been greatly appreciated. The resident archivists, including Rebecca Hawtrey, have expertly guided me through their collections.

I would like to pay particular tribute to Mike Sadler. This book would have been far more difficult to write without his help and friendship. He, and his daughter Sally, have been more than contributors. Mike's first-hand memories (often of little-covered subjects such as his trip to America in 1945 and his post-war expedition to Antarctica) have offered new and exciting perspectives. I am deeply grateful to both of them.

Special thanks, also, to Jane Storey, daughter of John Tonkin, who has been immensely generous with her father's archive. Tonkin recorded a detailed account of his experiences for the benefit of his family, and Jane has allowed me complete access He also took many photographs which appear throughout. The cover photo, taken in the midst of the fighting on Sicily, is one of these.

David and Fiona Gurmin have been extremely kind in providing me with material relating to Mick, whose journey from fake SAS to real SAS is an exciting revelation. Having discovered Mick's name and story in the National Archives, I engaged in some internet detective work which revealed that Mick's surname was shared by the present-day owner of a taxi company. I called the taxi number and got through to David – who found himself talking to an annoying stranger asking lots of inappropriate questions about his parentage. Luckily David turned out to be Mick Gurmin's son.

I have been fortunate to work with some tremendous people while writing this book. Arabella Pike, Katy Archer and Sam Harding from William Collins have been extremely supportive, anticipating problems and making my job far easier. Mel Haselden has been a wonderful picture editor. I have hugely enjoyed our days together in various libraries and archives. My agents Jim Gill and Amber Garvey have been solid and encouraging – as ever. I would also like to thank three people, each of whom sat beside me for a few days as time grew short. Marc Goldberg, the author of *Beyond the Green Line*, a devastating account of his time as a combat soldier, brought his analytical skills to the job of research; Henry Wood joined me at the Imperial War Museum and the London Library; and Victor Grant came to the Royal Air Force Museum and to Cambridge to speak to Mike Sadler. I wish them both the best of luck with their academic careers. Finally, I would like to thank Claire Price, who has offered immense support and proved to be a gifted editor as well as a reliable sounding board.

I am well aware that, in writing this illustrated history of the SAS, I am standing on the shoulders of impressive individuals. Gavin Mortimer, for example, has written superbly about all aspects of the SAS, SBS and LRDG, as well as many other related and unrelated subjects. He interviewed large numbers of SAS veterans across the world and, in 2004, published *Stirling's Men*, a deeply immersive narrative of the wartime SAS. Damien Lewis has written a series of thrilling and superbly researched books about the SAS of this period, most recently *SAS Brothers in Arms.* Gordon Stevens has also carried out numerous interviews (many of them filmed) with wartime members. Some of these were turned into an oral collection – *The Originals: The Secret History of the Birth of the SAS in their Own Words.* Many of these interviews are now held by the Imperial War Museum in both transcribed and audio form. In 2016, Ben Macintyre published the first ever authorized history of the SAS – *SAS: Rogue Heroes.* It has since been turned into both a television documentary and a BBC drama. There have also been two modern biographies of David Stirling, very different in approach but worth reading by Alan Hoe in 1994 and Gavin Mortimer in 2022. (I would also add that I am greatly looking forward to Tony Rushmer's upcoming biography of Reg Seekings.)

So far as my sources are concerned, I have found valuable material in both predictable and unexpected places. The SAS archive has a tremendous cache of official documents, interviews, accounts and memoirs. As well as the War Diary and the full set of *Mars and Minerva* (the journal of the SAS), I have had access to recorded interviews (with Keith Killby, Jim Smith and Arthur Huntbach, among many others), service records (including Mick Gurmin's), diaries (such as Cecil 'Jacko' Jackson's), files relating to numerous operations, and unpublished accounts (ranging from Jack 'Busty' Cooper's to Reg Seekings' partial wartime memoir). The archive also contains a huge collection of previous SAS books and memoirs. Perhaps the most authoritative has been *The SAS and LRDG Roll of Honour, 1941–1947* compiled by ex-Lance Corporal X, QGM. Taking thirteen years to complete, this three-volume project records and commemorates all SAS and LRDG casualties of the Second World War. It is a tremendous achievement.

Many published personal memoirs have been useful. The most immediate and evocative are *Parachute Padre* by Fraser McLuskey, *Born of the Desert* by Malcolm Pleydell, *Anything but a Soldier* by John Hislop, *To War with Whitaker,* a collection of Hermione Ranfurley's diaries and *Enter Trubshaw,* a 1944 collection of Ian Fenwick's cartoons. The story of Polar explorer Quentin Riley being trumped by the SRS in Augusta is in *Attain by Surprise* by John Nutting.

Among other excellent published sources are *One of the Originals* by Johnny Cooper, *When the Grass Stops Growing* by Carol Mather, *The General Salutes a Soldier* by J.V Byrne, *Gentleman Jim* by Lorna Almonds-Windmill, *SAS Men in the Making* by Peter Davis, *SAS Trooper* by Charlie Radford, *SAS and the Met* by Harold 'Tanky' Challenor, *In Action with the SAS* by Roy Close, *Phantom was There* by RJT Hills, *War in the Islands* by Adrian Seligman, *Eastern Approaches* by Fitzroy Maclean, *The Life of My Choice* by Wilfred Thesiger, *The Moon's a Balloon* by David Niven, *WWII Writings* by A J Liebling, *No Drums No Trumpets* by Alec Le Vernoy, *Four Studies in Loyalty* by Christopher Sykes, *SAS with the Maquis* by Ian Wellsted, *A Dinner of Herbs* by John Verney, *Geoffrey – Being the Story of 'Apple' of the Commandos and the Special Air Service Regiment* by JEA, *Jock Lewes* by John Lewes, *Fire from the Forest* by Roger Ford, *The Regiment* by Michael Asher, *Operation Bulbasket* by Paul McCue, *SAS Zero Hour* by Tim Jones and *Danger Has No Face* by James Hutchison – an account of the author's plastic surgery but, frustratingly, containing no corresponding 'before' and 'after' photographs.

Some unpublished memoirs were harder to find – but well worth the effort. For example, Admiral Sir Walter 'Tich' Cowan's improbable autobiography – *The Wheel of Fortune Through Seventy Years* – can be found at COW/17/6 in the National Maritime Museum archives. And William Oakes, the son of former SAS member Freddie Oakes, has very kindly provided me with *Wireless Worked Wonderfully Well,* Freddie's informative and entertaining memoir of the period.

I visited many archives and libraries while researching this book. I would particularly like to thank Jane Rosen and her superb team at the Imperial War Museum Reading Room for their help. A number of excellent photographs, drawing and sketches are held inside document files in the archive – and many of these are reproduced in this book. (They include the picture of the *other* SAS, the South African Survey, which is held within the private papers of JWS Castelton at 17356). There are also superb unpublished memoirs, such as JH Patterson's type-written autobiography (including his chilling memories of Celle) which is at 13225. Frank Jopling's LRDG diaries are in Box 15/9 of 15623. The letters from Jock Lewes to his father are at 17403. Malcolm Pleydell's diaries and letters are at 337, while Vivian Street's account of his escape from an Italian submarine is at 16370. JP Cochrane and his POW diary (and Charles Bonington's illustrated history) are at 19040 while Jimmy Brough's memories are at 24562 along with reports of interviews (with Bob Bennett, Pat Riley, Jim Almonds, Dave Kershaw and others) that were carried out in preparation for a feature film about the regiment that was never made.

The Imperial War Museum Sound Archive has been equally valuable. It holds interviews with, among others, Johnny Wiseman (20337), Carol Mather (19629), Douglas Arnold (17826), Johnny Cooper (17826), Jim Reid (30063), Arthur Batten (27802) and Brian-Scott Garrett (16741) whose account of Operation Bigamy offers fascinating insight into the work of the SAS through the eyes of an outsider.

The story of SIG and Martin Sugarman's interview with Maurice Tiefenbrunner are held in the AJEX archives. I accessed them at the Jewish Museum in London. Sugarman's article on the subject – *The SIG: behind the lines with Jewish Commandos* – is in Volume 35 of Jewish Historical Studies.

A considerable amount of the material in this book has been sourced at the National Archives in Kew. The Operation Abeam file (at WO 169/24904) explains the involvement of Mick Gurmin in Dudley Clarke's deception scheme. WO 169/24847 and FO 1093/252 offer further information about Clarke. The ULTRA message viewed by Churchill warning the Germans of the SAS's planned attack on German aerodromes in June 1942 is at HW 1/648. Further details of the broken American code are at HW 1/646, HW 1/652 and HW 1/653. The file relating to Theodore Schurch's court martial for treachery is at WO 71/1109. Reports on the formation of 'L' Detachment are at WO 218/173 and WO 201/785 while Robert Summers' vivid account of Operation Chestnut is at WO 218/98. Among numerous other files of interest are those relating to the murders of SAS members (TS 26/418, FO 916/895, WO 309/660, WO 235/560 inter alia).

While writing this book I have spent a great deal of time in the London Library and the British Library. Sections were also written in the beautiful Rose Main Reading Room at the New York Public Library. I am very grateful to the hard-working staff members of all these institutions.

In the end, this is a book about the people who came together to inspire, create and embody the wartime Special Air Service. It tries to bring these individuals to life and to explain what they did and how and why they did it. Any mistakes, errors or failings are, of course, my responsibility alone.

Joshua Levine, London, 2023

PICTURE CREDITS

Due to the circumstances in which they were taken, many of the photographs used in this book are not of the highest quality. Some are stills from films which are nearly a century old; some show the only known pictorial records of members of the SAS; and some were taken during dangerous operations. We hope that you appreciate their inclusion in this book as an important historical record of this time.

Part One: The Idea opening image taken from the SAS Regimental Association Archive
2: Troopers and horses, SAS Regimental Association Archive
4: Mick Gurmin, SAS Regimental Association Archive
4: Dudley Clarke, The Picture Art Collection/ Alamy
5: Horseplay, SAS Regimental Association Archive
6: *Parade* extract, The National Archives, ref. WO169-24904.
6: Two images showing local men 'ready to descend', SAS Regimental Association Archive
8 and 181: Mick Gurmin, SAS Regimental Association Archive
8: Gurmin and Smith, SAS Regimental Association Archive
9: Letter, SAS Regimental Association Archive
9: Fake SAS stamp, SAS Regimental Association Archive
10: Dudley Clarke in Madrid, National Archives, ref. FO1093-252
12: 'Paratroops Hit Nazis' 19 June 1941, Daily Mirror/Mirrorpix
13: T.E. Lawrence, IanDagnall Computing/ Alamy
14: Camels © IWM
14: Poster, public domain
15: Hejaz Railway, 1908 © IWM
15: Deep cutting near El Akhthar © IWM
16: Train, image from gbfilms.com/11th-november-1917
17: Lowell Thomas, Marist Archives and Special Collections, New York (Ref.1508.1b)
17: T.E. Lawrence by William Patrick Roberts, © Ashmolean Museum/Estate of John David Roberts. By permission of the Treasury Solicitor/Bridgeman Images
18: Colonel Blimp, Bill Brandt/Getty
20: Ralph Bagnold, Churchill Archives, Cambridge (Ref. BGND E55)
20: Sun compass, National Army Museum
21: Desert film stills © Royal Geographical Society/Courtesy of the BFI National Archive
22: Bagnold's dinner, from Ralph A. Bagnold, *Sand, Wind & War: Memoirs of a Desert Explorer*, University of Arizona Press (1990)
24: Mussolini declares war, Alinari/TopFoto
25: Wavell in the desert, Fotosearch/Getty
26: New Zealand members of LRDG, from Ralph A. Bagnold, *Sand, Wind & War: Memoirs of a Desert Explorer*, University of Arizona Press (1990)
27: LRDG life 1941, IWM 15623
28: Chevrolet trucks, from W.B. Kennedy Shaw, *Long Range Desert*, Collins (1945)
31: Boer Commandos, CBW/Alamy
33: Clarke © W.A.Jones Collection
33: Niven, Hulton Archive/Getty
33: Laycock, Central Press/Getty
34: Evelyn Waugh, Hulton Archive/Getty
34: Randolph Churchill, Bettmann/Getty
35: Jim Almonds and Pat Riley, SAS Regimental Association Archive
37: HMS *Glenroy* © IWM
38: Sir Walter Cowan, photograph by Walter Stoneman/National Portrait Gallery
39: HMS *Aphis* © IWM
41: Eureka landing craft © IWM

42: 'Tich' Cowan SAS Regimental Association Archive
45: 'Jock' Lewes, SAS Regimental Association Archive
50 and 51: David Stirling, SAS Regimental Association Archive
52: Parachute training, SAS Regimental Association Archive

Part Two: The Desert opening image taken from the SAS Regimental Association Archive
56: SAS volunteers emplaning © IWM
58: Bob Lilley and Reg Seekings, SAS Regimental Association Archive
62: Joe Duffy and Ken Warburton, SAS Regimental Association Archive
64: Bonnington's painting, IWM 19040
66: Shepheard's Hotel (top), SAS Regimental Association Archive
66: Shepheard's Hotel (bottom), courtesy of grandhotelsegypt.com
66: Parachute wings, SAS Regimental Association Archive
67: Jock Lewes still from 'Meet The Oxford Crew', British Pathé Ltd
67: Who Dares Wins, SAS Regimental Association Archive
68 and 70: Selected stills from 'Paratroops In The Middle East', British Pathé Ltd
72: Bristol Bombay, SAS Regimental Association Archive
74: Paddy Mayne, SAS Regimental Association Archive
75: The Fiasco!', IWM 19040
76: Aftermath of Operation Squatter, SAS Regimental Association Archive
77: David Lloyd Owen, SAS Regimental Association Archive
79: Sadler (left), SAS Regimental Association Archive; Sadler (right), image provided by Mike Sadler
84: Paddy Mayne, SAS Regimental Association Archive
88: Fraser, Chambers and Schott, SAS Regimental Association Archive
91: Annotated photo, SAS Regimental Association Archive
94: Hermione Ranfurly (left), © Illustrated London News Ltd/Mary Evans; Ranfurly (right), TopFoto
96: Inspection, SAS Regimental Association Archive
100: Paddy Mayne, SAS Regimental Association Archive
101: David Stirling, SAS Regimental Association Archive
104: Blitz Buggy, SAS Regimental Association Archive
108: The Churchills, PhotoQuest/Getty
109: Fitzroy Maclean, Popperfoto/Getty
110: The South African Survey, IWM 17356
111: Malta, SAS Regimental Association Archive
112: Reconnaissance photo, SAS Regimental Association Archive
113: Four SIG members, © Martin Sugarman at AJEX Jewish Military Museum
117: Graham Rose and Jimmy Storie, SAS Regimental Association Archive
121: Maurice Tiefenbrunner images © Martin Sugarman at AJEX Military Jewish Museum
125: Bonner Fellers, Bettmann/Getty
126: Most Secret Ultra Message, The National Archive, ref. HW1-648
128: Jeep images, SAS Regimental Association Archive
130: Armed jeeps and Stirling, SAS Regimental Association Archive
131: Jeep in amusement park, image courtesy of the author
134: Malcolm Pleydell, SAS Regimental Association Archive
137: Bob Bennet, SAS Regimental Association Archive
139: Fire, SAS Regimental Association Archive
142: Sandy Scratchley, SAS Regimental Association Archive
148: Notes from Curchill and Stirling, SAS Regimental Association Archive
149: Bill Cumper, from Jonathan Pittaway, *SAS RHODESIA*
154: Richard Ardley, Special Forces Roll of Honour website
158: Bob Mélot, SAS Regimental Association Archive
161: Benghazi party images, SAS Regimental Association Archive
164: Bernard Montgomery, Pictures from History/Getty

169: Theodore Schurch, The National Archive, ref. WO204-13021
170: Schurch statement, The National Archive, ref. WO71/11097
170: Committing a Civil Offence, The National Archive, ref. WO71/11097
171: Major General Vivian Wakefield Street, IWM 64335
174: Freddie Taxis, Special Forces Roll of Honour website
176: German soldiers pose, SAS Regimental Association Archive
177 and 291: Mike Sadler portrait, image provided by Mike Sadler
178: A.J. Liebling, agefotostock/Alamy
179: 'A reporter at large', SAS Regimental Association Archive
181: Gurmin (left), image provided by John Tonkin's daughter, Jane Storey
182: Road, SAS Regimental Association Archive
183: Various images, SAS Regimental Association Archive

Part Three: Europe opening image taken from the SAS Regimental Association Archive
186: 'C' Squadron, image provided by John Tonkin's daughter, Jane Storey
188: Johnny Wiseman, Bill Fraser and John Tonkin, image provided by John Tonkin's daughter, Jane Storey
188: Dougie Eccles, The SAS and LRDG Roll of Honour 1941–47
190–191: images provided by John Tonkin's daughter, Jane Storey
191: SRS men sitting on the barrel of a captured gun, SAS Regimental Association Archive
192: Italian soldiers and prisoners, images provided by John Tonkin's daughter, Jane Storey
193: The scene outside a farmhouse, image provided by John Tonkin's daughter, Jane Storey
197: Armstrong Whitworth Albemarle © IWM
200: *Ulster Monarch*, SAS Regimental Association Archive
200: Twin Vickers guns, image provided by John Tonkin's daughter, Jane Storey
200: View towards Augusta, image provided by John Tonkin's daughter, Jane Storey
202: An Augusta main street, image provided by John Tonkin's daughter, Jane Storey
204: Relaxing in a camp near Mount Etna, images provided by John Tonkin's daughter, Jane Storey
209: John Tonkin and Paddy Mayne, image provided by John Tonkin's daughter, Jane Storey
212: Ian Fenwick frontispiece, from Ian Fenwick, *Enter Trubshaw*, HarperCollins (1944)
212: Ian Fenwick, SAS Regimental Association Archive
214: Cartoons from Ian Fenwick, *Enter Trubshaw*, HarperCollins (1944), pages 20; 15; 22; 24; 107; 106
215: Dave Kershaw and Ian Fenwick, SAS Regimental Association Archive
216: Monty inspects the Phantoms in April 1944, © IWM
218 and 219: Aircrew and Stirling, 190 & 620 Sqns Archive
220: Supply containers dropping from a Halifax, from David Oliver, *Airborne Espionage*, Sutton Publishing (2005), page 70
229: Tonkin in France, image provided by John Tonkin's daughter, Jane Storey
231: Violette Szabo, TopFoto
233: Maingard's gasogene trucks; 'Twm' Stephens dressed as French man; and other, images provided by John Tonkin's daughter, Jane Storey
234: With the Maquis; Bulbasket; and surprised in sleeping bags, images provided by John Tonkin's daughter, Jane Storey
237: Camouflaged jeep; Tonkin with Maingard; and Forêt de Verrières camp, images provided by John Tonkin's daughter, Jane Storey
238: A supply drop, SAS Regimental Association Archive
239: Weaver making cigarettes, image provided by John Tonkin's daughter, Jane Storey
240: Operation to cut railway line, image provided by John Tonkin's daughter, Jane Storey
241: Preparing the landing strip, images provided by John Tonkin's daughter, Jane Storey

243: Grave and Saint-Sauvant memorial, images provided by John Tonkin's daughter, Jane Storey
247: Houndsworth party, SAS Regimental Association Archive
248: Fraser McLuskey, SAS Regimental Association Archive
248: Officiating a service, SAS Regimental Association Archive
252: Keith Killby, from Camp 59 Survivors website
253: James Hutchison after plastic surgery, from James Hutchinson, *Danger has no Face*, Arrow Books (1978)
256: Derrick Harrison, SAS Regimental Association Archive
256: James 'Curly' Hall, The SAS and LRDG Roll of Honour 1941–47
257: Liberation Day, SAS Regimental Association Archive
258: Mike Sadler at the wheel of a jeep, SAS Regimental Association Archive
260: Jeeps, John Tonkin, images provided by John Tonkin's daughter, Jane Storey
261: Members of 2nd SAS, SAS Regimental Association Archive
262: Buffalo crossing the Rhine, image provided by John Tonkin's daughter, Jane Storey
262: View from inside Buffalo, image provided by John Tonkin's daughter, Jane Storey
262: Freddie Oakes, image provided by William Oakes
264: Entering Belsen, image provided by John Tonkin's daughter, Jane Storey
266: Carrying the deceased, Keystone/Getty
268: German guard, image provided by John Tonkin's daughter, Jane Storey
268: The Beast of Belsen, Shawshots/Alamy
269: Irma Grese and Josef Kramer, Shawshots/Alamy
271: John Cochrane Diary frontispiece, IWM 19040
272: John Cochrane caricatures, IWM 19040
273: John Cochrane: 'We're Fee Men!!!', IWM 19040
274: Bonington's W/C painting/plane and parachute, IWM 19040
274: Mick Gurmin's POW card, SAS Regimental Association Archive
275: 'British Heros Here', Michigan University, Clark Historical Library
276: The SAS are welcomed to America, images provided by Chris Rooney from the Special Forces Roll of Honour website
277: Martha Vickers, Jimlop collection/Alamy
277: Mike Sadler and others, image provided by Mike Sadler
278: The division that tried to surrender to John Tonkin, image provided by John Tonkin's daughter, Jane Storey
279: Bob Boxall and Davrell Morris, The SAS and LRDG Roll of Honour 1941–47
282: Tonkin in Norway, images provided by John Tonkin's daughter, Jane Storey
287: Sadler and Tonkin in Antarctica, image provided by John Tonkin's daughter, Jane Storey
288: Paddy's funeral, SAS Regimental Association Archive
289: Stirling portrait at White's Club, used with permission of Jamie Coreth and White's Gentleman's Club
291: Mike Sadler, then and now, images provided by Mike Sadler and the author

INDEX

Note: page numbers in italics denote references to images; an 'n' after a page number denote references to notes

REPORT ON OPERATION "BULBASKET", BY CAPT. TONKIN.

6 Jun Advance party consisting of myself, Lt. Crisp, and Jedburgh team dropped successfully at Q21 3192 at 0137 hrs. We made contact immedi- ly with the Resistance elements and at 0200 hrs. contacted SAMUEL. He advised against staying in that area, so on night 6/7 Jun I moved South East to recce area Q5973. That night the Maquis cut Lot 1 in 54 places.

7/8 Jun Lt. Stephens and 8 ORs dropped successfully on DZ Q 5082. The Eureka was lost.

9 Jun Moved by truck to U 8756 and located new DZ at U 8355

11 Jun Located 11 petrol trains at U 6203. In the evening, a large German con- voy, estimated at least one division, was seen moving up LIMOGES- POITIERS road via LUSSAC. Considerable flap owing to proximity of division to DZ. I decided to bring in main party, however. Fires were lit at 0001 12 Jun. Only one a/c located DZ. The drop was successful except for container lights which lit up in sky. We moved to a camp at U 8658. On the DZ that night, we observed the results of the bombing - a large flame.

12 Jun. Enemy using LIMOGES-POITIERS railway, so Lt. Stephens attacked and half destroyed a bridge, rail over road at U 9054. Estimated it would take at least three days to repair. Enemy convoy was still passing. I informed Brigade, and Lt. [illegible] mines on road in area U 8740. Sgt. Jessiman inform[illegible] patrols were out and that Capt. [illegible] he did not contact me [illegible] previously [illegible]

Cpl. Stephenson (Phantoms)
L/C Baker
Tpr. Mullen
Tpr. Smith
Tpr. Ashley
Tpr. Armitage (Phantoms)
Tpr. Aspin
Tpr. Biffin
Tpr. Brophy
Tpr. Budden
Tpr. Bell (Phantoms)
Tpr. Brown
Tpr. Cummings
Tpr. Eades
Tpr. Fielding
Tpr. Guard
Tpr. Grey
Sgt. Jessiman
Tpr. Keeble
Tpr. Livingstone
Tpr. McNair
Tpr. McLeod
Tpr. Ogg
Tpr. O'Neill
Tpr. Pascoe
Tpr. Phillips
Tpr. Plumb (Phantom)
Tpr. Richardson
Tpr. Ryland
Tpr. Smith W
Tpr. Spooner
Tpr. Simmons
Lt. Morris
Lt. ~~Morris~~ Weaver
Lt. Surrey-Dane

Sabu 42

Sabu 36
Sabu 39

Returned to England 10th August.
Missing believed captured 3rd July
"
Returned to England 7th August
Missing believed captured 3rd July
Returned to England 7th August
Missing believed captured 3rd July
Missing 11th June.
Missing believed captured 3 July
"
Returned to England 10th August.
" 7th "
"
Missing believed captured 3rd July.
Returned to England 7th August
Missing believed captured 3rd July
"
"
Returned to England 7th August
Missing believed captured 3rd July
Returned to England 7th August.
Missing believed captured 3rd July
Wounded and missing, 3rd July
Injured in jeep crash 25 June, ta[illegible]
to hospital 26th June.
Seriously wounded, believed capt[illegible]
3rd July.
Missing believed captured 3rd Ju[illegible]
Returned to England 7th August.
Missing believed captured 3rd Ju[illegible]
"
Returned to England 7th August.
Missing believed captured, 3rd J[illegible]
"
Returned to England 7th August.
"
" " " 10th "

-0-0-0-0-0-0-0-0-0-0-0-0-0-0-0-0-0-0-